(

Environmental Policy

ENVIRONMENTAL POLICY

Transnational Issues
and National Trends

Edited by
Lynton K. Caldwell
and
Robert V. Bartlett

Q

QUORUM BOOKS
Westport, Connecticut • London

Library of Congress Cataloging-in-Publication Data

Environmental policy : transnational issues and national trends /
edited by Lynton K. Caldwell and Robert V. Bartlett.
  p.   cm.
Includes bibliographical references and index.
ISBN 1-56720-079-6 (alk. paper)
  1. Environmental policy. I. Caldwell, Lynton Keith.
II. Bartlett, Robert V.
GE170.E5769   1997
363.7—dc20   96-26268

British Library Cataloguing in Publication Data is available.

Library of Congress Catalog Card Number: 96-26268

ISBN: 1-56720-079-6

First published in 1997

Quorum Books, 88 Post Road West, Westport, CT 06881
An imprint of Greenwood Publishing Group, Inc.

Printed in the United States of America

The paper used in this book complies with the
Permanent Paper Standard issued by the National
Information Standards Organization (Z39.48–1984).

10 9 8 7 6 5 4 3 2

Copyright Acknowledgment

The editors and publisher gratefully acknowledge permission to
quote from the following:

For material from *Policy Studies Review*, vol. 12, nos. 3–4
(Autumn-Winter 1993). Copyright © 1993, Policy Studies
Organization. Used with permission.

CONTENTS

TABLES

PREFACE

Policy is a word of several meanings depending upon context. A common meaning, as defined by the *Oxford Reference Dictionary*, is "a course of action adopted by a government or party or person." The content of policy in government is almost always complex, often contradictory, and subject to various changes and interpretations. For any aspect of government there may be many policies, depending on the purpose of the lawmakers, the commitment of the administrators, and the breadth of the field through which policies are applied. In the journal *Technical Forecasting and Social Change* 40 (1941), Joseph F. Coates identified sixteen sources of environmental problems in the twenty-first century. The numbers could be increased by reference to additional problems that have been latent for many years, but now are appearing on our time horizon.

The following articles examine nine different contexts of public environmental policy in North America. Each is concerned with a different object of policy for some aspect of the environment, but because of the particular problems addressed and the differing subject-matter contexts are not examined comparatively. This breadth and diversity of context is a basic reason for the difficulty in addressing problems of policy for the environment in a general or coherent manner. Generalizations are only possible at a high level of abstraction— more philosophical than operational and, with respect to the environment, weak in practical appeal.

The purpose of these essays is to provide a cross-sectional view of a variety of environmental issues that create policy problems. They should help to clarify why the attempt of the U.S. Congress to adopt a basic environmental statute (the National Environmental Policy Act of 1969), dealt with principles, qualitative goals, and action-forcing procedures that cut across all environment-affecting statues and missions. NEPA was intended to provide a template against which specific environmental polices and decisions could be evaluated. In a different political context, the Canadian Environmental Protection Act seeks an integration of policy between the provinces and the federal government in Ottawa. Consistency with principle rather than uniformity in practice was the rational objective of NEPA. But the public, the environmental organizations, and the politicians tend to be issue-specific in their approach to environmental policy. Accordingly, environmental politics has been largely a process of "brush fire fighting." The broader environmental principles that, if applied, might reduce or prevent "brush fires" arouse little political concern.

The "practical" approach to environmental policy has therefore been categorical. The essays in this volume reflect this topical division of environmental policy and some attempts to integrate the parts with a more inclusive national policy. No attempt, however, has been made to impose a pattern or overall comparative design on the essays. Each stands by itself. Collectively they provide selective pictures of how various aspects of environmental policy have evoked differing legislative and administrative treatment.

In every case the conceptualization of the environmental problem and the approach to its solution have been changing. The problems are targets which are not only moving in time, but cross customary boundaries, as science and societal circumstances change the way in which environmental problems are perceived.

This volume offers no blueprint or prognosis of environmental policy in the twenty-first century. It does offer insight into trends that will influence the future shape of policy. The topics are necessarily selective. To include all areas of environmental policy would require a multivolume work and there is no agreed upon way in which such an extended collection of case studies could be integrated. But the scope and complexity of the policy are should be kept in mind be readers as these selective aspects of environmental policy are presented here.

We were unable to include a chapter on Australia. There are, however, several books available on Australian environmentalism. A volume in some respects complementary to this one is *Federalism and the Environment: Environmental Policymaking in Australia, Canada, and the United States*, edited by Kenneth M. Holland, F.L. Morton, and Brian Gallian (Westport, Connecticut: Greenwood Press, 1996).

ACKNOWLEDGMENTS

Beyond assistance received by the individual contributors to this book, the editors appreciate the roles played in its production by the following persons: Dean A. James Barnes, Professor Roy Shin, and Cynthia Mahigian Moorhead of the School of Public and Environmental Affairs, Indiana University, Bloomington; Michael Parrish of the Business/School of Public and Environmental Affairs Library, Indiana University, Bloomington; the librarians of the Reference and Government Documents Departments, Indiana University, Bloomington; Stuart Nagel, Publications Coordinators, Policy Studies Organization, and Allan Rosenbaum, editor of *Policy Studies Review*. Earlier versions of some, but not all, of the papers in this book were published initially in *Policy Studies Review*, (12)3–4 (Autumn-Winter 1993). All have been revised and extended, and articles by Dunlap, Kennett, and Saunders are entirely new. The assistance of Paul S. Weiland of the School of Public and Environmental Affairs was indispensable in putting the manuscripts into publishable form. We also thank Pamela Carriveau for assistance on the index.

INTRODUCTION

The principle purpose of an introduction is to assist the reader to understand more readily what a book has to offer—to make explicit its purpose—and to acknowledge its limitations. Toward this objective three observations may be helpful to readers of this book. *First*, environment as a concept and relationship is virtually unbounded in scope and content. Its outer limits are cosmic; its inner limits seem infinitely small. Within the recent two years four encyclopedias of the environment have been published and all differ selectively in their coverage. All writings on the environment may be presumed to be selective in content. The papers brought together in this book focus selectively on policies relating to a diversity of environmental issues, identified as particular matters of general public concern.

"Policy" is hardly a precise term, but we use it here as defined by the *Oxford Reference Dictionary* (1986) as "a course of action adopted by a government or party or person." The policy issues discussed in this volume are those affecting entire societies and increasingly encompassing all mankind. These subjects of environmental policy involve matters of choice and decision that necessarily become objects of governance at all sectors of society—local, regional, national, transnational, intergovernmental, and nongovernmental. Courses of action ultimately involve institutions and processes of political government through which societal decisions are made. There are, of course, forces of governance beyond the formal limits of government. But our focus here is on those actions in which governmental institutions are the decision-making actors.

Environmental policy in our time has become a moving target for description and analysis. The rate of change in every aspect of modern society has been accelerating during the last century and shows no prospect of diminishing in the foreseeable future. New discoveries in science, and innovations in technology, create new opportunities but also new problems. Circumstances change and with them also changes the attitudes and beliefs of people respecting their environment. All of these lead to changes in popular demands upon government reflected in new public policies. Changes in policies relating to the human environment and the biosphere have been especially numerous and rapid since the 1972 United Nations Conference in Stockholm. In consequence, writings on environmental policy today address situations that tomorrow may be replaced by new problems and choices.

We can be reasonably sure that the trends described in this book will continue, but not without variation, including opposition; intentions declared in laws and treaties are not always honored in action. And although the trend in environmental policy seems clear, there is no assurance that societal inertia and short-term perspectives will not delay the realization of environmental protection objectives in time to prevent an irreversible decline in environmental quality. These considerations should make clear to the readers that books on environmental policy can seldom do more than report the circumstances pro tempore.

The globalization of environmental policy has followed the transnational expansion of commerce and trade, made possible by advances in science-based technology. Today the accessibility, rapidity, and reliability of communication and transportation have revolutionized interactions among peoples and organizations. Environmental consequences of this new age of accessibility have permitted the expansion of knowledge, the accumulation of national wealth, and an unprecedented expansion of human populations and their domesticated animals and plants. The quality of life for many people has been enhanced, at least for the present and immediate future. But environmental consequences have largely been disastrous. The capacity of natural systems to process and neutralize the residual products of modern civilization have been exceeded. The consequence has been the contamination of air, water, and soil, and the reduction of the restorative capabilities of over-stressed species and ecosystems often to the point of extinction. Global climate change and thinning of the radiation protective ozone shield are also consequences, requiring transnational cooperation to protect life on earth. There are also consequences for human attitudes and beliefs concerning the human condition and its relationships to the natural world and to mankind's managed environment. The concept of a world of limits and the planetary biosphere are gradually becoming major factors in mankind's post-modern paradigm.

The foregoing observations describe the context in which the chapters that follow should be read. They offer selective examples of the policy response to public perceptions of need for environmental protection. No claim is made for comprehensiveness. For this, many more papers at higher levels of generalization would be necessary. But to fully comprehend general trends, recourse to specific instances is needed so that the realities of human action and experience are not lost in abstract generalizations which, however valid, may appear disconnected with everyday life.

1

ENVIRONMENT AS A PROBLEM FOR POLICY

Lynton K. Caldwell

To understand public policies and their administrative implementation, an appreciation of their underlying concepts, assumptions, and circumstances is required. To ignore these fundamentals is to risk superficiality in analysis and error in conclusions. Yet getting down to basics is often rejected as diversion from the goal of analysis. It deviates from a "straight to the point" approach, adds cost and time to investigation, and may not interest practical-minded analysts.

Even so, this chapter will be prefaced by a reminder of some basic factors that make environmental policy problematic. Among these are: (1) incompatible concepts of relationships between nature and humanity—notably conflict between perceived facts and values, and, closely related (2) inadequate appreciation of the complexities of nature and of interactive relationships between humans and nature, (3) sectoral subdivisions of knowledge, (4) situations and motivations in environmental politics, (5) fractionated structure of laws and administration, (6) internationalizing of environmental and economic policies, and (7) short-range time horizons. The ramifications of perceived environmental issues include the risk of unintended consequences of particular policy decisions. As exemplified by the chapters in this volume, humans deal with specific issues selectively. They have not yet learned the difficult act of policy synthesis among elusive but interactive relevant issues. The scope of environment as a field of knowledge has expanded greatly in recent years, and since 1994 at least four encyclopedias have been published to encompass it.[1] Thus the novelty, scope, and interactive complexity of environmental issues have become a problem for conventional public policymaking. Policies are most comprehensible in proportion to their simplicity. Environmental issues are seldom simple and characteristically involve degrees of synthesis that to be adequately understood require more information than ordinary common sense usually provides.

SOME BASIC CONSIDERATIONS

The word policy in the broad sense suggests the making of a decision. Policy has several different connotations, but all carry the implication of choice.[2] Were there no choice, there would be little occasion for policy. Decisions would be wholly directed by circumstances. Action without alternatives mandated by events external to the actors is hardly policy in any meaningful sense. The excuse—"we had no choice"—is seldom taken seriously as an extenuating circumstance. Choices are made by people, not by circumstances, although circumstances may define the necessities and parameters of choice.

Environment as a focus for policy presents decision-makers with multiple sets of problems that may complicate choice among alternative courses of action. This circumstance in public affairs is hardly unique to the environment—complexity characterizes nearly every problem of public policymaking. It is concomitant with modern life. But the broadly encompassing scope of major environmental problems and their interrelationships with other policy and problem areas make rational solutions exceptionally difficult, and their outcomes often uncertain. The difficulty is heightened by the ethical and evaluative nature of many environmental choices. Quantification, an indispensable tool of scientific analysis, may have limited applicability, especially where values are significant. Only in very specific and limited terms is it possible to deal with environmental policy as a single problem. As a general sector of public policy, "environment" summarizes a bundle of interconnecting problems of differing dimensions and significance—and uncertainties.

Among other sectors of policy with which environmental issues are often adversely involved, are those grouped together under the terms economics and rights. In actuality, the substance of many of these sectors of policy is self-centered and behavioral—economics or rights being invoked to justify or defend a private interest. A major task of public policymaking therefore is reconciling valid environmental objectives with opposing policy positions by evaluating alternative choices and probable outcomes. But the task is complicated by the particular interpretations placed upon the terms environmental, economic, and rights—none of which have universally accepted definitions. Many propositions regarding their relationship rest upon assumptions unverifiable in the actual world—and some can be shown to be untrue. This ambiguity of meaning presents difficulties in the formation of strategies for the related issue of sustainable development, which itself has no clear and universally accepted meaning.

Substrate of Environmental Policy

Environmental policy problems (as distinguished from actual events) arise from two basic orientations toward nature, each inducing a different political response. The first (biocentric) is inherent in human ecological-evolutionary relationships with nature. The second (anthropocentric) is sometimes called an "exceptionalist" view of the human relationship with nature—man being the measure of all things. Both orientations present problems for policymakers, but the first has been present since the emergence of humanity, whereas the second has escalated to hubris as a consequence of the way in which human ingenuity and industrial technology have developed. The basic differentiating factors distinguishing these points of view are the contrasting paradigms or beliefs about the relationship between humankind and the natural world. The differentiating question is the extent to which the human species is exempt from the natural limits governing all other forms of life.

The conceptual foundation for comprehensive environmental policy incorporates a holistic concept of man-in-biosphere—not man apart.[3] This biocentric point of view is inconsistent with the ethical, social, and religious doctrines of exceptionalism that have been especially dominant in modern times.[4] The assumption that the earth was made for man is built into the foundations of Western ideologies. Insofar as this anthropocentric view of life interprets the man-to-earth relationship as responsible custody and stewardship, it is consistent with conserving and ecological policies up to a point. That point (which is not fixed) is reached when human ambition or behavior impairs the sustainability of the biosphere. The Western paradigm of human domination is now challenged by deep anthropology, ecology, and by ecofeminism, which all take a less hierarchical and more latitudinal view of life on earth.[5] Many traditional societies have never conceived of human life outside of nature.

Relationships with Nature

Even before the beginning of written history, human life (like all other life) required coping with processes and events inherent in nature. Human society was at risk from natural forces often beyond human comprehension and largely beyond human control. Geophysical events such as earthquakes, volcanic eruptions, floods, droughts, and violent storms required societal responses that might be regarded as equivalent to social policies.[6] In the preindustrial era, options for coping were limited largely to adaptation or migration. These responses may not have corresponded to policymaking as we commonly understand it today but, nevertheless, decisions on behalf of the society were, in effect, policies implemented by its leadership. Institutions emerged in response to environmental situations and many became agents of policy. For example, historian Karl Wittfogel hypothesized that the despotic regimes of the ancient orient arose out of the necessity to manage the distribution of limited water supply—an adaptive response to a continuing environmental problem.[7]

Where an environmental problem was localized, but unmanageable, migration of people was often the only available alternative. There are various instances in the ancient world of cities moving from one location to another, sometimes for causes in the natural environment, but also often for reasons of defense and security.[8] In his commentary on the "Site of a City," a Roman architect and engineer, Marcus Vitruvius Pallio, emphasized the importance of environmental influences especially relating to health.[9] He recounts the petition of the town of Old Salpia in

Apulia, asking the Senate and the Roman people for permission to remove the town from a site that appears to have been afflicted by malaria. The migration option has been much diminished as human populations have occupied the inhabitable earth. Nevertheless, refugees from ecologically/economically "bankrupt" countries create policy problems for the countries in which they seek asylum.

Response to major environmental problems has become a transnational concern of national policy when the consequences of environmental disaster cannot be contained within national boundaries. Transboundary atmospheric deposition of contaminants (e.g., acid rain and radioactive fallout) is an example. No clear distinction in consequence separates environmental problems inherent in nature from environmental problems induced by human behavior.[10]

Hazards of Human Behavior

Unintended environmental consequences resulting from "intentional" human behavior are often politically difficult for policymakers. Unlike the perils to people who inadvertently place themselves at risk by settling on a riverine flood plain, or the slopes of a volcano, people can create environmental problems through intended efforts to exploit or manage nature. Rivers that are dammed, straightened, diverted, or treated as sewers may create unintended downstream environmental problems. Upstream deforestation, over-grazing, or unconserving cultivation may cause soil erosion, siltation harmful to water quality, and increased likelihood of flooding. Pursuit of economic enrichment, growth, and jobs has often led to exploitive degradation of the environment, man-made as well as natural. While historically these consequences have been largely unperceived and unanticipated, today they are more widely understood and often are perceived as environmental problems requiring national or international policy responses.

The development of industrial technology and the exponential increase in human populations have greatly expanded the impact of human activities on the environment. Many of these impacts have resulted from objectives believed to be beneficial. Many have added to the quality of human life (e.g., water purification and air conditioning) and others have been intended to protect against hazards in nature (e.g., pesticides and weather reports). If technological remedies generate new hazards, government may be importuned to prevent or control them also. Thus, a major problem for policymakers is how to deal with the pluses and minuses of technological innovation.[11]

Information on which to base policies responding to man-made problems has been sought through technology assessment, impact analysis, risk analysis, and cost-benefit estimates. The numerous and complex interrelationships of present-day technologies present policymakers with difficult problems of fact finding and evaluation. To formulate these problems and to determine how they might be dealt with often requires technical and scientific expertise on a scale not previously found in many government agencies or in the private sector. And problems induced by human behavior also may raise questions of values and ethics for which science provides no answers but to which policy must respond. Thus, science-based analysis (e.g., environmental or technological impact assessment) may clarify a problem, but does not necessarily determine a policy choice.

A public function of technoscientific expertise is to apply analytic methodologies to environmental problems. The first objective is identification and formulation of the problem, its causes, scope, and probable consequences. Second, based on this knowledge, is the delineation of the appropriate alternatives or feasible responses, and assessment of their impacts on both people and the relevant environments. Implementation of alternatives involves choice among administrative procedures that have implications for governmental structures, legal prescriptions, and political acceptability. The final result of these interrelating developments has been the emergence of a distinctive and growing dimension of public policy that increasingly involves both science-based analyses and interactions between various levels of government, and that today is becoming global in scope.

Whether policy problems relating to the environment are results of either passive or active human behavior, their resolution invariably has an impact on people and their governments. The impacts may be indirect, resulting, for example, in forbidding settlement on flood plains or on coastal areas subject to severe storm damage, or in preventing building on sites that might become vulnerable to environmental disruption (e.g., by avalanches, landslides, or land subsidence), or place other environments at risk.

Even where there is no direct physical hazard, the economic and other personal objectives of some people might be curtailed to satisfy broader social objectives— for example, protection of public health and welfare, and preservation of scenic areas, of historical and religious sites, and of prime agricultural land. Areas of major importance to the advancement of scientific investigation, or ecosystems that are vulnerable to damage by human activities may be put out-of-bounds for development (e.g., the Antarctic continent, bioreserves, and national parks or monuments).

Nature, even in its most violent manifestations, becomes a problem only as people are, or may be, affected directly or even indirectly. Of course, there are scientific environmental problems that (as defined) may appear to have nothing to do with people. But indirectly and by implication even the most abstract scientific problems may lead to answers that affect the way in which people see the world. The so-called Copernican revolution in the perception of the solar system radically changed a paradigm that had prevailed in Western Europe for at least 1,000 years. Changing views of the way the world works may also lead to changes in human behavior.[12] A problem for the policymaker is the fact that people do not uniformly change their beliefs or behaviors. Environmental policies accordingly involve mediation and often compromise between differing values and differing interpretations of factual evidence.

Comprehending Environmental Problems

The logical consequence of seeing environmental problems as people problems is recognition of the difference in how people understand and evaluate environmental relationships. Any analysis or classification of environmental circumstances will invariably simplify reality. Conventional scientific findings alone may fail to influence the intensity, the scope, or the consistency of popular perceptions, and perceptual differences influence the politics, objectives, and methods of environmental policymaking. These influences are not only derived from peoples' view of their relationships to their environment, but are also joined to evaluations of the risks, the costs, benefits, and methods proposed for addressing a problem. The numbers of people concerned, the extent and accuracy of their information, and the intensity of their beliefs about policy alternatives are factors that may determine the political feasibility of policy choice.

To alter environmental circumstances, or to adapt to them, are especially problematic alternatives when responsive measures would redirect, limit, or prevent action preferred by politically influential groups or individuals. Conflicts in purpose and behavior lead to political conflicts and to dilemmas for policymakers. As a facetious example, a U.S. Secretary of the Interior sought to protect private enterprise in the production of chlorofluorocarbons (CFCs) by advising people to protect themselves from solar radiation, penetrating a thinning stratospheric ozone layer, by wearing sun glasses and increasing the use of sun lotion. But neither the public generally nor the scientific community accepted this alternative, and the United States signed and ratified a treaty to reduce and terminate the production and use of CFCs—chemicals that had extensive and profitable uses.[13]

There does appear to be a spectrum of opinion that within its range could indicate probable political choices among policy alternatives. Table 1.1 is a schematic of popular perceptions regarding environmental impairment that, however, should be viewed as subject to qualifications when applied to individuals. These empirical observations are not derived from scientific analysis, but may be as close to defining the variants of public opinion as any method is likely to attain.

Level I perceptions interpret environmental impairments as largely isolated phenomena, incidental but inevitable in the course of life. Environmental disruptions are seen as accidents, miscalculations, or consequences of human ignorance, indifference, irresponsibility, or neglect. Policy strategies are relatively few and not far-reaching. They include admonition, education, indoctrination, and a few legal sanctions such as anti-litter laws and prohibition of public nuisances (such as untended fires in the open, or noxious odors). Policy at Level I is essentially cautionary or cosmetic. Its concern is characteristically expressed through community cleanup and paintup campaigns, through planting trees, cultivating flower boxes, establishing and improving public streets and parks, and enforcing municipal safety and sanitary ordinances. These actions have been widely and traditionally accepted, and while important as civic policies, are largely incidental to basic environmental problems.

Level II perceptions similarly see environmental problems as largely inadvertent, caused by inadequate or inappropriate organization and management of economic and public affairs—notably in relation to technology. Governmental intervention to prohibit environment-impairing behaviors, standard-setting for effluent discharges and emissions, automobile emission controls, and land use

Table 1.1
Interpretations of Environmental Impairment

Perceived Causes	Explanations	Remedies
I. Incidental: harmful behaviors occurring in the normal course of human activities	Errors in judgment: dereliction, ignorance, carelessness, alcohol and drug abuse	Exhortation: ad hoc responses, cleanup campaigns, indoctrination, education, and penalties
II. Operational: misdirected policy, flawed program planning and execution, and bureaucratic intransigence	Ineffective management: insufficient or incorrect information, poor morale or operating procedures, avarice and corruption	Correction: improved procedures, impact assessments, independent review of proposals, standards, enforcement, and incentives
III. Systemic: impairment inherent in technology economic systems; unsustainable and exploitive economic practice	Built-in hazards: narrowly focused policies failing to assess full dimensions of environmental consequences; policies based on unwarranted assumptions	Reorientation: basic changes in beliefs and behavior systems; redesigning institutions and development of alternative technologies, elimination of harmful products and procedures

regulations exemplify activities at this level of perception and interpretation. This is the level at which most governmental and intergovernmental environmental policy is presently developed and administered. It is exemplified in the environmental resolutions of the U.N. conferences on the environment (notably Stockholm and Rio), in declarations by environmental protection organizations, in environmental directives of the Commission of the European Union, and in the environmental statutes of most modern governments.

International treaties and comparable agreements are negotiated largely at this level of perception, as, for example, conventions for prevention of oil pollution at sea, prohibition of international trade in endangered wildlife, and regulation of the transport of hazardous materials. The objective at this level is to rectify behavior without attempting to alter basic economic or societal institutional arrangements.

At Level III a break point is reached between conventional and radical interpretations of environmental dereliction, its causes and cures. Radical, in this context, does not imply customary left-of-center positioning. Radical, as used here, implies an effort to uncover the roots of environmental degradation, and seek to remedy basic causes. Level III marks the major division within the environmental movement between people who believe that action sufficient to achieve sustainable environmental conditions is possible within the present socioeconomic-technological order (socialist and capitalist), and those who identify this order as the ultimate cause of deteriorating environmental conditions.

Level III perception regards the attrition of environmental quality and the degradation of the biosphere as inherent in the assumptions, goals, and values of modern technological society and its growth oriented, economistic priorities. Remedial measures attempted by conservationists and preservationists as seen from the perspective of "deep ecology" are superficial and temporizing, ultimately to be overwhelmed by the combined pressures of population growth, indiscriminate economic development, and technological determinism.[14]

The denominator common to various Level III interpretations of humankind's environmental predicament is the systemic character of the problem.[15] Within the environmental movement there may be greater agreement that the modern industrial-technoeconomic order is inherently environmentally degrading, than agreement over what kind of system should replace it. Opinions range widely. Some few call for a one-world political order superseding national sovereignty. Environmental policy is seen as an essential element in a worldwide egalitarian redistribution of wealth, technology, and political power.[16] Still others perceive the ultimate possibility of an authoritarian world system of "iron governments" compensating for the inability of people, untutored, to avoid degradation of their environments through lack of restraint necessary to attain a sustainable economy.[17]

From a more pragmatic and conservative point of view, remedy is sought in progressive adaptation and innovation in institutional arrangements. The preferred approach to a transnational environmental problem from this perspective is a flexible, open-ended arrangement that encompasses the present diversity of nations in a common effort to deal with the problem with such modifications of national policies as are needed to coordinate effective protective measures. This preference allows for a worldwide transnational regime for critical global problems while retaining national sovereignty and administrative responsibility. But it is not evident how nations can proceed toward this object without curbing the population growth that drives growing demands upon a limited environment, without restraining excessive consumption of materials and resources, and without efforts adequate to discover new sources of food and renewable energy.

Progression of policy through these levels leads toward more intrusion into some personal preferences, lifestyles, and economic practices. The interposition of government in human behavior is positive for some people and negative for others. In this era of advancing information and communication technology, confirmed knowledge is an important ingredient of policymaking toward greater behavior control. For example, scientific epidemiological studies with statistical significance have led to restrictions on cigarette smoking that would not have been feasible 30 years ago. Similarly, many regulations affecting the manufacture and distribution of consumer products reflect findings of scientific investigation. Societal response is not necessarily political in intent, but it may be in effect. Voluntary changes in personal behavior may be induced by confirmed knowledge, yet not all claims of confirmation are accepted. Even among scientists, weight of evidence or of expert opinion has been rejected by a minority who deny the reality of stratospheric ozone depletion, the "greenhouse" global warming effect, the effects of acid rain, or the addictive properties of nicotine.

No fixed or firm line separates these levels of perception. Depending on the environmental problem, each of these interpretations or combinations of them may have validity. Moreover, policy response is not confined to action by government. The commercial market may be expected to adapt to public expectations if they are sufficient in scope and strength to affect economic transactions. Non-government volunteer organizations have increasingly become initiators of policies. In a information intensive society these initiatives, and the findings that support them, are widely disseminated and command the attention of perceptive public and corporate officials.[18] Scientific findings may initiate changes in beliefs, values, and behaviors that if systemic and pervasive, could reduce the need for governmental control.

Perceptions of the way the world works systematically form the paradigms that shape or influence the beliefs and behaviors of people regarding environmental relationships. The beliefs expressed and the objectives adopted by the 1992 U.N. Conference on Environment and Development (UNCED), and the degree of rhetorical acceptance by national delegates, may be taken as indicators of largely unpredicted worldwide perceptual change. But the extent to which the Rio commitments will be realized in political action is still unpredictable. Even so, well-founded efforts to foresee the possible consequences of considered action should be important elements of future policymaking.[19]

It should be added, however, that there are people who regard alleged environmental problems as unreal, or as surrogates for more far-reaching social change. Among humans there is a great capacity for denial to protect cherished myths and threatened interests. There is a level of perception at which environmental impairment is denied, is alleged to be exaggerated, or claimed to be self-corrective, either by market forces or by natural processes over time. Frequently, these negative assessments coincide with personal or group interests, usually economic or libertarian.

Political Difficulties in Environmental Policymaking

Given this range of perceptions, the question arises is policymaking for the environment more difficult than is policymaking in other areas—for example in education, health, criminal justice, or defense? Or are environmental problems no more difficult but merely different? No clear and ready answer is likely to be credible. All major policy areas have their own diverse problems and occasions for political conflict. Yet a case may be made that there are distinctive characteristics of environmental problems that make them difficult to resolve without raising other political issues in the process (e.g., human rights, property rights, economic growth). Based on the foregoing identification of the substrate of environmental problems, the case will be argued here that, as a policy area, the environment presents problems that are distinctive in complexity and ramification. These difficulties would be diminished were there a consensus on basic values consistent with the way the natural world works. But this is not the case. The dominant values in modern society are economic and egocentric, and their modification to protect environmental quality and sustainability has yet to be achieved.

Political problems in other areas may be as acute and divisive as any in the environment, but some may more often be resolved by policy decisions. Resolution is more likely where clear-cut yes-and-no decisions are possible and enforceable, and where value conflicts are not irreconcilable. Some environmental issues can be settled decisively—but too often perceived responsibility for the immediate problem is attacked, whereas the basic causal circumstances remain unexamined and persistent, frustrating future policy objectives.

A conspicuous case-in-point in the United States is the cleanup of dangerously contaminated sites under the Comprehensive Environmental Response, Compensation, and Liability Act, also known as "Superfund."[20] Legal complications in fixing liability absorb resources intended for remediation. Among policies that address symptoms but fail to deal effectively with causes are strict emission standards for automobiles offset by increasing numbers of motor vehicles on the highways. Regulations often restrain conditions from becoming worse but do not address the basic cause of the problem—namely, the increasing combustion of polluting fuels. The multiple-use mandate for federal public lands presents numerous cases where an ostensibly rational policy choice generates a large number of conflicting ecological, economic, recreational, equitable, and legal alternatives relating to the environment.[21]

There are at least six circumstantial factors in modern society that create problems for environmental policymaking. They are mind-sets or beliefs and behavioral or institutional expressions of belief that influence choice and environmental policymaking. Although not in themselves overtly political—that is, they are not, per se, political issues—they are nonetheless sources of difficulty in political decisionmaking and environmental policy choice. Internalized within the human mind, these perceptions are interconnecting and interacting in the choices that people make. The aggregate interactions of belief and behavior are expressed as cultural interpretations of natural phenomena. If in the mind-set of most people the natural world were perceived in an informed, prudent, and conserving manner, there would be relatively fewer environmental policy problems. Following is a summary of circumstantial factors that environmental policymakers must take into account. In each of these factors there are psychological and cultural predispositions that are seldom articulated in policy debate.

(1) Incompatible concepts of human relationships to the natural world expressed in conflicts between perceived facts and values. Differences in human attitudes toward environmental relationships are derived from religious beliefs, cosmologies, perceived economic interests, and especially from information ranging from scientific findings to culturally transmitted tradition (myth and folklore). Moreover, the mind-set of people is strongly influenced by their cultural and economic circumstances.

The experience of "modern" people has inclined them generally to an economistic or technocratic view of relationships with nature.[22] The concept of natural resources has displaced nature in a commercial technological society. Thus the conservation of natural resources has proceeded on assumptions unlike those that now dominate the environmental movement. An example would be belief in the necessity of endless growth.

Differing bases of judgment allow for the incompatibility of choices and the intensity of feelings that characterize many environmental disputes. Factual evidence alone may be inconclusive when subject to differing interpretations reflecting different values.[23] Familiar examples are logically incompatible differences over the "taking" of private land for public purposes, or alternatively over the generous leases or concessions to private interests in exploiting public lands for private advantage. Incompatible conclusions are especially intense in disputes over the relationship between population growth and its environmental impacts.

For some people a more fundamental and intractable value objection to modern environmentalism is faith in biblical Old Testament dominion theology—the belief that God instructed man to have dominion over nature and to subdue the earth.[24] Not all environmental policy measures are incompatible with this belief (e.g., doctrine of stewardship). Nevertheless, it can limit the scope and implementation of environmental policy.

Facts (including scientific facts) do not speak for themselves—someone always interprets the facts and may evaluate both their significance and ethical implications. Political decision-makers usually prefer factual simplicity—or the appearance of factual simplicity. Complex explanations strain the patience of the news media and the public that want simple, direct answers to political questions. Inquiring reporters to the contrary, most people do not want to be troubled with all of the facts, their relative weighting and evaluation.

(2) Multiple, complex, and interrelating elements in nature and their inadequate or erroneous perception by humans. A major reason for incompatible concepts of environmental relationships is the difficulty in identifying interconnecting and causal relationships among natural and man-made phenomena. We have already noted that there are politically significant differences in perceptions and values relating to nature. Perceptual differences have become more significant as modern society becomes more differentiated, more interdependent, and more specialized in occupations and interests. Science-based technology has vastly increased human ability to exploit and manipulate nature, while understanding the opportunities and risks involved has become correspondingly more important. The costs of error are greatly increased, and words like Chernobyl, Bhopal, Sandoz, Seveso, and Prince William Sound are symbolic of man-made environmental disasters brought about, in part, by failure to exercise prudence and to be guided by assessments of the risks involved in the exploitation of natural resources. They also have implications for national and international environmental policy.

(3) Sectoral subdivisions of knowledge. The discipline-oriented structure of education today makes little provision for understanding the widely acknowledged unity of science or of nature. The achievements of modern science have been essentially reductionist. A common mind-set in both academia and government—notably among some natural resource managers and physical scientists—suggests disinclination to conceptualize or implement a holistic or synthesizing approach to understanding nature or environmental relationships.

Depending upon their educational and occupational perspectives, people differ in their assessment of environmental phenomena. Experience alone does not always inform attitudes. Psychological fixation often narrows the choices that people make. Following natural disasters causing loss of life and property, people will often try to rebuild on flood plains, earthquake faults, and other demonstrably hazardous areas. Professional foresters historically have tended to see trees as crops to be culled and harvested. In the United States this tendency is exemplified by the placement of the Forest Service in the Department of Agriculture. Miners regard it as wrong to prohibit the extraction of minerals to meet the material needs of people and the economy because of alleged damage to the natural environment. Agricultural policy in most countries has sought to promote yields, with priority over other considerations (e.g., soil conservation and biological diversity).

A consequence of these narrow-focused views is that almost any professed policy for environmental enhancement or protection will be greeted by objections from groups whose economic or professional interests are adversely affected. Elective politicians often take up the causes of disaffected constituents and try to prevent or impede objectionable legislation, regardless of wider and longer-term benefits to society. The single-track perspective derived from educational and professional indoctrination is a factor that commonly causes an environmental problem to become a political problem when remedial solutions are proposed.

(4) Situations and motivations in environmental politics. The situations and motivations that influence the behaviors respectively of politicians, administrators, and environmental protectionists are factors basic to environmental policymaking. The mind-sets or predispositions that influence the choices made by environmental policymakers ought therefore to be ascertained in efforts to shape environmental policies. In addressing environmental problems it is safe to generalize that the incentives that motivate politicians, administrators, and protectionists are likely to be different.

The circumstances in which elective politicians are characteristically placed motivate their efforts to maximize the basis of their political security. This often leads them to seek compromise among contending interests. When these interests have differing—even incompatible—measures of value, the basis for compromise may be difficult to find. For some, environmental policy objectives (e.g., protection of endangered species and ecosystems) make it so that no real compromise may be possible. A typical political strategy to keep control of an environmental issue is to try to satisfy the protectionist with rhetoric and implied (but not specific) promises. Meanwhile, economic, technocratic, and bureaucratic interests may be pacified with quiet concessions.

The motivations of administrative professionals are normally consistent with the assumptions and values inculcated by their profession. When government is faced with changing public expectations, or when policy preference is inconsistent with professional canons, political controversy is likely to result. During the decades since 1950, government agencies and programs relating to natural resources and the environment have become focal points of policy conflict. Faced with conflicting expectations and demands derived from incompatible assumptions, administrators with responsibilities for environmental policymaking must cope with problems that seldom have technical solutions.

Outside of formal government the principal actors in environmental politics are organized economic and professional interests and volunteer membership organizations. Paradoxically, the motivations that are the political strength of non-governmental environmental organizations are often also their policy weaknesses. Their political influence and financial support depend largely on voluntary dues-paying members. This circumstance causes these organizations to focus on events that arouse their constituents—and these tend to be immediate or approaching threats to some specific aspect of the environment. Urgent appeals to save this endangered species or to stop that dam are more productive of popular support than are broader issues of environmental policy. Thus the environmental protectionists tend to fight "brush fires" in preference to more fundamental legislative and constitutional measures that would prevent or reduce the "brush fires" but probably would not arouse their clientele and would alarm and consolidate opposing interests.

(5) A governmental structure for policy and administration that serves and perpetuates a fractionated approach to environmental problems. The administrative structure of government in the United States (and largely elsewhere) reflects a special interest (and often obsolete) approach to public policy. The federal departments of Agriculture, Commerce, Labor, Interior, and many departments in state governments were created with a view to serving the interests of those groups in society that promoted their establishment. Each agency has its own legislation, structure, and definition of mission. Often these client-structured agencies have been at cross-purposes with one another in their policies regarding the implementation of environmental objectives.

Resolution of these bureaucratic conflicts has never been easy nor wholly successful. Many of the agencies owe their first allegiance to the committees of the Congress that authorized their establishment and appropriate their funds. The legislative record shows very little interest in holistic approaches to policy of any kind. The structure of the Congress and of the executive branch makes policy reconciliation or synthesis difficult to achieve and unrewarding to most legislators or administrators who might attempt to pursue structural reform. Only at the presidential level would there be any credible prospect of harmonizing and reconciling agency policies—notably those pertaining to the environment. The National Environmental Policy Act of 1969 established criteria for policies affecting the environment and created a Council on Environmental Quality in the Executive Office of the President to oversee implementation of this legislation. But this quasi-independent council lacked presidential support and numerous White House advisors sought its abolition. A succession of presidents since Franklin D. Roosevelt has sought reorganization of the administrative structure of the executive branch at the "cabinet" level, but to little effect. Organized economic interests have succeeded in defeating changes that would lessen their ability to influence the policies of the agencies that they see as their official representatives.

(6) The internationalization of environmental policy. There is another aspect of governmental structure in which environmental issues become problems for policy. These are transnational issues which, to be addressed effectively, may require reconsideration of the doctrine of national sovereignty, and recognition of extraterritorial agreements as sources for public laws. A long-established principal of international law holds that treaty commitments ratified by national governments should be honored by implementation (pacta sunt servanda). Since establishment of the United Nations in 1945, international intergovernmental organizations have increasingly become sources of international law. The influence of international intergovernmental organizations has often been indirect, but they have frequently provided forums in which international treaties are negotiated. The U.N. Conference on the Law of the Sea is an example. Treaties were also outcomes of the 1972 Conference on the Human Environment and the 1992 Conference on Environment and Development. Resolutions of the U.N. General Assembly, reports of the International Law Commission, and opinions of the World Court have influenced the enactment of national legislation as have findings or proposals of U.N. Specialized Agencies.[25]

Under Article IV of the Constitution of the United States, consummated treaties become "the supreme law of the land." In other nation-states the status of treaties in national law is similar. National legislation may be required, however, to implement treaty provisions. Historically, treaties have covered a wide range of issues (e.g., commercial, maritime, military, jurisdictional). Environmental agreements and notably those requiring worldwide adherence have added a further dimension to international law (e.g., law of the sea, climate change, ozone layer). It is now hardly an exaggeration to speak of legislation by treaty. National legislators may be confronted with a problem of policy when required to ratify or to implement a transnational agreement that many of their constituents have not requested and do not understand. Transnational agreements may expand or restrain international law and policy. The need for policy responses to transnational issues—environmental among others—now occurs with a frequency that may be described as a trend. Problems of reconciling national policies with international agreements are exacerbated when international commitments and national policies conflict or have potential to conflict. In the United States political disputes have arisen over the effect of the General Agreement on Tariffs and Trade (GATT) and the North American Free Trade Agreement (NAFTA) on the nation's environmental laws.

Beyond the "hard" international law of binding treaties there is a "soft" law of international declarations, resolutions, and reports.[26] The sources of this soft law are usually international conferences, statements issued after meetings by high-level public officials (e.g., heads of state and environmental ministers), recommendations of scientific bodies, and resolutions by international non-governmental organizations. These expressions are intended to influence policy and, although they may not have an official character, may nevertheless help shape the agendas of national governments. They may be harbingers of new policies and agreements. At the same time, multinational economic interests act to influence policy, often to restrain or deflect national and international environmental policies that would restrict their opportunities or increase their costs or liabilities.

(7) The perception of time. The time factor is too often overlooked in efforts to ascertain existing predispositions toward policy choices. Especially in periods of rapid change adding uncertainties for the future, there is a tendency to deal with issues on a here-and-now basis. There are expectations that the future will be "different"—but its shape uncertain. Moreover, opportunities for reform in government and business fall within time periods limited by law or by circumstance, and many a proposal for organizational change has been lost in the adjournment of a congress, the expiration of a budget authorization, or the end of a presidential term.

Time is measured by differing periodicities. Lifetime is the measure of greatest concern to most people. Shorter intervals of time are measured by fiscal years, terms of appointment or election, budget cycles, contract obligations, and target dates for various projects. Environmental policy issues (e.g., climate modification, soil depletion, or demographic change) are complicated by the fact that their effects tend to be transgenerational, not felt at the time when responsive policies should be adopted if they are to be effective. Response to many environmental problems requires a long view into the future whereas political policy tends to focus on here and now.

Scientific findings are now influencing time-horizons to a somewhat greater extent than heretofore. Yet there are many areas of scientific inquiry where concern for long-term consequences of present policies is discouraged, regarded as premature, or unsuitable for scientific research. Issues in agriculture, demography, climate change, and genetics are among those subject to resistance or denial by influential sectors of society. Persons who put faith in self-evident truths are likely to regard scientific inquiry into their beliefs as unwarranted, irrelevant, and unnecessary. But, depending on its focus, science-based technology has both condensed and extended time-horizons. Time can now be understood in many dimensions, and a task of policy is to apply the measure of time that is appropriate to the environmental circumstance—from the most minute to the most extended intervals.[27]

CONCLUSION

Among the conclusions deduced from this analysis of the problematic nature of environmental policymaking are these.

First, and most obviously, environmental problems are created by the interactions of people with the natural systems of which they are a part. Natural phenomena may result in environmental problems for people because of where they are or what they are doing. An avalanche, earthquake, flood, or volcano is not in itself a problem. It becomes one only when people are involved. Thus environmental problems are people problems.

Second, many but not all environmental problems may be avoided or mitigated by informed, prudent policy and timely action. But cultural bias and perceived self-interest often cause preventive or remedial measures to be rejected or evaded. If they believe it is in their own self-interest, organized special interests will pressure government to implement legislation regardless of adverse environmental consequences.

Third, future-oriented policies that restrain current ambitions or expectations may be politically hazardous to their sponsors. In a political system in which money can be dispensed by organized economic interests to elect their advocates and defeat their adversaries there is an obvious incentive to refrain from biting the hand that feeds.

Fourth, it follows from the foregoing conclusions that problems of the environment are neither wholly technical nor scientific. They may be explained or clarified by science, but are primarily problems of human concept, purpose, and behavior. Technical measures may be employed in avoidance or mitigation. But choice in their selection depends on information, will, rationality, and popular acceptance. The diversity of perceptions, expectations, and values in the world today limits the chances of finding a common denominator on which to build popular consensus.

Fifth, the implications of these conclusions suggest changes in the substance and organization of education at all levels of learning. These changes should not jeopardize specialization nor the focused missions of the disciplines. But they do involve provision for meta-disciplinary concepts of science and the environment, along with a synthesis of related knowledge for a more comprehensive and coherent understanding of the place of mankind in the natural world. Science is needed to identify the limits as well as the opportunities inherent in nature. What is learned in colleges and universities, in the common schools, in the news and information media, in the community, and in religion will ultimately affect public opinion and the choices made by public decision-makers.

It may not be an exaggeration to say that the survival of postmodern society may depend upon public leadership toward a fundamental societal change in belief regarding the requisites for a sustainable future for human life on earth. Misinformed and misdirected conservatism may destroy the conditions that it wished to conserve. Changes in the environment and in knowledge (especially in the area of technology) continue to exceed public understanding of their implications. Our policies and institutions have been based, to a large extent, upon assumptions and objectives that cannot be sustained indefinitely. Events may coerce society into a more adaptive response to changes for which it is responsible. But this remains to be seen.

NOTES

1. *Environmental Encyclopedia*, edited by William P. Cunningham et al. (Detroit, MI: Gale Research International, 1994); *The Encyclopedia of the Environment,* edited by Ruth A. Eblen and William Eblen (Boston: Houghton Mifflin, 1994); *The Environment Encyclopedia and Directory,* no editor given (London: Europa Publications, 1994); and *Conservation and Environmentalism: An Encyclopedia,* edited by Robert Paehlke (New York: Garland, 1995).

2. Stuart Nagel, *Public Policy: Goals, Means, and Methods* (New York: St. Martin's Press, 1984).

3. There are numerous publications addressing this theme, see, for example, Barbara Ward and Rene Dubos, *Only One Earth, the Care and Maintenance of a Small Planet* (New York: Norton, 1972).

4. Clarence Glacken, *Traces on the Rhodian Shore: Nature and Culture in Western Thought from Ancient Times to the End of the Eighteenth Century* (Berkeley: University of California Press, 1967). See also Arnold Toynbee, *Mankind and Mother Earth* (Oxford: Oxford University Press, 1976).

5. Rosemary Radford Ruether, *Gaia and God: An Ecofeminist Theology of Earth Healing* (San Francisco: Harper, 1992).

6. Gilbert F. White and J. Eugene Haas, *Assessment of Research on Natural Disasters* (Cambridge MA: MIT Press, 1975).

7. Karl A. Wittfogel, *Oriental Despotism: A Comparative Study of Total Power* (New Haven, CT: Yale University Press, 1957). Wittfogel may have over-extended his thesis. Communitarian control of irrigation has also developed. Even so, centralized authoritarian control has characterized large-scale hydraulic systems. Factors of scale and culture may be involved. See Julian Haynes Stewart, ed., *Irrigation Civilizations: A Comparative Study* . . . (Washington, DC: Pan American Union, Social Science Section, 1955).

8. Nancy H. Demand, *Urban Relocation in Archaic and Classical Greece: Flight and Consolidation* (Norman, OK: University of Oklahoma Press 1990).

9. [Marcus] *Vitruvius—The Ten Books on Architecture,* translated by Morris Hicky Morgan (Cambridge, MA: Harvard University Press, 1914), 21.

10. The costs of working against nature are set out by Earl Finbar Murphy in *Man and His Environment: Law* (New York: Harper & Row, 1971).

11. A response by the Congress of the United States was creation of the Office of Technological Assessment by the Technology Assessment Act of 1972–86.5 SAT. 797. But this agency was unfunded by the 104 Congress in 1995.

12. Thomas Kuhn, *The Structure of Scientific Revolutions* (Chicago: University of Chicago Press, 1962); Lynton K. Caldwell, *Between Two Worlds: Science, the Environmental Movement and Policy Choice* (Cambridge: Cambridge University Press, 1992); Willis Harman, *Global Mind Changes: The Promise of the Last Years of the Twentieth Century* (Indianapolis, IN: Knowledge Systems, Inc., 1988).

13. Richard E. Benedick, *Ozone Diplomacy: New Directions in Safeguarding the Planet* (Cambridge, MA: Harvard University Press 1991).

14. B. Devall and G. Sessions, *Deep Ecology* (Salt Lake City: G.M. Smith, 1985); and Jacques Ellul, *The Technological Society* (New York: Knopf, 1964).

15. For systemic analyses of disasters see Charles Perrow, *Normal Accidents: Living with High-Risk Technology* (New York: Basic Books, 1984). See also Gilbert F. White, *Natural Disaster: Local, National, Global* (New York: Oxford University Press, 1974); and J. Eugene Haas, Robert W. Kates, and Mortyn J. Bowden, *Reconstruction Following*

Disaster (Cambridge, MA: MIT Press, 1977). For a more recent analysis, see Edward Tenner, *Why Things Bite Back: Technology and the Revenge of Unintended Consequences* (New York: Knopf, 1964).

16. Richard Falk, *This Endangered Planet: Prospects and Proposals for Human Survival* (New York: Random House, 1971).

17. Robert L. Heilbroner, *An Inquiry into the Human Prospect: Updated and Reconsidered for the 1980s* (New York: Norton, 1980).

18. Aaron Katz, "Toward High Information-Level Culture," *Cybernetica*, 7(3), 201–43 (1965).

19. Lindsey Grant, *Foresight and Decisions: The Horseman and Bureaucrat* (Lanham, MD: University Press of America, 1988).

20. Don J. DeBenedictis, "How Superfund Money is Spent," *American Bar Association Journal*,78 (September 1992), 30. See also Thomas Church and Robert Nakamura, *Cleaning Up the Mess* (Washington, DC: The Brookings Institution, 1993); and Daniel Mazmanian and David Morell, *Beyond Superfailure* (Boulder, CO: Westview Press, 1992) for analyses of Superfund.

21. See Michael D. Bowls and John V. Krutilla, *Multiple-Use Management: The Economics of Public Forest Lands* (Washington DC: Resources for the Future, 1989). See also George C. Coggins, "Of Succotash and Vacuous Platitudes: The Meaning of 'Multiple Use, Sustained Yield' for Public Land Management," *University of Colorado Law Review*, 53 (1981), 229–80; and Michael Blumm,"Public Choice Theory and the Public Lands: Why 'Multiple Use' Failed," *Harvard Environmental Law Review*,18 (1994), 405–32.

22. Nicholas Berdyeav, *The Fate of Man in the Modern World*, translated by Donald A. Lowrie (London: Student Christian Movement Press, 1935), 78–9. "Economism" ascribes a primacy of economic processes and development over all other values.

23. Giandomenico Majone, *Evidence, Argument and Persuasion in the Policy Process* (New Haven, CT: Yale University Press 1989), 8.

24. Harvey Cox, "The Warring Visions of the Religious Right," *Atlantic Monthly*, 276, (5) (November 1995), 59–69.

25. The role of treaties and other agreements in national and international environmental policy is extensively documented in Lynton K. Caldwell, *International Environmental Policy: From the 20th to 21st Century*, 3d ed. (Durham, NC: Duke University Press, 1996). See also Philippe Sands, ed., *Greening International Law* (London: Earthscan, 1993).

26. W. E. Burhenne et al., *International Environmental Soft Law* (Boston, MA and Dordrecht, Netherlands: Martinus Nijhoff, 1995). (Published under the auspices of the International Council of Environmental Law.)

27. There is a substantial literature on time and humanity. Time and change have greater significance than our commonsensical notions perceive. See Julius T. Fraeser, *Time, the Familiar Stranger* (Amherst, MA: University of Massachusetts Press, 1987).

2

PROGRESSIVE RATCHETING OF ENVIRONMENTAL LAW: IMPLICATIONS FOR PUBLIC MANAGEMENT

Rosemary O'Leary and Tae Joon Lah

One of the problem-making tendencies in environmental policymaking has been an incremental approach to regulation and control. Either because the full dimensions of an environmental problem are not perceived or because political resistance compels step-by-step action, environmental controls tend to be applied progressively, beginning with nominal, largely ineffectual, retroactive declarations. Following failure to attain their objectives, laws are toughened and extended year by year until the severity of their sanctions begins to defeat their intended effects. The fractionated state of environmental law, focused on specific problems of pollution and subject to changes in interpretation, have made observance and enforcement difficult. The National Environmental Policy Act of 1969 could assist a unification of environmental policy; unfortunately, presidents and congresses have not chosen to use it to this purpose. Meanwhile, because environmental protection per se is relatively new to public law and policy, and has few roots in the common law, private citizens aggrieved by political obstruction of their expectation have appealed to the courts for relief and compensation. Conservative courts have granted this relief under the "taking" clause of the Constitution. Extraordinary measures in constitutional law may be necessary to resolve an impasse in public policy resulting from conflict between public interests and private rights as interpreted by the judiciary.

Environmental laws pervade every area of our society. They affect the air we breathe, the water we drink, and the food we eat. Increasingly, environmental laws have come to pervade many areas of public management. Examples of affected functions include the purchase of land, the operation of schools, wastewater collection and treatment, refuse disposal, the operation of hospitals, land use planning, road maintenance, water supply and delivery, the operation of parks, and the operation of airports. This "ratcheting" of environmental laws is prompting nothing less than a fundamental change in public administration around the world and is likely to affect future generations for years to come.

This chapter focuses on the progressive ratcheting of environmental laws and the impacts of these laws on U.S. public management in three areas: clean water, regulatory takings, and hazardous waste cleanup. (For the purposes of this chapter, ratcheting is defined as "to raise to progressively higher levels" [*Webster's*, 1991].) A comparison with the emerging European experience in hazardous waste is offered.

The dominance of environmental laws that is the subject of this chapter has not always been the case. The first 120 years of government within the United States saw no major environmental legislation (Advisory Commission on Intergovernmental Relations, 1981). The first major U.S. environmental law, the Refuse Act, was promulgated in 1899 as a means of keeping navigable waters clear of refuse that might block ships. Nearly fifty years later, the second major environmental statute, the Water Pollution Control Act (WPCA) of 1948, became law. The 1950s brought the enactment of two more important environmental laws: the Air Pollution Control Act of 1955 and the 1956 amendments to the WPCA.

Beginning in the 1960s, the situation started to change as the tide of environmental laws began to swell. Eleven major federal environmental laws were enacted in the 1960s, while seventeen were enacted in the 1970s. By the 1980s, the tide had turned into a flood as an amazing forty-eight environmental bills became law. In 1990, Congress passed significant amendments to the Clean Air Act, as well as amendments to the Clean Water Act. As of the writing of this chapter, major changes in the Clean Water Act, the Safe Drinking Water Act, the Superfund Act, and the Resource Conservation and Recovery Act were being considered by Congress.

Examining the dramatic rise in federal environmental laws in the United States, one author wrote:

What we see looking back is that pollution control is a new subject . . . of law. All have been freshly invented. A large and very complex system has been built over the past 20 years, its separate parts built separately and sometimes without much awareness of the whole structure. (Novick, 1986)

Most environmental laws have brought increased responsibilities to the 83,000 state and local governments that comprise the United States. Increasingly, the duty to implement these laws is falling on state and local governments in what some call "the shift and the shaft": Environmental responsibility is shifted downward without the needed funds to implement the programs the laws mandate.

As responsibilities have shifted downward, environmental laws have been ratcheted "upward," presenting increased demands in the area of environmental compliance for all government entities. In the area of clean water, where municipalities have become mini-water pollution control agencies, the ratcheting occurred in amendments to the Clean Water Act, in court decisions interpreting that statute, and in regulations promulgated by the U.S. Environmental Protection Agency (EPA). In the case of hazardous waste cleanup, the original ratcheting occurred in the statute designed by Congress, but subsequent judicial decisions ratcheted the requirements and the punishments for violating those requirements even higher. In the case of regulatory takings, which is essentially a constitutional question, the ratcheting has taken place primarily in federal courts.

In Europe, there are no identical matches to U.S. law in the areas of municipal liability for water protection or regulatory takings. The closest match is the emerging hazardous waste law in the European Union (E.U.). For reasons discussed below, however, the proposed E.U. hazardous waste scheme probably will not yield public management challenges as stringent as those experienced by U.S. public managers today. Let us now examine three cases of the progressive ratcheting of environmental laws and the concomitant impact on public management.

CASE ONE: THE MUNICIPALITY AS MINI-WATER POLLUTION CONTROL AGENCY

An area of environmental law that affects hundreds of public administrators concerns increasing responsibilities of municipalities under the Clean Water Act. In the past, municipalities needed only to be concerned about their own water pollution. Today, these local government entities have become mini-water pollution control agencies. As such, they are responsible not only for their own wastes, but must control industrial discharges to all publicly owned treatment works (POTWs) and prohibit illegal discharges into separate municipal storm sewer systems.

Pursuant to the Clean Water Act, municipalities that discharge wastewater from POTWs must apply for and adhere to a National Pollutant Discharge Elimination System (NPDES) permit. In order to obtain such a permit, large-municipality POTWs—defined as those that treat more than five million gallons per day—must agree to accept and implement a number of new responsibilities, including identifying and educating industrial users about all pertinent regulations, inspecting industrial users and monitoring their actions, investigating industrial users' violations of pretreatment standards, and prosecuting any violations by industrial users [40 CFR sections 403.8(f) and 403.9(b)(1990)].

Moreover, for years there had been virtually no regulation of stormwater management under the Clean Water Act. Congressional action in 1987, coupled with a series of court cases filed by the Natural Resources Defense Council (see *Natural Resources Defense Council* v. *Costle*, 1977; *Natural Resources Defense Council* v. *United States Environmental Protection Agency*, 1992; *Natural Resources Defense Council* v. *United States Environmental Protection Agency*, 1995), have further ratcheted stormwater management requirements. For example, under current storm sewer laws, municipalities with large separate storm sewer systems (defined as serving a population of 250,000 or more) or medium separate storm sewer systems (defined as serving a population of 100,000 or more but less than 250,000) must, again, apply for and comply with a NPDES permit for stormwater discharges from the system. One condition of such a permit is the control of discharges into the storm sewer system. Other conditions include writing a stormwater quality plan, identifying and listing all potential industrial stormwater dischargers, inspecting and monitoring all discharges into the storm sewer system, prosecuting any violations, and analyzing how all of this will be paid for [40 CFR section 122.26(d)]. These new requirements affect 225 cities and counties plus 100,000 industrial dischargers. Smaller municipalities are targeted in phase two of these requirements, but as of the writing of this chapter, proposals were being discussed that would ease the regulatory burden on smaller communities, either through congressional legislation or through EPA regulations ("Fix for Phase II," 1995).

Furthermore, Congress and the EPA have increased the likelihood that a municipality will be sued for noncompliance with such laws. First, the EPA, states, and citizens may all file suits against a municipality for noncompliance with the Clean Water Act. Hence, an action may come from several sources. Second, action can be brought against a municipality not only for noncompliance with the letter of the law, but for not enforcing the law as stringently as the EPA or the state thinks it should be enforced. This subjective call may be made after the fact with little guidance given to the municipality that might prevent such problems.

If a municipality acting as a water pollution control agency is the subject of an enforcement action, sanctions range from a phone call for minor violations to three years in prison and fines of $50,000 per day for criminal violations (33 U.S.C. 1319). Typically, a municipality will agree to take certain actions to remedy the problems and to prevent them from recurring. Ordered actions under the Clean Water Act may include the municipality filing suit against an industrial violator, meeting deadlines for the compliance of all who discharge into the POTW, or shutting down the violating industry.

The potential impacts on public management of such ratcheting provisions are great. First, performing the tasks of a water pollution control agency can be costly and resource intensive, depending on the size of the municipality and the environmental challenges facing it. In many instances, new ordinances must be passed giving the local government the necessary legal enforcement powers. Such efforts initially require legal expertise and, later, the efforts of engineers, inspectors, and additional clerical staff. Many times, costly infrastructure improvements are needed. In one study, for example, the deputy director of the Sacramento, California Department of Public Works concluded that it would cost that city two billion dollars to implement the "best method of compliance" with the newly ratcheted stormwater management requirements ("Numerical Effluent Limits," 1991). In another instance, the state of Wisconsin, prepared to process only 5,000 industrial permit applications, received 17,000 (Rubin et al., 1992). In yet a third instance, the state of Virginia announced that it could not comply with the law because of budget cuts (Rubin et al., 1992).

Second, by imposing more and more demands upon municipalities, Congress and the EPA reduce citizen discretion and managers' options. As local choices narrow and mandates grow, the chances of taking action that might prompt lawsuits increase. This creates a difficult environment in which to work, especially where local government managers are judged by "20/20 hindsight."

Finally, should a municipality be found liable for violating the Clean Water Act, monetary penalties may be more than city coffers will bear. Special taxes or fees may be needed to support such sanctions. Other local government programs may need to be terminated in order to pay the required penalties. "The federal government is forcing local governments to spend money on a problem that may not stack up priority-wise," said the executive director of the urban drainage and flood control district in Denver (Rubin et al., 1992). The superintendent of Shreveport, Louisiana, summed up this difficulty by pointing out that his city had problems getting funding from the taxpayers for important crime programs. "Imagine what they'd say if we . . . [asked for] a tax on rain," he said ("Numerical Effluent Limits," 1991).

These requirements have been the subject of recently proposed congressional legislation that would amend the Clean Water Act. As of the writing of this chapter, however, no bill had passed both the House and the Senate and at least one Washington insider had commented that a Clean Water Act rewrite was one of two environmental measures with the "worst chances" of being passed during the 104th Congress ("Senate Approach," 1995). Clearly the development of the municipality as a mini-water pollution control agency has immense implications for public management.

The Clean Water Act is not the only area where there has been a significant ratcheting of environmental laws with an impact on public management. Let us now examine a second area of intense ratcheting, this time by the courts: regulatory takings.

CASE TWO: LIABILITY FOR REGULATORY TAKINGS

Another important example of the ratcheting of environmental laws that affects many public functions is liability for regulatory takings. The idea of regulatory takings is not a new one. The Fifth Amendment of the Constitution clearly states that private property shall not be taken for public use without just compensation. In 1922, U.S. Supreme Court Justice Oliver Wendell Holmes wrote, "while property may be regulated to a certain extent, if regulation goes too far it will be recognized as a taking" (*Pennsylvania Coal Co.* v. *Mahon*, 1922). What is new is the use of the concept of regulatory takings in actions where a government entity has been enforcing an environmental law. Through a series of court decisions, government liability for regulatory takings has been ratcheted to a new high. Another way of examining this issue is to look at liability for regulatory takings as a way of discouraging the progressive ratcheting of environmental laws by punishing those who implement those laws.

In deciding whether there has been a regulatory taking without just compensation, the courts examine two aspects of a case. First, the courts look at whether the government regulation at issue fails to substantially advance a legitimate governmental interest. Second, the courts look at whether the implementation of the government regulation deprives the owner of all economically viable uses of the land. Consider the following cases:

- In 1991, a federal court of appeals held that the mere passage of the Surface Mining Control and Reclamation Act of 1977 effected a regulatory taking without just compensation of property owned by the Whitney Benefits company. The passage of the act, the court reasoned, prevented the mining of hundreds of acres containing coal and thus deprived the mining company of all economic use of its property, even though no mining permit had been applied for by the company. The court ordered the U.S. government to pay the company $60,296,000, plus prejudgment interest from August 3, 1977 (*Whitney Benefits* v. *United States*, 1991).
- In a case decided the year before, a court found that the residential and commercial development of 12.5 acres on Long Beach Island, New Jersey, was prevented by the enactment of the New Jersey Wetlands Act and certain wetlands provisions of the federal Clean Water Act. Finding that such action was a regulatory taking without just compensation, the court ordered the U.S. government to pay the developer $2,658,000 plus interest from the date of the taking, May 5, 1982 (*Loveladies Harbor, Inc.* v. *United States*, 1990).
- In a third case, a court found that the denial of a permit by the U.S. Army Corps of Engineers to Florida Rock Industries to mine ninety-eight acres protected under the Clean Water Act constituted a regulatory taking without just compensation. The court reasoned that the denial of the permit deprived Florida Rock Industries of all economically viable uses of its land. The federal government was ordered to pay $1,029,000 plus interest from the date of the taking, October 2, 1980 (*Florida Rock Industries, Inc.,* v. *United States*, 1990).
- On June 29, 1992, the U.S. Supreme Court announced its decision in the case of *Lucas* v. *South Carolina Coastal Council* (1992), in which the pivotal issue was whether the implementation of the South Carolina Beachfront Management Act (1989) was a regulatory taking of property. While narrowly drafted, the decision has implications for the future of public administration, especially in the areas of budgeting and finance.

In 1986, David H. Lucas, the petitioner, purchased two vacant oceanfront lots on the Isle of Palms in Charleston County, South Carolina, for $975,000 with the intention of building single-family residences. In 1988, the South Carolina Legislature enacted the Beachfront Management Act, which had the effect of prohibiting the construction of any permanent structure, including a dwelling and excepting a small deck or walkway, on the Lucas property. Lucas filed suit in the Court of Common Pleas, asserting that the restrictions on the use of his lots amounted to a taking of his property without just compensation. The lower court agreed with Lucas, maintaining that the state act rendered the land "valueless," and awarded him the amount of $1,232,387.50 as just compensation for the regulatory taking. Upon appeal, the Supreme Court of South Carolina reversed the lower court's decision, maintaining that the regulation under attack prevented a use seriously harming the public, and so no regulatory taking occurred (*Lucas* v. *South Carolina Coastal Council*, 1991).

In a six-to-three decision, the U.S. Supreme Court reversed the holding of South Carolina's highest court and remanded the case for further action. In its decision, the U.S.

Supreme Court articulated several pivotal principles. First, it emphasized that regulations denying a property owner of all "economically viable use of his land" will require compensation without inquiry into the public interest being advanced in support of the restraint. Next, the court said that the fact that a regulation addresses or prevents a "harmful or noxious use" cannot be used to negate the rule that total regulatory takings must be compensated by government entities.

Finally, the U.S. Supreme Court threw back the issue of whether a taking occurred in this specific instance to the South Carolina courts. The court maintained that the lower courts must examine citizens' historic understandings regarding the content of the state's power over the "bundle of rights" they acquired when they took title to the property in question. The pivotal question, then, became whether the restrictions in a state regulation merely explicate what already inheres in the property title, or whether the state regulations are subsequent decisions that eliminate all economically beneficial uses of the property. On remand, Lucas was awarded full value for the taking of his property.

- A recent case provides an even greater opportunity for property owners to access the federal courts to seek compensation for regulatory takings. In *Dolan* v. *Tigard* (1994), the owner of a plumbing and electrical supply store, Dolan, applied to the city of Tigard for a permit to redevelop the site to expand the size of the store and to pave the parking lot. The city, pursuant to a state-required land-use program, had adopted a comprehensive plan, a plan for pedestrian/bicycle pathways, and a Master Drainage Plan. The city planning commission conditioned the granting of the permit with the requirements that Dolan dedicate (convey title) to the portion of her property lying within the 100-year floodplain for improvement of a storm drainage system and that she dedicate an additional 15-foot strip of land adjacent to the floodplain as a pedestrian/bicycle pathway. The Planning Commission declared that the required floodplain dedication would be reasonably related to the owner's request to intensify use of the site given the increase in impervious surface, and that the creation of the pedestrian/bicycle pathway system as an alternative means of transportation would lessen the forecasted increase in traffic congestion.

The Court sought in its analysis to determine whether the degree of the exactions demanded by the city's permit conditions bore the required relationship to the projected impact of the store owner's proposed development. After reviewing various doctrines that state courts had used to guide such analyses, the Court enunciated its own test of "rough proportionality," and stated, "no precise mathematical calculation is required, but the city must make some sort of individualized determination that the required dedication is related both in nature and extent to the impact of the proposed development." The Court decided that the city had not made any individualized determination to support its requirement that the land be transferred to the city (rather than set aside as greenspace while Dolan retained ownership), and concluded that the findings that the city had made did not show the required reasonable relationship between the floodplain easement and the owner's proposed new building. The Court also decided that the city had not met its burden of demonstrating that the additional number of vehicle and bicycle trips generated by the store expansion reasonably related to the city's requirement for a dedication of the pedestrian/bicycle pathway easement. The Court said that the city must make some effort to quantify its findings in support of the dedication for the pedestrian/bicycle pathway beyond the conclusionary statement that it could offset some of the traffic demand generated.

Dissenting Justices accused the Court's majority of proposing that "the federal judiciary micromanage state decisions of this kind," and predicted that the Court was "extending its welcome mat to a significant new class of litigants." The Court's decision places a responsibility on state and local regulators to provide more detailed analyses to support their determinations. It will also most likely be followed by additional litigation as the lower federal courts hear challenges to regulatory requirements that disappointed property owners claim do not meet the test of "rough proportionality." The lower federal courts will become more involved players in defining what kinds of evidence they expect to see from state and local regulators before agreeing that the test is met.

At one time more than 200 takings cases were pending in the court of claims (O'Leary, 1992); the number is growing. It is estimated that many of these concern environmental and natural resources regulations. Other statutes affected to date include the Clean Water Act, the Endangered Species Act, and the Wilderness Act. The surge of such cases in recent years has many speculating on the effects of such a trend. Environmental groups charge that the holdings of these cases may destroy years of hard-fought incremental progress in protecting the environment. Some government regulators agree, adding that the trend could devastate already ailing government budgets, especially if proposed federal legislation is enacted that would require the payment of such judgments directly out of the coffers of the federal agencies that promulgated the regulations in question. Affected land owners argue that this development is merely just compensation for years of losses triggered by environmental regulations and is no different than being reimbursed for the taking of property to be used for roads and parks.

The major public administration implications of liability for regulatory takings are twofold. First, because takings law is still developing and takings determinations are made on a case-by-case basis, it is difficult for public administrators to act proactively to minimize the chances of such suits. In most of these instances the government acted legitimately to preserve the general environment. It would have been difficult, and in some instances impossible, to predict the ensuing effects of the environmental laws on many specific properties as well as the reaction of the courts. Second, the fiscal implications of this trend obviously are quite grave. While the mere promulgation of a regulation is not enough to trigger regulatory takings liability (since the property must be shown to have been affected), the issue of who will pay for such takings is an important one that will not go away. Clearly, the regulatory takings trend has the potential of changing public administration as we know it today.

CASE THREE: HAZARDOUS WASTE CLEANUP

On October 21, 1976, Congress enacted the Resource Conservation and Recovery Act (RCRA), substantially amending the Solid Waste Disposal Act. In the ensuing eight years, RCRA was amended ten times. With each amendment, the requirements of the act, as well as the liabilities for noncompliance, were intensified. The Comprehensive Environmental Response, Compensation, and Liability Act (CERCLA, also known as Superfund) was enacted in 1980 to address hazardous waste issues not covered by RCRA. CERCLA established a "Super-fund" to enable the federal government to clean up hazardous waste disposal sites. It ratcheted liability for hazardous waste site cleanup by expanding the class of private parties who may be held liable, including site owners and operators, waste transporters, and generators.

Government organizations are increasingly being held liable under federal laws for hazardous waste cleanup costs, primarily because of their roles as generators or transporters of hazardous waste or as owners/operators of facilities that receive hazardous wastes. Cleanup costs have reached well into the millions of dollars. Even if not a liable party to a cleanup, governments may incur substantial legal and oversight expenses.

Consider the following hazardous waste lawsuits involving governments:

- In *United States* v. *Stringfellow* (1989), the state of California had taken an active role from 1950 through 1973 in locating, supervising, and regulating an industrial waste facility in the Jarupa Mountains near Glen Avon. In 1974, the state took control of the site to contain wastes that were migrating offsite. In 1983, EPA and the state brought suit against thirty-one defendants who generated or transported wastes dumped at the site. During the trial, it was determined that the generator-defendants could assert a counter-claim against California for part of the cleanup costs since the state acted as a "quasi-private consultant" in the operation of the landfill. On June 2, 1989, a jury found the state guilty of negligence in its consultant role. Estimates of the state's liability range from $450 million to $750 million (Bingenheimer, 1989). As of the writing of this chapter, the site still had not been totally cleaned up.
- In the late 1980s, the city of Corvallis, Oregon, was notified by the EPA that the United Chrome Products plant south of town was Oregon's worst hazardous waste site. Soil and water around the plant had been contaminated with chromium during twenty-eight years of chrome-plating operations. Because the city owned the land on which the former plant stood, the EPA held the city responsible for cleanup of the site. In 1989, the city filed a $19.7 million lawsuit against United Chrome Products to force the company to pay for the cleanup, which should be completed by the year 2000 (City of Corvallis, 1989).
- When the EPA began cleaning up four Superfund sites on the east coast in the mid-1980s, 476 parties were sued as generator-defendants in an effort to recoup EPA expenses. The defendants included the town of Barnstable, Massachusetts; the Barnstable High School; the Barnstable Public School System; the Barnstable Water Company; and the Barnstable Dump. Total cleanup costs were estimated at $52 million. Half of the defendants, including all the Barnstable defendants, were determined to fall under EPA's de minimis policy for small-volume generators of hazardous waste. (The main concept behind de minimis settlements is to assess those who contributed a minimal amount of waste to a site for response work based on such factors as toxicity and amount of waste.) Together the de minimis parties settled with the EPA for $11 million [53 *Fed. Reg.* 28 (1988)].
- GAF Corporation had dumped industrial wastes in the Colesville municipal landfill, operated by Broome County, New York, in 1973 and 1974. Thirteen years later, Broome County and GAF Corporation agreed, in a $6 million consent agreement, to share the cleanup costs. The state of New York reimbursed the county for 75 percent of its cleanup costs as part of an unusual state law that allowed such an arrangement as long as the county took the lead in conducting the cleanup ("Enforcement," 1987).

These are just a few of the many examples of hazardous waste cleanup suits involving governments and government organizations. A 1991 survey sponsored by the International City Management Association concluded that approximately 51 percent of U.S. municipalities and counties own their own landfills (Good et al., 1991). Of the approximately 1,200 Superfund sites on the EPA's National Priority List, 25 percent involve municipalities or municipal wastes. Of those, about one in five sites is a municipal landfill. The EPA expects the number to increase in the future. The current average cost of cleanup of a Superfund site is more than $25 million; the Environmental Protection Agency projects this amount will exceed $40 million.

A study by the Congressional Budget Office (1990) concluded that more than 2,300 facilities owned by federal agencies handle hazardous wastes or contain hazardous waste contamination. That same report found that more than 7,100 properties formerly owned by federal agencies may incur financial liabilities from contamination problems. The United States owns a third of the nation's land, making it a major "potentially responsible party," or PRP, under hazardous waste law. There are more than 1,000 federal facilities on the EPA's Federal Agency Hazardous Waste Compliance Docket. Many of these sites are old mining, oil, and gas sites owned by the U.S. Department of Interior and the U.S. Department of Agriculture. Department of Defense installations also have been cited for hazardous waste contamination.

CERCLA Liability

It has been written that the parameters of CERCLA have been determined not in the EPA's interpretation of the act through rule promulgation, but in the courts (see, e.g., O'Leary, 1993), with each decision ratcheting the liability of responsible parties higher and higher. For example, nowhere in CERCLA is the term "strict liability" used. (A strict liability statute is one that imposes liability without requiring a showing of intent.) Soon after the passage of CERCLA, however, EPA attorneys adopted a strategy of arguing that a reasonable interpretation of the Superfund statute demanded that it be read as imposing strict liability on hazardous waste generators, transporters, and disposers. Since then, courts have universally held that CERCLA imposes strict liability, meaning that a waste generator, such as a city or state, may be subject to liability even if it has not departed in any way from the standard of reasonable care and has not violated any environmental laws [42 U.S.C. 9601 (32)]. (For representative cases see *United States* v. *Ward*, 1985; *United States* v. *Mirabile*, 1985; *United States* v. *Conservation Chemical Co.*, 1985; and *United States* v. *Tyson*, 1986.)

Additionally, where injury is indivisible (i.e., where it is not clear whose wastes caused what damage), courts have agreed with the EPA argument that liability is joint and several. Joint and several liability means that the federal government can proceed against any one or a group of potentially liable parties for the total costs of the cleanup, for which each is jointly or individually liable. If such liability is established, traditionally the only remedy for the defendants has been to seek contribution from other responsible parties through legal action.[1] (For representative case law defining "indivisible," see *United States* v. *NEPACCO*, 1984, and *United States* v. *Dickerson et al.*, 1986. For representative case law concerning joint and several liability see *United States* v. *Mirabile*, 1985; *United States* v. *SCRDI*, 1984; and *United States* v. *Chem-Dyne Corp.*, 1983.)

Nowhere in CERCLA is the term "joint and several liability" used. In fact, that term was expressly deleted from drafts of the statute (126 Cong. Rec. S14964 [November 24, 1980s]; 126 Cong. Rec. H11787 [December 3, 1980]). The legislative history of CERCLA that surrounds the deletion of terms shows an expressed congressional intent that the appropriate scope of liability be determined under common law principles, "where a court performing a case by case evaluation of the complex factual scenarios associated with eh multiple-generator waste sites . . . [can] assess the propriety of applying joint and several liability on an individual basis." Based on such common law principles, courts universally have found that each of the responsible parties whose actions have led to a distinct or single harm for which there is a reasonable basis for apportionment should be individually subject to liability only for the portion she or he has caused. Conversely, where harm is not apportionable, as when many companies have dumped wastes into a landfill, each individual entity or person may be found liable for the entire harm.

Moreover, the EPA has convinced the courts that it (or any other plaintiff) need not prove that a defendant's actions were the cause of environmental threat or harm in question. Courts have held that CERCLA requires no more proof than showing that a generator sent out hazardous wastes for disposal, that the wastes ended up at a site at which a release or threatened release of any hazardous substance necessitated responds action, and that wastes of the type the generator disposed of are present at the site (see *United States* v. *Ottati and Goss*, 1988; *United States* v. *NEPACCO*, 1984; *United States* v. *Dickerson et al.*, 1986).

Although CERCLA initially defined a "person" subject to hazardous waste cleanup liability as including the "United States Government, [a] State, municipality, commission, political subdivision of a State or interstate body," this definition was further clarified in 1986. In the Superfund Amendments and Reauthorization Act, Congress added a section clarifying that a state "shall be subject to the provisions of this Act in the same manner and the same extent" as any nongovernmental entity. The Supreme Court has noted that this amendment withdraws any state immunity that may have been previously implied (*Pennsylvania* v. *Union Gas*, 1989, discussed below). Local governments also are not immune from suit. (For representative cases concerning municipal landfills, see *South Macomb Disposal Authority* v. *United States Environmental Protection Agency*, 1988; *New Castle County* v. *Hartford Accident and Indemnity Company*, 1988; and *City of New York* v. *Exxon Corporation*, 1988.)

RCRA Liability

RCRA regulates hazardous wastes from their initial generation to their ultimate disposal—from "cradle to grave." There are several major sections of

RCRA that have ratcheted the requirements that are of particular importance to governments. These sections concern on-site storage of hazardous wastes (42.U.S.C.6922–6925), a manifest system for tracking hazardous wastes from generator to transporter to disposal facility (42 U.S.C.6922–6923), and minimum standards for hazardous waste disposal, enforced through a permit system for disposal facilities (43 U.S.C. 6924–6925).

Pursuant to RCRA, when presented with evidence that the past or present handling, storage, treatment, transportation, or disposal of any waste may present an "imminent and substantial endangerment," the EPA may bring suit against any entity that has contributed to the situation. Possible defendants include past or present generators, transporters, and owners or operators of treatment, storage, or disposal facilities. In such a situation, the EPA may order a government entity to restrain from specific activities, may order the government to take specific actions as deemed necessary by the agency, or both. The EPA may also take appropriate administrative actions [42 U.S.C. 6973(a)]. Any state or local government that violates a court order under such circumstances may be subject to fines of up to $5,000 for each day that the violation or noncompliance continues [42 U.S.C. 6973(b)].

If convicted of violating any other applicable requirements of RCRA, a state or local government may face civil penalties of up to $25,000 per day [42 U.S.C. 3008(g)]. Criminal penalties can be as high as $50,000 a day [42 U.S.C. 3008(d)(7)(A)]. Upon a second criminal conviction, the fine is doubled [42 U.S.C. 3008(d)(7)(A)]. Additionally, the act contains penalties for the offense of "knowing endangerment" for which an organization may be fined up to $1 million [42 U.S.C. 3008(e)]. Leverage over federal facilities that pollute may be found in certain circumstances under the Federal Facilities Compliance Act of 1992 as well as other statutes.

The Supreme Court Acts

The gravity of the ratcheting of potential liability for hazardous waste cleanup can be seen clearly in a case decided by the U.S. Supreme Court in 1989, but subsequently reversed in 1996. The pivotal issue in *Pennsylvania* v. *Union Gas* (1989: 109 S.Ct. 2463) was whether a state that contributed to a hazardous waste discharge can be sued by a private party in an effort to recoup a portion of the costs of cleaning up the site. Pennsylvania asked the Supreme Court to interpret a 1986 amendment to the federal Superfund Act when it appealed a lower court decision that a state can be sued by a private party for hazardous waste site cleanup costs.

The case began in 1980s when the Commonwealth of Pennsylvania, carrying out flood control measures, excavated at a site formerly owned by Union Gas Company, to which the state held an easement. Workers struck a large deposit of coal tar that began to seep into a nearby creek. The EPA immediately ordered a cleanup, which Pennsylvania and the United States jointly carried out. The U.S. government spent an estimated $1.4 million on the cleanup, which included reimbursing Pennsylvania for its costs.

As is typical in such a case, the federal government then sued Union Gas in district court for recoupment of costs incurred in cleaning up the spill. Union Gas responded by denying liability and filing a complaint against Pennsylvania, alleging that the Commonwealth had "negligently caused, or contributed to, the discharge" and should therefore share a portion of the cleanup costs. Pennsylvania defended itself by asserting that the Eleventh Amendment of the Constitution had been interpreted by courts as a grant of sovereign immunity to the states in federal court.

The court agreed with Union Gas that Congress had provided clear language in amendments to CERCLA that had just become law, rendering states liable for monetary damages for hazardous waste cleanup and that such action is within congressional powers. The five-to-four decision forced Pennsylvania to later defend itself against a Union Gas lawsuit seeking to recover cleanup costs. The decision, however, was reversed in 1996 when the Supreme Court held that Congress lacks the power under the Commerce Clause to override the state's Eleventh Amendment immunity from lawsuits by individuals (*Seminole Tribe of Florida* v. *Florida*, 1996). As of this writing, the implications of the 1996 decision for United States environmental law, which concerned the legality of the Indian Gaming Regulatory Act, remain to be seen.

There are important implications of the ratcheting of governments' liability for hazardous waste cleanup. As congressional pressures on the EPA to recoup Superfund monies and to clean up waste sites grow, so too will the pressures to file suit against governments. Simply put, as Congress ratchets so shall it force the EPA to do likewise.

The issues of who will pay and how they will pay are significant. Liability for hazardous waste cleanup may severely curtail important governmental functions as programs are extinguished to provide funds for hazardous waste cleanup costs. Further, local governments may be reluctant to provide traditional services, such as refuse control and landfill space, for fear of liability. Finally, such liability undoubtedly will be considered in bond ratings that evaluate solvency, affecting state and local governments' ability to borrow funds for projects and services.

Proposed Hazardous Waste Liability Ratcheting in Europe

Of course, the United States is not the only country ratcheting its environmental laws. In Europe, the leaders in environmental law have been Germany and the Netherlands, although the E.U. (before 1993 the European Community) has proposed some general unifying directives. While the European experience in hazardous waste law is different than that of the U.S. experience, it is nonetheless significant for public managers. Let us now examine the proposed progressive ratcheting of hazardous waste law in Europe.

Directive 75/442, the legislation that shaped the member states' schemes for waste management in the European Community, was first enacted in 1975 and revised in 1991. Another piece of legislation that specifically addresses toxic and dangerous waste, Directive 78/319, was adopted in 1978. The amended Directive

75/442 on Waste and Directive 78/319 on Toxic and Dangerous Waste specify the following permitting requirements:

- the types and quantities of waste to be disposed of;
- the general technical requirements;
- the precautions to be taken;
- the suitable disposal sites; and
- the disposal methods.

The directives also require the waste to be disposed of without endangering health or the environment. Particularly, the participating nations should ensure that the waste is disposed of:

- without creating risk to water, air or soil, or flora or fauna;
- without causing a nuisance by noise or odors; and
- without adversely affecting countryside or places of special interest.

The unique feature of the E.U.—consisting of fifteen independent nations—has prompted environmental regulation to take on two different forms of harmonization: economic harmonization of the community and harmonization of the member states' national laws with the E.U. directives. On the one hand, by providing directives, the E.U. attempts to reduce disparities among the laws of the member states, and create equal conditions of competition for its member states. However, by not specifying details in the directives, the E.U. hopes to provide for greater harmonization of member states' national laws. Unlike the United States' RCRA, for example, both directives 78/319 and 75/442 do not address specific standards or requirements other than those mentioned above. While RCRA regulates hazardous waste from the cradle to the grave, E.U. directives leave regulatory requirements in the hands of the member states.

In spite of the relatively greater discretion given to the member states, when directives specify obligations the member states should fulfill, the participating nations should stick to the specific E.U. rules. The member state that does not abide by the E.U. directives will have to pay a high price, even though directives are not necessarily binding. The case of the *E.C. Commission* v. *Belgium* (1990) clearly shows the individual member state's responsibility to follow the larger community directives.

The *Belgium* case concerned Directives 75/439 on the Disposal of Waste Oils, 75/442 on Waste, 76/403 on the Disposal of Polychlorinated Biphenyls and Polychlorinated Terphenyls, and 78/319 on Toxic and Dangerous Waste, which all require that every three years each member state send a report to the Commission on the implementation of the individual directive. The E.C. brought an action against the country of Belgium because it failed to fulfill its obligations by not forwarding reports required by the above mentioned directives to the Commission in the prescribed periods. Belgium was ordered to bear the costs. In this respect, it should be noted that the court held that a member state may not rely on national provisions, practices or circumstances of its internal legal order to justify noncompliance with its obligations under E.C. law.

The difference in the specificity of environmental laws between the United States and the E.C. was expected to be reduced dramatically when the E.U. proposed new civil liability provisions in 1991. As mentioned previously, CERCLA, coupled with RCRA, has shaped the environmental liability schemes in the United States since 1980s. In the E.U., before the directive was proposed, individual states had an unequal range of liability schemes. The E.C.'s (now E.U.'s) proposal in this regard attempts to impose more rigorous and specific requirements on its member states. Under the proposed directive, strict, joint, and several liability are imposed to all responsible producers of the waste that bring about damage, or impairment of the environment.

Like other environmental harm-related directives, this proposed directive is based on the "polluter pays" principle. A simple twist made in the proposed directive is that the *producer* of the waste that did harm to the environment is liable for the damage. As McCann (1992) pointed out, the proposed directive seeks to make this principle serve as the basis for a uniform liability scheme for the E.U., substituting existing liability schemes of the member states. The directive is still pending. Once this proposal is finalized, however, the fifteen partaking nations in the E.U. would most likely not see as severe a ratcheting of environmental laws as has occurred in the United States given the diversity in E.U. nations.

What the E.U. attempts to achieve through the proposed directive is to ensure that waste be under the control of legitimate authorities by encouraging responsible behavior of producers. Only when the waste is taken care of by the authorized waste disposal facility, the producer of the waste is free from liability. If the producer cannot be identified, the person who had "actual control" of the waste at the time of "incident" is liable. The authorities then must find ways to appropriately take care of the waste. Dissatisfied public interest groups, the victims adversely affected by the waste either physically or economically, and governmental authorities can all file a lawsuit for damages and reimbursement of cleanup costs under the proposal.

Despite the different scale, the United States' CERCLA and the E.U.'s proposed directive share a similar basis that makes some comparison possible: both address civil liability for damage caused by waste. While both CERCLA and the proposed directive impose strict, joint, and several liability, the European scheme provides more leeway from liability in a few aspects.

According to the provisions of the proposed directive, the person who had actual control of the waste at the time of damage can pass liability back to the producer of the waste, if that person finds out who the producer is. This is not the case under CERCLA—both could be held liable. Also, though the producers are the focus of liability under the proposed directive, they are not liable if the incident occurs after the waste has been delivered to a legitimate authority. Under CERCLA, the producers potentially would be liable in the exactly same situation. As mentioned previously, CERCLA designates four categories of potentially responsible parties and any combination of them may be strictly, jointly, and severally liable. Whereas the proposed Directive has the equivalent of the four liable parties, the focus is on producers.

Another difference in the provisions is that under CERCLA, liability occurs when there is a "release or threat of release" of "listed hazardous substances" [42 U.S.C. 9607(a)-(b)]. Potential liability is great under CERCLA in the sense that the terms "release" and "hazardous substances" are defined broadly. Further, the waste doesn't even have to inflict damage to the environment; rather, threatened release suffices. In comparison, the terms used in the directive, "damage and impairment of the environment," are more restrictive than the terms "release of hazardous substances." Still another difference is that under the proposed directive liability is not retroactive, whereas it is interpreted as retroactive under CERCLA.

A goal of the proposed directive is to provide a fair, reliable, and reasonable scheme of compensation of damage. Unlike CERCLA, in which responsible parties are fully liable for damages for restoration, the proposed directive provides a provision that the liable party is relieved from reimbursing the cleanup costs if "the costs substantially exceed the benefit arising for the environment" or if there are available alternatives at a "substantially lower cost." In terms of the cleanup standards, CERCLA does provide standard procedures, but it is the EPA who finally determines how clean is clean. The proposed directive is vague on this issue and leaves the cleanup standards to the member states. However, the directive requires that the member states provide specific remedies.

CONCLUSION

This chapter has examined the impact on public management of the progressive ratcheting of environmental laws in three different scenarios. Municipalities in the United States have become mini-water pollution control agencies, undertaking enormous environmental regulatory responsibilities. Liability for regulatory takings in the United States already has had a major impact on public coffers. Governments in the United States are being sued for hazardous waste cleanup, where expanded liability affects the operation of hundreds of government functions, from landfills to vehicle maintenance shops, to the purchase of land. It is predicted, however, that even with the current E.U. proposals, similar results will most likely not evolve as stringently as in the U.S. situation. These are only three of hundreds of possible cases demonstrating the impact of the ratcheting of environmental laws in legislatures, environmental agencies, and the courts. A substantial number of examples also exist in the private sector, as businesses struggle with increasing environmental regulation.

Our environmental laws serve an important function: to protect public health and the environment. Strong and vigorous environmental laws are needed. What can be done, then, to maximize the positive effects of our environmental laws and minimize the negatives? Where does the problem lie?

The primary source of the problem is our nation's incremental approach to environmental law making. Step by step, year by year, well-meaning legislators pass environmental law after environmental law, ratcheting requirements higher and higher. Rarely does Congress examine the cumulative effect of environmental laws, the regulations that implement environmental laws, or judicial decisions interpreting those laws.

Our environmental laws must be reexamined and refined. Our environmental problems must be prioritized using political, economic, legal, and health inputs, utilizing a holistic approach, not a piecemeal, incremental one. In addition, a greater emphasis on pollution prevention in our laws is essential. This will not be an easy task, for our environmental problems are growing more challenging—and the resulting public management decisions more difficult—every day. Yet, we must begin such an examination at once if our governments are to adequately serve the public interest and implement important public programs. Clearly, the progressive ratcheting of environmental laws will affect public management for years to come.

NOTE

1. Exceptions to this rule include the "innocent landowner" defense and the EPA's de minimis policy.

REFERENCES

Advisory Commission on Intergovernmental Relations. (1981). *Protecting the Environment: Politics, Pollution and Federal Policy.* Vol. 7 of *The Federal Role in the Federal System: The Dynamics of Growth.* Washington, D.C.: Government Printing Office.

Bingenheimer, K. (1989, June 19). "Jury Rules California Liable for Cleanup." *Waste Tech News*, p. 1.

City of Corvallis, Oregon. (1989). "The City: Special Report—United Chrome." Corvallis, OR: Author.

City of New York v. *Exxon Corporation*, 697 F. Supp. 677 (1988).

126 *Cong. Rec.* S14964 (Daily ed., November 24, 1980s).

126 *Cong. Rec.* H11787 (Daily ed., December 3, 1980s).

Congressional Budget Office. (1990). *Federal Liabilities Under Hazardous Waste Laws.* Washington, DC: Government Printing Office.

Dolan v. *Tigard*, 114 S.Ct. 1395 (1994).

E.C. Commission v. *Belgium*, I E.C.R. 2391 (1990).

"Enforcement: GAF, New York County Agree to Site Cleanup." (1987, May 1). *BNA Environment Reporter.*

Federal Register. (1988). 53, p. 28.

"Fix for Phase II of Storm Water Program Should Get 'Highest Priority' Official Says." (1995, September 15), *BNA Environment Reporter*, p. 922.

Florida Rock Industries, Inc. v. *United States,* 21 Cl.Ct. 161 (1990).

Good, D., Kissel, J., Mullins, D., and O'Leary, R. (1991). "The Solid Waste Crisis." Washington, DC: International City/County Management Association.

Loveladies Harbor, Inc. v. *United States,* 21 Cl. Ct. 153 (1990).

Lucas v. *South Carolina Coastal Council,* 502 U.S. 966.

Lucas v. *South Carolina Coastal Council,* 112 S.Ct. 2886 U.S. LEXIS 4537, 60 U.S.L.W. 4842 (1992).

McCann, Michael R. (1992). "CERCLA & The European Community's Civil Liability Proposal: A Comparison of American and European Law Pertaining to Liability for Environmental Harm Caused by Hazardous Wastes," *Journal of Environmental Law* 2: 146–69.

Natural Resources Defense Council v. *Costle,* 568 F.2d 1369 (1977).

Natural Resources Defense Council v. *United States Environmental Protection Agency,* 966 F.2d 1292 (1992).

Natural Resources Defense Council v. *United States Environmental Protection Agency,* No. 95–0634 (1995).

New Castle County v. *Hartford Accident and Indemnity Company,* 685 F. Supp. 1321 (1988).

Novick, S. M. (1986, January). "The 20-year Evolution of Pollution Law: A Look Back." *The Environmental Forum,* pp. 12–8.

"Numerical Effluent Limits for Storm Water Impossible to Achieve, NAFSMA Members Say." (1991, November 1). *BNA Environment Reporter,* p. 1658.

O'Leary, R. (Spring, 1992). "Upcoming Supreme Court Decision in *Lucas* v. *South Carolina* Should Clarify Direction of Regulatory Takings Trend," *Natural Resources and Environment,* 6, 4, pp. 63–4.

_____ . (1993). *Environmental Change: Federal Courts and the EPA.* Philadelphia: Temple University Press.

Pennsylvania Coal Co. v. *Mahon,* 260 U.S. 393 (1922).

Pennsylvania v. *Union Gas,* 109 S.Ct. 2463 (1989).

Rubin, D. K., Powers, M. B., Setzer, S., and Bradford, H. (1992, September 21). "U.S. Faces a Draining Experience," *Engineering News Record,* p. 1.

Seminole Tribe of Florida v. *Florida,* 116 S.Ct. 1114 (1996).

"Senate Approach to Bipartisan SDWA Bill May Be Model for CWA Rewrite, Aide Says." (1995, November 10). *BNA Environment Reporter,* p. 1192.

South Macomb Disposal Authority v. *United States Environmental Protection Agency,* 681 F. Supp. 1244 (1988).

United States v. *Chem-Dyne Corp.,* 572 F. Supp. 802 (1983).

United States v. *Conservation Chemical Co.,* 619 F. Supp. 162 (1985).

United States v. *Dickerson et al.,* 640 F. Supp. 448 (1986).

United States v. *Mirabile,* 14 Env't Law Rep. 20992 (1985).

United States v. *NEPACCO,* 579 F. Supp. 843 (1984).

United States v. *Ottati and Goss,* 22 ERC (BNA) 1736 (1984).

United States v. *SCRDI,* 21 Env't. Rep. Cas. 1756 (1984).

United States v. *Stringfellow,* No. 83–2501 JMI (1989).

United States v. *Tyson,* 25 Env't. Rep. Cas. 1899 (1986).

United States v. *Ward,* 618 F. Supp. 884 (1985).

Webster's Ninth New Collegiate Dictionary. (1991). Springfield, MA: Merriam-Webster, Inc.

Whitney Benefits v. *United States,* 926 F.2d 1169 (1991).

3

RETHINKING THE ROLE OF RISK ASSESSMENT IN ENVIRONMENTAL POLICYMAKING

Audrey M. Armour

A problem in policymaking for prevention of harm to persons and the environment concerns the probability of harm occurring, that is, the measure of risk involved. Policymakers have almost always sought to calculate the risk involved in proposed courses of action. Their methods have often been irrational and their estimates erroneous. Explicit analysis of risk to society, and systematic methods for estimating it emerged with the advent of science as more reliable procedures for prediction and decision making. However, as with many other forms of analysis, the assessment of risk has carried its own risk—namely, an undue reliance on logical quantitative techniques that fail to address the root causes of public concern and apprehension. Common sense assessments of risk tell us more what risks people regard as acceptable and what risks arouse anxiety and protest. Carnage from accidents on the nation's highways arouse much less apprehension than nuclear accidents even though actual risk from automobiles is much greater than injury or death from nuclear reactors. The following paper makes the case that the art and science of risk assessment will fall short of social and political realities until the psychological and cultural aspects of risk receive more adequate attention.

In everyday terms, the concept of "risk" is relatively straightforward. A "risk" is the chance of injury, damage, or loss. Who hasn't had to grapple, at one time or other, with whether to "take a risk" on something and expose oneself to the possibility of facing some kind of negative consequence? In the context of environmental decision making, however, risk remains a baffling concept, as does "risk assessment." Should there be stricter regulations to reduce the potential health risks of cadmium dust and fumes in factories? Does a proposed hazardous waste management facility pose an unacceptable risk to the environment and nearby population, as opponents of the facility contend? What are the risks associated with recombinant DNA research and should such research be regulated? These are the kinds of questions for which policymakers turn to risk assessment experts for answers.

The use of risk assessment in public policymaking can be traced back several centuries to the efforts made by public health officials to predict life expectancy and the probability of death from various life-threatening diseases. In the early 1900s, when the use of pesticides became popular among farmers and when pharmaceutical companies began producing a wide variety of innovative drugs, this medical focus was expanded to encompass concerns about the health hazards associated with the ingestion of man-made chemical compounds.

But it was not until the late 1960s that risk assessment really began to exert a more pervasive and profound influence on public policymaking processes. As reports of various adverse and often unanticipated consequences of new technologies, industrial processes, and large-scale engineering projects made their way into the popular press, the public's post-war enthusiasm for science and technology began to give way to a nagging sense of unease about the insidious side of modern progress. Politicians and government officials came under increasing pressure from consumer associations and public interest groups, as well as the scientific community to enact more stringent regulations governing the production and use of chemicals. They were also pressured to take more account of environmental risks in making decisions about the development and implementation of new technologies and new facilities, especially those regarded as inherently hazardous such as nuclear power plants or waste treatment facilities. Risk assessment, with its promise of scientific rigor and objective analysis, came to be seen by policymakers as a way of determining the need for regulatory control or, when conducted within the context of a comprehensive environmental assessment, a way of deciding upon the overall acceptability of a proposed course of action.[1]

It has been assumed that a sound assessment of risk will tell policymakers all they need to know to make appropriate risk management decisions. But this has seldom been the case. Experience reveals that the way in which risk assessors approach an environmental risk problem and the way in which policymakers and other layperson make risk management decisions are quite different. Thus, risk assessment studies have often proven to be disappointing for everyone involved, and sometimes more of a hindrance than a help. Indeed, they can be counterproductive, exacerbating rather than allaying fears and fueling rather than resolving sociopolitical conflict.

It would be unfair, however, to lay the blame for this on risk assessors. That policymakers look to risk assessment to resolve such issues reflects both a lack of understanding of the limitations of the science of risk assessment and a long-standing inability and/or unwillingness to deal directly with the political aspects of environmental risk. Until this changes, dealing with matters of risk in environmental policymaking will remain the frustrating endeavor that it is regardless of whatever improvements risk assessors might make in their science.

THE "SCIENCE" OF RISK ASSESSMENT

Risk assessment is a process of identifying and evaluating the potential for injury, damage, or loss to human health and the environment as the result of exposure to the effects of a chemical, technology, or project. Generally, to assess risk, four types of analyses have to be undertaken: hazard identification, exposure assessment, dose-response evaluation, and risk characterization.[2] Since the purpose of such studies is to aid decision making, there is a fifth essential analytic component, namely risk management.

The objective of hazard identification is to determine if a hazard exists—that is, if a set of circumstances exist with the potential to cause harm. If a chemical were being assessed, such factors as the expected dose level, the potential for exposure, and the duration of exposure would be taken into account in determining if the chemical were hazardous. It should be noted that the adverse effects alone are not what makes a chemical hazardous; its presence in the environment is what counts. "A very toxic chemical with no exposure potential is not hazardous to the environment" (Ramamoorthy and Baddaloo 1991, 397). If the object of assessment were a hazardous waste landfill proposal, then all of the chemicals that could enter into the environment from the landfilling activities would be listed along with their known potential adverse human health effects (that is, their known toxicity).

Exposure assessment would be undertaken to determine the actual likelihood, intensity, and duration of human exposure to the hazards identified, taking into account either the worst-case situation or a reasonable maximum exposure (RME) scenario.[3] The aim would be to derive an estimate of the total possible exposure. In the case of the hazardous waste landfill, this task would involve calculating the amount of each chemical likely to be placed in the landfill and the amount that could become ambient in the environment, using data obtained from historical records or gathered at similar facilities. Then, all of the pathways by which the contaminants could reach people and be ingested by them would be identified. In addition, the risk assessor would take into account the functional characteristics and limitations of proposed landfilling technology as well as the kinds of regulatory controls that could be applied to prevent or reduce the potential exposure of the chemicals. This analysis, in and of itself, often exerts a positive influence on the ultimate design and operation of a facility such as a hazardous waste landfill, leading to changes that make it safer than it would have been otherwise.

The task of dose-response evaluation is to determine the relationship between the estimated magnitude of exposure and the probability of occurrence of adverse health effects in an exposed population. In essence, the objective is to derive an estimate of the potency of the chemical exposure. Factors such as the age, sex, and any other characteristic of the potentially exposed population that define its relative vulnerability (e.g., pregnant women, hypersensitive individuals) would be included in the analysis.

In risk characterization, the total exposure estimate calculated in the exposure assessment is multiplied by the potency estimate developed in the dose-response evaluation to derive a final estimate of the risk for a given population. Simply put, probability times consequence equals the calculated risk. In the case of the hazardous waste landfill, where numerous chemicals are involved, the calculated risk for each chemical would be combined to obtain an estimate of the total risk.

At this point, risk management considerations would enter the process. Given the estimation of the probability of harm, effort would be directed toward risk limitation, that is, identifying and assessing the effectiveness of measures necessary to reduce the risk. In some instances, such as in the case of nuclear installations, effort would be directed toward reducing the risk as far below the regulatory limits as possible (in conformance with the "as low as reasonably achievable" principle [ALARA]—taking social and economic factors into account). The consideration of risk management strategies would involve taking into account not only regulatory requirements and current technologies but also the costs associated with risk reduction and the point at which a return on further investment would be negligible.

The timing of each of these analyses and the level of detail pursued will vary depending upon whether the risk assessment is undertaken as a discrete exercise (as would be the case in the assessment of a proposed chemical application) or as an integral part of a larger project planning process (such the siting of a hazardous facility). In the latter situation, the risk assessment would be conducted in phases, first at a generic level to assist in the selection of those technological options and/ or siting alternatives meriting further study, and then at a more detailed level to identify the preferred technology and site location and assist in refining the design and operation of the proposed facility so as to minimize potential risks.

Needless to say, the overall reliability of the risk characterization analysis is crucial to the development of sound risk management strategies. And the key determinant of the reliability of the risk characterization is the results of the earlier analyses. The more problems there are in the earlier phases of the risk assessment process, the more dubious the final analysis is likely to be. Therein lies the rub. Although the science of risk assessment has come a long way over the past several hundred years, it is still beset with numerous methodological problems that continue to undermine its credibility and usefulness as an aid to decision making.

For example, hazard identification is clearly limited by what is known (or at least suspected) about the potential toxicity of the chemicals being assessed, especially their synergistic effects. It is also limited by the often unavoidable uncertainty surrounding estimates of the probability of accidental releases of harmful substances. This is particularly the case when there is not a lot of historical data to draw upon, such as when new or relatively new technologies (e.g., rDNA) are involved (Talcott, 1992).

Similarly, exposure assessment is limited by the accuracy of estimates of the quantities of contaminants likely to be released into the environment, which in turn is dependent upon the availability of data regarding actual releases of toxic substances. In addition, although many sophisticated computer models have been developed to assist in tracing exposure pathways, it is still questionable how well such models simulate real environmental conditions.

Even more problematic is the fact there is a lot of disagreement regarding how to define "the worst-case scenario." The criteria for "worst" are largely subjective (Wartenberg and Chess, 1992). Some argue that it should be defined as total failure in the containment of contaminants while others prefer to consider a more "realistic" scenario of partial failure. The matter is clearly a critical one since the analysis of the worst case heavily influences the final estimation of risk. Although emphasis is now shifting to "reasonable maximum exposure" as the basis for exposure assessment, the determination of "reasonable" requires professional judgment, as noted in a risk assessment guidance manual put out by the U.S. Environmental Protection Agency (1989). And given the relative recency of this approach, it may be some time before there is a reliable consensus on what those professional judgments should be.

The difficulties associated with hazard identification and exposure assessment, however, pale in comparison to those associated with dose-response evaluation. Because of the ethical and practical limitations of using people as test subjects, much of the current knowledge of the properties of chemicals and their effects on biological systems has been and continues to be derived from experiments with laboratory animals. The commonly accepted procedure in establishing dose-response relationships has been to expose lab animals to increasing doses of the chemical of concern in order to determine a "no-observed-adverse-effect-level" (NOAEL) for the chemical. If data identifying a NOAEL are unavailable, a "lowest-observed-adverse-effect-level" (LOAEL) is sometimes used as the basis for determining a safe threshold dose. The dose-response data from the high exposure level is then extrapolated to levels relevant to human (or other species') exposure to obtain a quantitative evaluation of the potential risk to human (or other species') health. To add an extra margin of safety, for non-carcinogenic toxins, the regulatory standard is usually set at 100 times below the experimentally determined NOAEL. The application of such a safety factor is necessary since the range of susceptibilities in a human population is likely to be much wider than in a genetically homogeneous test animal population. For suspected carcinogenic toxins, many regulatory agencies have adopted the approach that there is no justifiable safety margin and thus, in the absence of proof to the contrary, there is no threshold below which there is no risk to human health.

Obviously, one key assumption underlying all of this is that the response of laboratory animals to toxic substances can be extrapolated to other species, in particular the human species. The validity of this assumption is a continuing source of controversy in the risk assessment field. This is especially the case for carcinogens, since there are solid data for only a few carcinogens that support animal to human extrapolation (Wartenberg and Chess, 1992, 19). Moreover, since lab animals are usually given higher doses of suspected carcinogens than humans would normally ingest, and only a small number of lab animals are subjected to such tests, and single rather than synergistic effects of chemicals are the focus of analysis, many scientists question the reliability of the extrapolations that are made, the incorporation of a safety factor notwithstanding. And, for the same reasons, they question the validity of the "no threshold" premise. Indeed, a not uncommon view put forward in the context of regulatory review is that the numerous limitations of laboratory animal testing not only often results in overestimations of the potency of some carcinogens but also in labeling as carcinogens substances that may actually be harmless.

It is these kinds of problems that led one analyst to conclude that sizable uncertainties are associated with risk assessments:

A full assessment of how much or how little is known about the quantities of harmful substances released from different sources, the concentrations of these substances in the environment, and the toxicity of these substances would reveal that actual environmental risks could be higher or lower than estimated risks by factors ranging from tens to hundreds or more. If such uncertainty were characteristic of an individual's income over a one-year period, that income could plausibly range between $5,000 and $500,000, or even between $500 and $5 million. (Talcott 1992, 10)

Risk assessors have responded to this uncertainty by basing their risk assessments on conservative assumptions so as to yield an overestimation of the risk. For example, in assessing the potential human health risk associated with a proposed hazardous waste treatment facility, they may assume that all the food a person may consume over a lifetime will come from the geographic area with maximum potential for contamination (e.g., within the airshed or watershed of the facility). Or they may assume that a person will live at the fence of the facility property every day, twenty-four hours a day, for a whole lifetime. Producing conservative assessments of risk, however, is a double-edged sword. While this approach helps the scientists to deal with uncertainties, it often does little to allay the public's fears and may even do exactly the opposite. Having put forward an overestimation of risk, it can be very difficult to convince those likely to live next to a proposed hazardous waste treatment facility that the "real" risks are actually lower than the "conservative estimates" imply. And, the more the scientists try to explain their assumptions and qualify their work, the more their assessment of risk will be held suspect.

When all is said and done, however, the one aspect of risk assessment that remains the most troubling is that the fundamental questions—what level is safe? and is the risk an acceptable one?—too often cannot be answered by the experts. The fact is that the laboratory procedures used by risk assessors do not yield data on what level is safe. They only provide data on the levels where problems are observable. And given this, on what basis should the acceptability of a calculated risk be judged? By reference to existing regulatory standards that themselves may be based on inadequate data? By balancing risks against projected benefits? By comparison to other risks that are now tolerated by society? At present, there is no consensus on the matter, which means that the risk assessors and/or policymakers stand a good chance of making the "wrong" choice.

Risk assessors are very much aware of the limitations of their science and they counsel each other to make all assumptions and uncertainties explicit. This may offer the scientists involved some measure of comfort but it does little to help the policymaker who, regardless of the uncertainties involved, is expected to decide whether to ban or restrict a product or proposed project. Whatever course of action he or she takes will be open to criticism. There are those who would expect the policymaker to be prudent in the face of tenuous risk assessments and impose stringent standards. And there are others, concerned about the effect of overregulation on the market system, who would berate such a course of action as economic folly.[4]

Thus, at the end of the day when the risk assessment results are in, policymakers usually find themselves not much further ahead than they were at the beginning. Given the uncertainties involved in any assessment of risk, it was inevitable that risk assessment would come to be used as yet another weapon in the battles between regulators and chemical manufacturers or facility proponents and the public, each side with its bevy of risk assessment experts laying claim to the "real facts" of the matter and pressuring for a ruling in their favor. If it were simply a matter of adjudicating disputes among scientists, the problem would not be so daunting for policymakers. However, this is seldom the case.

LAY VERSUS EXPERT PERCEPTIONS OF RISKS

The demand for risk assessment grew out of the public's concern about the environmental and health hazards of technology and development activities. Yet, for many members of the public, risk assessment generally falls well short of addressing their concerns.

Risk assessment is a method that adheres to the precepts of rational planning and decision making—alternative courses of action should be compared and evaluated against desired ends, using specified criteria, so that the best course of action can be selected. Such rationality is widely regarded as not only logical but also better than other approaches to decision making in leading to decisions that are both relatively objective and ultimately in the interests of the "common good." As the eminent planning theorist Andreas Faludi (1973: 37–38) once noted "the procedure used by an intelligent decision-taker in determining the practical desirability of any one of a number of proposals is . . . the rational planning process" and "the definition of an intelligent proposal as one that can be reconstructed as having resulted from a rational planning process is primary to any other one."

It is well recognized that, in practice, no planning and decision-making process is ever completely rational. Lindblom (1965, 1973) clearly articulated the limitations of rational decision making in his discussion of "the science of muddling through." He proposed that, in reality, policymakers conduct "successive limited comparisons" rather than carry out comprehensive analyses in deciding on alternative courses of action. Lindblom elevated this to a method labeled "disjointed incrementalism." Etzioni (1973) argued that policymakers practice both rationalism and incrementalism—the former in making fundamental policy decisions that set basic directions (a broad scan is made of all possible options) and the latter in preparing to act on fundamental decisions (a detailed examination is made of a few options). He labeled his model of planning and decision making "mixed scanning." Nonetheless, as Faludi has noted, the aim of most agencies and organizations is to be as technically rational in their planning and decision making as possible.

In the context of assessing risks, the operative assumption has been that such rationality, with its force of scientific fact, will help to legitimize public policy decisions. This assumption is proving to be a shaky one. There is often a wide gulf between the scientists' assessment of the risks associated with a proposed product or project and the public's, a situation exacerbated by the fact that, when it comes to identifying and assessing risks, scientists and laypersons talk different languages.

Many professionals question the epistemological basis of risk assessment science, that is, the idea that "rational" decisions about risk should be based on knowledge derived from empirical studies and that, as often happens in the risk assessment process, the ratio of measurable benefits to costs should determine the merits of a course of action (McClennan, 1983; Breheny and Hooper, 1985). They would argue that the assessment of risk is not amenable to such analysis:

the fundamental uncertainties about the nature and extent of the risks inherent in many technological choices often defy systematic analysis. Sometimes the efforts to quantify risks and benefits have simply masked real uncertainties. Often the estimation of risk has ignored the nonquantifiable, fragile values—the emotional distress or the disruption of social relationships—that are associated with technological risks. (Nelkin, 1985: 14–15)

The more popular stance, however, has been to deride the public's view of risk and to argue that lay people's perceptions are "irrational" and must be changed. Proponents of risk assessment often contend that a useful purpose of risk assessment is to help the public to understand better the "real" risks involved—an objective that has become nearly impossible to achieve with the application of conservative assumptions and overestimations of risk.

It has only been in the last couple of decades that there has been a concerted effort to focus research on people's perceptions of risks and to account for apparent differences in the way laypersons and experts assess comparable risks. Not unexpectedly, given the recency of the effort, certain shortcomings are evident in the quality of the research. For example, most of it is based on surveys of small, often highly specialized and/or unrepresentative groups of individuals. In addition, the common emphasis is on individual psychological traits (such as feelings of personal efficacy and self-reliance) rather than broader social variables such as occupation, marital status, organizational membership, and religion (Covello, 1983; Bachrach and Zautra, 1985). This latter shortcoming is particularly significant. Perceptions of risk are not just subjective but are socially structured. And in the context of public policymaking, it is the socially constructed definition of the risk situation, the shared beliefs of various members of the public, that provides the powerful motivation for sociopolitical action. Unfortunately, very little is known about the risk perceptions of "interests" as opposed to individuals.[5]

These shortcomings notwithstanding, current risk perception research provides sufficient evidence to suggest that there is a need to change approaches taken in evaluating environmental risks. This research has revealed that:

- There are substantial differences between the risk estimates of experts and laypersons and these differences result, in large part, from differences between the risk perceptions of experts and those of the public (Kasper, 1980; Slovic et al., 1983; Fischhoff, 1985).
- Technical experts and laypersons both perceive risk as a combination of probability and consequences but use different criteria and analytic methods to arrive at an evaluation of overall "riskiness" (Covello, 1983; Renn, 1983).
- Experts tend to assign equal weight to both probability and consequences in their estimations of risk (the same risk value is assigned to 500 accidents per year each involving one death as to one accident per year resulting in 500 fatalities), whereas laypersons tend to put more weight on consequences (the one accident and 500 deaths would be judged as more significant) (Covello, 1983; Renn, 1983; Rubin, 1986).
- Experts tend to measure consequences in terms of expected losses (measured quantitatively as annual deaths, dollars lost, or lost person-days of work) and to assume that willingness to accept a risk is a matter of the trade-off between expected losses and expected gains. Laypersons, on the other hand, use expected losses as only one criterion among many to judge potential consequences. They also assign importance to the qualitative attributes of the risk situation such as its voluntariness, catastrophic potential, likelihood to result in death, familiarity, and equity (Slovic, Fischhoff, and Lichtenstein, 1982; Covello, 1983; Advisory Committee on Nuclear Safety, 1985).
- Experts tend to focus on the properties of the risk per se (both quantitative and qualitative), whereas laypersons also include aspects of the context within which the risk is situated (most notably, the reliability and credibility of the proponent and regulatory bodies responsible for managing the risk) (Renn, 1983).

The main conclusion to be drawn from this research is that much of the public controversy that often surrounds risk assessments relates to the judgmental aspects of the exercise—those points in the process where decisions must be made regarding what variables to take into account, what evaluation criteria to use, how much weight to give these, and what overall conclusions to reach. When it comes to making these kinds of extra-scientific judgments, it has been shown that experts use the same thought processes that laypersons do, with similar consequences (Hammond et al., 1984, Fischhoff, 1985). While experts may have more technical knowledge than laypersons, experts have no particular claim to a special set of judgment skills. Unfortunately, this too often goes unacknowledged, with predictable consequences. The risk assessment experts and the risk-concerned public usually talk past one another:

Typically, analyses of "public understanding" turn out to be analyses of the public's failure to understand, and the unspoken assumption is that what experts have to say is, indeed, what most needs to be understood. The risk perception literature suggests that—at least from the point of view of the audience—this is emphatically not the case. What audiences most want to know about a risk and what experts most want to tell them may have fairly little to do with each other. (Sandman, 1986)

For ordinary citizens concerned about the health risks associated with chemicals to which they may be exposed, expert assessments of risks seldom express the way they feel about it personally. The language of technical rationality which pervades the risk assessment process unavoidably inhibits the communication that must take place between experts and citizens. First, it eschews personal knowledge. Insights and intuition born of life experience are discounted. Second, it eschews cognition by reason. Moral issues, such as the right to impose risks on some for the benefit of the "common good," tend to be brushed aside. Third, it eschews social constructions of reality. Issues of power and the structural relations between potentially affected interests (which underlie concerns about the fairness of imposed risks) are treated as peripheral matters. And fourth, in practice, such rationality usually constrains analysis to matters that can be quantified and discourages the examination of meanings, intentions, and values (de Neufville, 1986). Yet, for the people concerned about a potential environmental or health risk, it is precisely the matters that technical rationality denigrates that are often of critical concern.

What the public see in the relegation of risk to a matter of scientific analysis is an attempt by environmental policymakers to avoid confronting the "real" issues, that is, the ones that are meaningful for them. For the public, the issue of "risk" usually has less to do with calculable probabilities and cost/benefit ratios than with issues of social choice, power, and the accountability, credibility, and trustworthiness of corporate officers, government regulators, and public policymakers (Wynne, 1980; de Neufville, 1986; Lerner 1987).

The dichotomy between experts and laypersons in the assessment of risk is perhaps the area of greatest divergence in public policymaking processes on environmental issues, even greater than the rifts that often develop among scientists. For policymakers, this dichotomy is especially problematic for reasons that go well beyond the obvious—it exists within themselves. It is in the interplay between their rational decision maker self and their layperson self that they find a resolution to such issues. Unfortunately, this interplay is seldom acknowledged and made explicit. Nor is the fundamental fact accounting for the dichotomy acknowledged, namely that the notions of "risk" and "risky" are products of sociopolitical processes. How these terms are defined and explained necessarily reflects the value judgments of those doing the defining and explaining. In this regard, risk assessment could be said to be no more than the "illusion of technique" (Wynne,1980; Douglas and Wildavsky, 1982; Holdsworth, 1986; Rayner and Robin, 1987; Greer-Wootten, 1988). All of these realities were revealed in startling clarity in a recent decision about the siting of a hazardous waste management facility in the Province of Ontario.

THE CASE OF ONTARIO'S HAZARDOUS
WASTE MANAGEMENT FACILITY

In 1980, the Ontario Government established a new crown corporation, the Ontario Waste Management Corporation (OWMC), and gave it the responsibility to "research, develop, establish and maintain facilities for the transmission, reception, collection, examination, storage, treatment and disposal of [industrial hazardous] wastes" (Ontario Waste Management Corporation Act, S.O., 1981).

After ten years of work and $80 million in expenditures, the OWMC sought government approval for a site it had selected in the township of West Lincoln, a rural municipality located near Niagara Falls, as the preferred location for a centralized, fully integrated facility consisting of an incinerator, a physical/ chemical treatment plant, solidification plant, and landfill. It proposed that the initial capacity would be 120,000 t/a for the physical/chemical treatment facility and 30,000 t/a for the incinerator, while the ultimate capacity would be 240,000 and 60,000 t/a, respectively.

In arriving at this proposal, the OWMC carried out a comprehensive environmental impact assessment (EIA), guided by four goals: minimize risk to human health, minimize risk to the environment, minimize financial cost to OWMC and the people of Ontario, and enhance the waste management system in Ontario (service). The risk-related goals were given the highest priority and were reflected in two facility design principles: only proven technologies would be used (defined as "commercially demonstrated to perform reliably for a period of at least 12 months, on a scale and in a manner comparable with that required by the OWMC facility"); and the site chosen for its facility must afford natural protection, as well as that provided by the engineering design.

The Corporation's EIA work was integrated within a five-phase facility development process. Phase One focused on the identification of twenty-seven system options and criteria for evaluating them. These system options were reduced to three: a centralized versus decentralized system (more than one full service facility), a fully versus partially integrated (components at more than one site) system, and specialized regional facilities. Phase Two involved the identification of three generic technologies and a narrowing of the site search to one region of the province, the Golden Horseshoe around Lake Ontario, where most of the hazardous waste is generated. Phase Three dealt with the selection of first, twenty candidate areas and then, within these areas, 152 candidate sites. In Phase Four, the candidate sites were reduced to eight, which were then subjected to detailed comparative evaluation in order to select a preferred site and a preferred technology. The West Lincoln site was then subjected to detailed site assessment to identify, at an even greater level of specificity, potential risks and impacts, to develop risk and impact management strategies, and to determine the overall net effect and advantages and disadvantages of the proposed undertaking. Phase Five involved a three-year public hearing (February 1990 to September 1993).

In each phase, OWMC undertook extensive public consultation to obtain input to the identification of goals, principles, options, impacts, risks, and mitigation measures. It also circulated draft reports for public comment and government review. The Ministry of Environment coordinated the government agencies' review of OWMC's impact and risk assessment studies and, at the end of Phase Four, prepared a report that supported OWMC's proposal. It was in Phase Five, the public hearing, that everything unraveled. The Hearing Board rejected the OWMC proposal essentially on the basis of the way in which the OWMC had dealt with an environmental risk issue.

The board's decision sent shock waves through the professional community—up to this point, OWMC's impact and risk assessment work had been considered state-of-the-art. OWMC's risk assessment was carried out over several of the phases of the facility development process: in the evaluation of generic treatment technologies (e.g., incineration, physical/chemical treatment, solidification, biological treatment); in the evaluation of effluent and solidified residue disposal methods (e.g., landfill, salt mines, warehousing); in the evaluation of system options (e.g., centralized versus decentralized systems, fully versus partially integrated systems); in the assessment of candidate sites; and in the detailed assessment of the preferred site. In all cases except the last, the analyses of risk was more qualitative than quantitative, based on professional judgment of evaluation factors or concerns relevant to each of the four goals, although the depth of analysis increased as options became more clearly defined. The work done on the preferred site was quantitative and adhered strictly to the methodology described above.

In assessing generic treatment technologies, OWMC placed importance on those options that would give it the flexibility to treat all types of waste generated in Ontario, were proven technologies, and would treat the wastes to the maximum extent possible. Incineration, physical/chemical treatment, and solidification were determined to meet these requirements. Biological treatment was eliminated as a possible option.

In the assessment of generic effluent and solidified residue disposal methods, risk factors were ranked according to their relative priority based on severity, frequency/duration, and mitigation potential and used to compare the net effects of each option. The factors considered the most important were: exposure to contaminated surface water due to normal operations, exposure to contaminated groundwater due to normal operations, and personal injury accidents involving OWMC-related vehicles along access routes. Risk factors considered less important were: exposure to contaminated surface water due to upset conditions, and occupational health and safety during normal operations. Although all options were assessed to have "low risk" in the absolute sense, OWMC determined that disposal of solidified residues in a landfill or an existing salt mine were preferred to warehousing or disposal in a new salt mine. The existing salt mine option was judged to be preferred in terms of risk to surface water (under normal operations), groundwater (under normal operations), and transportation. It was judged to be equal to landfilling for the two other risk factors. When all goals were taken into account—risk, impact, cost, and service—landfilling of the solidified residues was selected by OWMC as the preferred option due to the high costs associated with disposal in an existing salt mine. The cost difference between landfilling and the salt mine option was estimated to be about $50 million, in favor of the landfill. Moreover, OWMC concluded that landfilling was a proven disposal method for hazardous waste whereas the salt mine option was not, a conclusion supported by the Ministry of the Environment technical staff.

In addressing system options, OWMC conducted three risk analyses: an assessment of chronic risks associated with air emissions and groundwater effects under normal facility operating conditions; an assessment of acute health risk to the public and facility workers due to air emissions from upset conditions; and an assessment of transportation risks including accidents resulting in physical injury or death and accidents resulting in spills of hazardous waste. OWMC determined that there was no clear preference for a centralized versus decentralized system with regard to chronic or acute risks. The assessment of transportation risks favored a decentralized system but the assessment of environmental impacts favored the centralized system. A fully integrated system was more preferred than a partially integrated one in terms of both risks and impacts. Specialized regional facilities were determined to be infeasible. Taking into account all predicted effects and possible mitigation measures, the OWMC selected a centralized, fully integrated system as its preferred system option.

In selecting a site for its proposed facility, OWMC first conducted a generic risk assessment of the candidate sites, using a single set of generalized parameters applicable to all candidate regions. Once a preferred site had been selected, OWMC expanded the risk analysis to include an evaluation of routine emissions that had not been included in the earlier site assessment as well as additional exposure pathways. It also incorporated into its assessment of risk various conservative assumptions and safety factors. OWMC concluded that the risk to human health and the environment were minimal and acceptable. Routine emissions to the atmosphere were not likely to cause adverse effects in exposed human or environmental receptors. Leachate from the landfill would not pose a significant risk to human health for two reasons: the extensive clay layer beneath the preferred site would isolate chemicals in the leachate from the groundwater for a period of at least hundreds or thousands of years, and the solidification process would effectively stabilize many contaminants, especially metals, thereby limiting concentrations in the leachate. Although there was some potential for some type of adverse effect as a result of a tank farm fire or a spill from a transportation accident, such events were expected to occur infrequently and mitigation measures would reduce potential risks.

The only significant concern identified in the assessment of the preferred site was the potential for chloride contamination. It was estimated that between 2,000 and 6,000 t/a of chlorides would be part of the solidified waste, a loading that could result in a concentration of 44,000 mg/l of chlorides in the leachate. After several hundred years, this concentration of chlorides would lead to an exceedance of the Province's "Reasonable Use Policy," which sets limits on the amount of degradation of groundwater that is acceptable. Most wells in the area draw water from the bedrock. However, the water from these wells generally suffers from problems of hardness and the presence of sulphites and iron. Chloride levels in the well water in the area vary from 18 mg/l to 80 mg/l. All of this affects the taste of the water and thus water from the wells is used primarily for livestock. At the time, OWMC did not regard the chlorides problem as a significant constraint to developing the West Lincoln site and proceeded to finalize their studies in preparation for the public hearing.

Not surprisingly, OWMC's work generated considerable public opposition. Within two months of the announcement of eight candidate sites, opposition citizen groups formed in each community. These groups then united to form a coalition known as the Group of Eight. The Coalition claimed that OWMC's assessment was flawed in its basic assumptions (especially the principle that the selected site must provide natural containment, a criterion that eliminated much of the province from consideration) and in the emphasis given to minimizing costs regardless of overall social costs. Opponents to OWMC's proposal characterized it as a "mega-facility" that concentrated all the risks and impacts on one small community. They argued that OWMC should have looked at alternative ways of meeting treatment needs on a regional basis, including the enhancement of existing facilities such as municipal fluid bed incinerations and cement kilns. They also maintained that OWMC should have considered "best available" technologies not just "proven" technologies. (Not everyone held this point of view. Early on in the process, numerous citizens expressed the view in public meetings that they did not want to be treated as "guinea pigs" for a new technology, a sentiment that influenced OWMC's preference for proven technologies.) In addition, opponents did not accept OWMC's position that the "absolute risks" were low for all disposal options or that the differences between the landfilling and salt mine options were as minor as OWMC portrayed them. It was not these arguments, however, that led the board to reject OWMC's proposal. Rather, it was the chloride issue.

The Hearing Board accepted OWMC's assessment that the total accumulation of risks and impacts at the West Lincoln site were "acceptable"—though significant locally, they were not of such a magnitude as to warrant not approving the site (The Joint Board, 1994, ix). The board also accepted OWMC's conclusion that, when all costs and benefits are taken into account, there would be net benefits to the province. However, the board rejected OWMC's assessment of alternative waste management systems and, in particular, its assessment of options to dispose of solidified residue. The board contended that OWMC had not proven that, in terms of environmental risk, it had found the optimum site and that its proposed undertaking offered the best ratio of advantages to disadvantages (The Joint Board, 1994, xi).

The board faulted the OWMC for not revisiting its earlier decision to eliminate disposal of solidified residue in an existing salt mine once it became apparent that there was a chlorides problem and significant costs associated with OWMC's preferred chlorides management method. OWMC didn't identify chlorides as an environmental risk problem until 1987, after it had conducted its detailed assessment of the preferred site. When it released its environmental assessment documentation in 1988 it was still considering what to do about chlorides. At the start of the hearing, OWMC put forward a Chlorides Management Plan, which involved diverting chlorides from the landfill. OWMC continued to study the problem and half way through the hearing informed the board that it had determined that the cost of chloride diversion would be between $12 and $28 million and that there was no guarantee that, even with diversion, chlorides would be sufficiently reduced to comply with the Ministry of Environment Reasonable Use Policy. It proposed a different approach to chlorides management that would involve landfilling chloride-bearing residues, establishing a contaminant attenuation zone of approximately 1,200 hectares, monitoring chlorides in groundwater over the life of the facility, and thereafter taking whatever further remedial measures may be needed. However, the Ministry of Environment then informed the OWMC that, to comply with its Reasonable Use Policy, OWMC would have to purchase the rights to the groundwater in the attenuation zone. The cost of this significantly reduced the advantage of the attenuation zone option. Moreover, the controversy that greeted the proposal made it apparent that it would likely be rejected on principle. By the mid-1980s sustainable development had become an item on the political agenda and OWMC recognized that, regardless of the already degraded quality and limited use of the groundwater beneath the proposed site, the risk of further contamination had to be eliminated, not just reduced and managed. Thus, near the end of the hearing, OWMC went back to the option of keeping chlorides out of the landfill and proposed a more comprehensive diversion strategy. It estimated that the cost of this approach to chlorides management would amount to more than $100 million over the life of the facility.

The board maintained that, "if OWMC had included the cost of chloride management in its evaluation of solidified residue options, the existing salt mine option would had to have been found to be preferred to landfill on a generic basis" (The Joint Board, 1994, 5–28). It maintained that, since minimization of cost was one of its four goals, the OWMC should have interrupted the hearing to reexamine its earlier decision on the salt mine option and proven beyond doubt that it was not a more cost effective way of managing the chlorides risk. In taking this position, the board discounted the emphasis OWMC gave to proven technologies as a preferred risk management objective in selecting landfilling instead of salt mines as the option for the disposal of residues.

The OWMC appealed the board's decision to the Provincial Cabinet but to no avail. During the hearing there was a provincial election and the New Democratic Party (NDP) swept aside the Liberal and Conservative parties to become the party in power for the first time in its history in the province. Philosophically, the NDP government did not support so-called "mega-projects" and it had already banned incineration as a waste management option for municipal garbage. Moreover, it had inherited a large deficit and canceling the OWMC project was seen as a good opportunity to save money.

What does it say about risk assessment in environmental policymaking when a proposed facility, regarded as needed, found to be acceptable in terms of its risks, and offering a net benefit overall, is rejected on the basis that the siting proposal may not be the "best" one? What does it say when, after ten years of study and two years into a public hearing, a proponent is expected to re-do its assessment simply to remove any doubt that the risk versus cost equation is "optimal"? One thing it reveals is how powerful a force the concept of "risk" can be in the decision-making process. This was evidenced in the effort and expense the OWMC was willing to undertake to address the risk of degradation, hundreds of years into the future, of a groundwater resource acknowledged to be naturally of low quality. It was also evidenced in the board's desire to have the salt mine option "revisited" some five years after OWMC had completed its studies just so that they could be assured that there wasn't some other "potentially preferred" option.

More importantly, it reveals that "risk assessment" can have little to do with the way in which decision makers address risk. The board did not find fault with OWMC's risk assessment methodology or its conclusions. It determined that OWMC had followed accepted procedures and had proven through logical systematic analysis that the risks of locating its proposed facility at West Lincoln were acceptable. It was on the basis of its own, more subjective, risk assessment that the board turned down OWMC's proposal. For the Board, the salt mine option intuitively seemed to be a better option, notwithstanding the Ministry of Environment technical staffs' views to the contrary. In the board's words, "The most significant advantage of a salt mine over a landfill is that a salt mine can contain the chlorides in the solidified waste residues" (The Joint Board, 1994, 5–21). This intuitive assessment gave it reason to doubt OWMC's proposal and that doubt became a pivotal point in their decision making. "The Board could not say that the ultimate conclusions (that the OWMC undertaking is preferred to the alternatives) would have remained the same had OWMC re-visited the evaluations involving the salt mines" (The Joint Board 1994, v). Note also that the board's way of dealing with the chlorides problem was to call for iteration—a revisiting of earlier decisions in the analytic process. As decision makers, the Board focused on how OWMC explored the risk issue. It wanted OWMC's (and its own) decision-making process to be painstakingly thorough, even if that meant re-doing ten years of work. As a proponent, OWMC's response to the chlorides problem was to focus on developing an acceptable plan to manage the chlorides at the West Lincoln site. It was concerned with solving the problem at hand.

The lessons learned in the OWMC case were perhaps summed up best in an editorial that appeared on November 28, 1994, in the [Toronto] *Globe and Mail* shortly after the Board announced its decision: "Facts and proportion seem to lose their efficacy when set against the term "environmental threat." Over and over, reasonable risk calculations are made victims of silly political ones." There is little doubt that the denial of OWMC's application reflected underlying political agendas. In the eyes of the public, OWMC had changed from a much-needed bold solution to an unwieldy risk-laden mega-project, a transformation reflecting a recession-bound societal concern with controlling government expenditures and promoting sustainable development. This political agenda fed into the political agendas of the board and the newly elected NDP government. In the board's mind, the OWMC proposal had to be proven to be the "best" or "optimal" solution not just an acceptable one. The board made it plain that, as a public body supported by the taxpayers of Ontario, the OWMC had a special onus to meet this requirement. And in denying OWMC's appeal of the board's decision, the newly elected provincial government conveyed its intention to move hazardous waste management and the government's role in environmental management in a different direction than that established by its predecessors.

THE POLITICS OF RISK ASSESSMENT

It would be naive not to question the political role of risk assessment in environmental policymaking, be it the extent to which "the science of risk ... serves as a control mechanism (hard or soft) for the maintenance of the status quo" (Greer-Wootten, 1988) or, as in the OWMC case, the extent to which the issue of risk is used to further political agendas.

Fundamentally, risk *is* a political issue. Decisions about environmental risks are decisions about the distribution of goods and bads in society. Each time a decision is made about "how safe is safe?" and "at what level should the risks be considered worth it?" some interests stand to gain and some stand to lose. The critical question then is who in society should participate in deciding matters of environmental risk? Whose values should prevail?

It has been suggested that the present distribution of risk in society reflects the present distribution of power and status (Douglas, 1986). There are studies that appear to lend support to this point of view. For example, a 1983 U.S. federal government study revealed a correlation between the location of hazardous waste landfills and the racial and economic status of surrounding communities—the majority of the population was black and poor (U.S. General Accounting Office, 1983). These findings were reinforced by the results of a similar study conducted in New Jersey, the state with the most hazardous waste production and Superfund sites (Greenberg et al., 1984). The study examined the social characteristics of communities with abandoned hazardous waste sites. A comparison was made between thirty-one towns in the state with at least four abandoned hazardous waste sites or one of the twenty-two first priority Superfund sites in New Jersey as of 1982. It was determined that communities whose population had a high socioeconomic status, contained fewer young, elderly and minorities, and which had increased substantially due to migration, were less likely to have abandoned sites. "The most consistent difference between DUMPS and NONDUMPS was socioeconomic status" (Greenberg et al., 1984, 390). At the same time, the researchers concluded that a community's political attributes—the presence of a strong form of government, planning boards, an environmental commission, voters who demonstrate strong support for environmental issues, or proximity to an important seat of political power—did not appear to make a difference. These attributes did not equate with political strength.

It is difficult if not impossible to prove or, for that matter disprove, that a particular facility siting decision was motivated by social bias. Indeed, the authors of the New Jersey study discussed above emphasized that "the finding of [social] effects in communities with abandoned sites does not mean that hazardous waste facilities were deliberately sited in areas of least resistance" (Greenberg et al., 1984, 389). They note that the facilities may simply have been sited nearest to the producers of hazardous waste.

Needless to say, the extent to which there is a direct cause-effect relationship between the present distribution of risk and the distribution of power and status in society is a matter of ongoing debate. For this reason, risk assessments inevitably raise concerns about distributive justice and the linkages between technology and science and power and social status in society. It cannot be otherwise.

Yet, this question is seldom explicitly addressed in public policymaking on environmental risks and even then it is unlikely to be policymakers raising the matter. What policymakers have failed to comprehend is that identifying and determining the acceptability of the risks associated with proposed chemical products, technologies, and development projects is first and foremost an exercise in social discourse, not scientific method. The basic questions that must be answered—on what basis should "risk" be defined? and is the risk "acceptable"?—are more political than scientific ones. This is not to say that science has no place in the political arena. Obviously, the social discourse on risk should be an informed one. But science and experts should not be placed at the center of the political debate, as has been the case with environmental risk issues. This simply results in pushing the central issues and key stakeholders, which includes policymakers, to the periphery. Whether this is an intended strategy on the part of policymakers keen to avoid having to deal directly with risk issues or an unintended one is difficult to discern. Regardless, the effect is the same.

The problem is that the sociopolitical infrastructure necessary for productive social discourse on risk is woefully lacking. In Habermas' terms, the system promotes distorted or impoverished communications. This can be traced to the irresistible tendency in today's planning and decision-making systems toward a bureaucratized exercise of power (McCarthy, 1979) and deference to expertise (Lerner, 1976). The ideals and values associated with technical rationality, coupled with the power that they exert in decision processes and bestow upon experts at the expense of layperson, not only prevent a meaningful exchange of ideas and concerns but also result in the marginalization of those whose lives are likely to be most affected by the decisions.

RETHINKING RISK ASSESSMENT

Three things can be said about risk assessment in environmental policymaking: the science is weak, layperson's concerns are not being fully or explicitly addressed, and important political issues are being pushed aside. Looked at in light of these realities, the approach policymakers have taken to dealing with environmental risks warrants reconsideration.

Risk assessment in environmental policymaking has been focused primarily on determining whether a proposed product, project or technology is safe. The main objective has been to characterize the potential hazard and produce a scientific calculation of "the risk" that would then allow a further calculation of overall costs and benefits. It is time to ask whether this is the appropriate focus.

It is logical, especially in the case of a suspected carcinogen, to give priority to scientific studies to determine the dose levels at which health hazards are apparent and to document the set of circumstances that create the potential for harm. It would be more logical still to conduct such studies as joint fact-finding endeavors involving all key stakeholders rather than, as is now the case, to engage in rancorous win-lose adversarial science battles. That said, it would nonetheless be prudent to ask whether such a study ought to be the starting point in every case. Confronted with an environmental risk issue, policymakers would be wise to ask is the answer to the question "what is the risk?" knowable to the degree of certainty needed to support regulatory action? Much of the controversy that accompanies risk assessment studies generally center on the reliability of the data and the plausibility of the conclusions. Is enough known about the potential toxicity of the chemicals to be studied to enable hazards to be identified and dose-response relationships evaluated? Is there consensus on how the scientific studies ought to be conducted? Is there agreement on the reliability of the models used to trace pathway exposures? Negative answers to these questions should cast doubt on the advisability of proceeding to rely on a scientific assessment of risk as the basis for decision making.

Stepping back even further from the risk assessment process, one might ask whether "what is the risk?" is in fact the key question. It seems to have been taken as a given that the whole point of risk assessment in environmental policymaking is to establish "the risk." It could be argued, however, that this is a rather myopic view of the matter. Social discourse about risk is more often than not discourse about values, trust, power, and equity.[6] Thus, should not as much emphasis if not more be placed on questions such as: on what basis should risk acceptability be judged?; to what extent are the environmental risks manageable?; what is the best approach to managing them? who should control the risk management process?; will the sharing of the risks be equitable?; and what would represent fair compensation for harm, should harm be done? Until these issues are resolved, or at least until more structured processes are in place by which to address them, answers to the question "what is the risk?", no matter how scientifically sound, will be continually challenged.

CONCLUSION

There is still a long way to go to develop effective means of addressing environmental risk in public policymaking processes. To date, the emphasis has been placed on the science of risk assessment in the hope that science will provide the needed answers to arbitrate risk-related disputes. This hope rests upon on a misperception of the role of risk assessment science in public policymaking. Until the concept of risk is broadened from a perceived scientific matter to encompass the notion of risk as a matter for social dialogue and more effort is directed toward putting in place the sociopolitical infrastructure needed to facilitate such dialogue, risk-related controversies will remain a bane in environmental policymaking.

What this calls for, in essence, is the modernization of democracy. Given the realities of contemporary society—the immense power of science and technology to change the world, the rapidity of change, the pervasive influence of modern bureaucracies, the global interdependence of economic systems, and the increasing complexity and scale of our systems of governance—it is little wonder that traditional decision-making approaches are proving problematic. Risk-related controversies in environmental policymaking can be traced to the intersection of science and politics. If such controversies are to be resolved more effectively and equitably then it is at this intersection that we must look for ways to change our processes of collective decision making.

Fortunately, it would appear that the potential for meaningful reform in the manner in which societal decisions about environmental risks are made is much greater today than it has been at any time in the past. The last decade has seen a proliferation of innovative experiments in democratic process. These include, among others, voluntary or invitational siting processes for hazardous facilities, citizen advisory committees, citizen policy juries, negotiated rule making, alternative dispute resolution, negotiated compensation, and multi-stakeholder consultation and policy dialogues.[7] The central premise of each of these experiments is an acceptance of the need for a more collaborative or partnership approach to decision making, one in which scientists, policymakers and citizens share both responsibility and accountability for seeking common ground and mutually acceptable solutions. This premise is the key to resolving issues of environmental risk and thus these experiments potentially have much to offer to the policymaker willing to rethink and reshape the role of risk assessment in environmental policy making.

NOTES

1. It is often difficult in the context of environmental policymaking to separate risk assessment from the much broader concern for environmental impact. Indeed, for many members of the public, environmental risk and environmental impact are perceived to be one and the same. Nonetheless, even in the context of environmental impact assessment, risk and hazard are usually regarded as distinct issues and assessed in their own right as one of several "disciplinary" analyses to be later integrated into an overall assessment of environmental impact. However, regardless of whether one is referring to a separate risk assessment study or the analysis of risk(s) within an environmental impact assessment study, the views expressed in this chapter regarding current approaches to the assessment of risk apply.

2. The Canadian Standards Association, a not-for-profit, nonstatutory voluntary membership association, defines risk assessment to be the process of risk analysis *and* risk evaluation. Risk analysis consists of scope definition, hazard identification, and risk estimation (which involves exposure assessment, dose-response evaluation, and risk characterization). Risk evaluation involves the consideration of the importance of the estimated risks and the associated social, environmental, and economic consequences in order to identify a range of alternatives for managing the risks. See: Canadian Standards Association, *Risk Analysis Requirements and Guidelines*, CAN/CSA-Q634–M91 (Toronto: CSA, November 1991).

3. The U.S. Environmental Protection Agency prefers the "reasonable maximum exposure approach" to the "worst-case scenario." See: U.S. Environmental Protection

Agency, *Risk Assessment Guidance for Superfund, Volume 1 Human Health Evaluation Manual (Part A), Interim Final* (Washington, D.C.: U.S. EPA, December 1989).

4. For example, Aaron Wildavsky, a political theorist at the University of California, Berkeley, argued that the socioeconomic cost of stringent regulations are not receiving sufficient attention in government's response to risk issues. His argument was that regulation limits market competition, which in turn limits economic growth, which in turn reduces the potential for improvements in human health. Simply put, wealthier is healthier. He suggested that risk analyses should be expanded to incorporate an assessment of lives lost because of regulation. See "Richer is Sicker versus Richer is Safer," in *Searching for Safety*, Aaron Wildavsky (Oxford: Transaction Publishers, 1988), pp. 59–75.

5. M. Gibbons and R. Voyer attempted to address this gap in their approach to technology assessment. They applied the concept of "actors"—those social groups that are (or should be) concerned with the development of a given technological program—in developing a definition of the technology assessment system and characterized decision making in this system in terms of the attitudes, concerns, and interactions of the actors. See: M. Gibbons and R. Voyer, *A Technology Assessment System: A Case Study of the East Coast Petroleum Exploration* (Ottawa: Science Council of Canada, Background Study No. 30, 1974). Their approach was extended in a study by Robert Keith, et al., *Northern Development and Technology Assessment Systems: A Study of Petroleum Development Programs in the Mackenzie Delta-Beaufort Sea Region and the Arctic Islands* (Ottawa: Science Council of Canada, Background Study No. 34, 1976).

6. This point has been made by various authors. See, for example, David Holdsworth, "Meaning, Risk and Social Context: Implications for Nuclear Waste Management," in *Hazardous Materials/Wastes: Social Aspects of Facility Planning and Management, Conference Proceedings* (Winnipeg, Manitoba: Institute for Social Impact Assessment, 1992), 259–266; Audrey Armour, *Socially Responsive Facility Siting* (Waterloo, Ontario: University of Waterloo, School of Urban and Regional Planning, Ph.D. Dissertation, 1990); S. M. Macgill and D. J. Snowball, "What Use Risk Assessment?" in *Applied Geography* 3 (1983), 171–192.

7. The Canadian federal government and two of ten provinces have experimented successfully with voluntary approaches to siting hazardous waste management facilities. Their experiments are documented in *Innovative Approaches to the Siting of Waste Management Facilities: A Guide to Nonconfrontational Siting Procedures*, Resources Futures International, ed. (Pittsburgh, PA: Air and Waste Management Association, 1992). Experiments with citizen advisory committees (also known as citizen liaison committees or study groups), citizen policy juries, negotiated rule making, alternative dispute resolution, and negotiated compensation are described in detail in *Fairness and Competence in Citizen Participation: Evaluating Models for Environmental Discourse*, Ortwin Renn, Thomas Webler, and Peter Wiedemann, eds. (Boston: Kluwer Academic Publishers, 1995). Multistakeholder consultation and policy dialogues are described in *Resolving Environmental Disputes: A Decade of Experience*, by Gail Bingham (Washington, DC: The Conservation Foundation, 1986).

REFERENCES

Advisory Committee on Nuclear Safety. (1985). *A Report on the Public Perception of Risk.* Ottawa: Atomic Energy Control Board.

Bachrach, Kenneth M. and Zautra, Alex J. (1985). "Coping with a Community Stressor: The Threat of a Hazardous Waste Facility." *Journal of Health and Social Behaviour* 26: 127–141.

Bingham, Gail. (1986). *Resolving Environmental Disputes: A Decade of Experience.* Washington, DC: The Conservation Foundation.

Breheny, M. and Hooper, A. (1985). *Rationality in Planning. Critical Essays on the Role of Rationality in Urban and Regional Planning.* London: Pion.

Covello, Vincent T. (1983). "The Perception of Technological Risks: A Literature Review." *Technological Forecasting and Social Change* 23: 285–297.

de Neufville, Judith Innis. (1986). "Usable Planning Theory: An Agenda for Research and Education." In *Strategic Perspectives on Planning Practice.* Barry Checkoway, ed. Toronto: Lexington Books.

Douglas, Mary. (1986). *Risk Acceptability According to the Social Sciences.* London: Routledge and Kegan Paul.

Douglas, Mary and Wildavsky, Aaron (1982). *Risk and Culture.* Berkeley, CA: University of California Press.

Etzioni, Amitai. (1973). "Mixed Scanning: A 'Third' Approach to Decision-making." In *A Reader in Planning Theory.* A. Faludi, ed, Oxford: Pergamon Press.

Faludi, Andreas. (1973). *Planning Theory.* Oxford: Pergamon Press.

Fischhoff, Barauch. (1985). "Managing Risk Perception." *Issues in Science and Technology* (Fall): 83–96.

Greenberg, Michael; Anderson, Richard; and Rosenberger, Kirk. (1984). "Social and Economic Effects of Hazardous Waste Management Sites." *Hazardous Waste* 1: 387–396.

Greer-Wootten, Bryn. (1988). "The Science of Locational Risk and the Risk of Locational Science." In *Complex Location Problems: Interdisciplnary Approaches,* Bryan Massam, ed.

Hammond, Kenneth R. et al. (1984). "Improving Scientists' Judgments of Risk." *Risk Analysis* 4: 69–78.

Holdsworth, David. (1986). *Rational Risk Assessment and the Illusion of Technique.* Toronto: Ontario Hydro.

The Joint Board. (1994). *The Consolidated Hearings Act. Ontario Waste Management Corporation Application, Reasons of Decision and Decision.* Toronto: The Joint Board (November).

Kasper, R. (1980). "Perceptions of Risk and Their Effects on Decision-Making." In *Societal Risk Assessment: How Safe is Safe Enough?* R. Schwing and W. Albers, eds. New York: Plenum.

Lerner, Allan W. (1976). *The Politics of Decision-Making: Strategy, Cooperation and Conflict.* Beverly Hills, CA: Sage Publications.

Lerner, Sally. (1987). *Risk Communication: A Problem of Credibility?* Waterloo, Ontario: University of Waterloo.

Lindblom, Charles E. (1965). *The Intelligence of Democracy.* New York: The Free Press.
_____ . (1973). "The Science of Muddling Through." In *A Reader in Planning Theory.* A. Faludi, ed. Oxford: Pergamon Press.

McCarthy, Thomas. (1979). *The Critical Theory of Jurgen Habermas.* Cambridge, MA: The MIT Press.

McClennan, Edward F. (1983). "Rational Choice and Public Policy: A Critical Survey." *Social Theory and Practice* 9 (Summer-Fall): 335–379.

Nelkin, Dorothy. (1985). *The Language of Risk.* Beverly Hills, CA: Sage Publications.

Ramamoorthy, S. and Baddaloo, E. (1991). *Evaluation of Environmental Data for Regulatory and Impact Assessment*. New York: Elsevier.

Rayner, Steve and Cantor, Robin. (1987). "How Fair is Safe Enough? The Cultural Approach to Societal Technology Choice." *Risk Analysis* 7: 3–9.

Renn, O. (1983). "Technology, Risk and Public Perception." *Angewandte Systemanalyse* 50–65.

Renn, Ortwin; Webler, Thomas; and Wiedemann, Peter, eds. (1995) *Fairness and Competence in Citizen Participation: Evaluating Models for Environmental Discourse*. Boston,: Kluwer Academic Publishers.

Resource Futures International. (1992). *Innovative Approaches to the Siting of Waste Management Facilities*. Pittsburgh, PA: Air and Waste Management Association.

Rubin, Norman. (1986). *Probability Times Consequences: Rational and Scientific, or Just Imprudent?* Toronto: Energy Probe.

Sandman, Peter. (1986). *Explaining Risk to Non-Experts*. Washington, DC: Annenberg School of Communications.

Slovic, P. et al. (1983). *Perceived Risk: Psychological Factors and Social Implications*. Les Arcs, France: NATO Advanced Study Institute.

Slovic, Paul; Fischhoff, Barauch; Lichtenstein, Sarah. (1982). "Rating the Risks: The Structure of Expert and Lay Perceptions." In *Risk in the Technological Society*. Christoph Hohenemser and Jeanne X. Kasperson, eds. Boulder, CO: Westview Press.

Talcott, Frederick W. (1992). "How Certain is the Environmental Risk Estimate?" *Resources* No. 103 (Spring): 10–15.

U.S. Environmental Protection Agency. (1989). *Risk Assessment Guidance for Superfund, Volume 1 Human Health Evaluation Manual (Part A), Interim Final*. Washington, D.C.: U.S. EPA (December).

U.S. General Accounting Office. (1983). *Siting of Hazardous Waste Landfills and Their Correlation with Racial and Economic Status of Surrounding Communities*. Washington, D.C.: U.S. GAO.

Wartenberg, Daniel and Chess Caron. (1992). "Risky Business: The Inexact Art of Hazard Assessment." *The Sciences* (March/April).

Wynne, Brian. (1980). "Technology, Risk and Participation: On the Social Treatment of Uncertainty." In *Science, Technology and Risk Assessment*. J. Conrad, ed. London: Academic Press.

4

THE NAFTA AND THE NORTH AMERICAN AGREEMENT ON ENVIRONMENTAL COOPERATION

J. Owen Saunders

Interactions between transnational free trade and environmental quality and protection now occupy an important place in international law and policy. It seems fair to say that the North American Free Trade Agreement (NAFTA) and the North American Agreement for Environmental Cooperation (AEC) represent a trend in international affairs and in national policy and administration. Where this is the only instance of protective environmental provisions following expanding transnational trade agreements, the AEC might be regarded as an exception. Its purpose was to overcome the opposition of environmental organizations in the United States that sought to prevent attrition of U.S. protective legislation on the precedent of the General Agreement on Tariffs and Trade (GATT) ruling in the Tuna-Dolphin controversy, narrowing the applicability of the U.S. Marine Mammal Protection Act. But a similar sequence of environmental protective legislation following free trade occurred earlier when transnational environmental agreements followed the formation of the European Community Committee and the European Union. National environmental legislation was strengthened and expanded to provide international consistency in the laws and policies under which trade was carried on. Legislation by treaty has been occurring in other areas of public policy. It provides a way of avoiding obstruction by the sovereignty dogma of issues requiring international cooperation. It tends to blur the distinction between the substance of national and international law.

NAFTA has both been attacked by environmentalists for its insensitivity to environmental issues and hailed as a breakthrough example of a "green" trade agreement. However one evaluates these conflicting views, the NAFTA is significant in that it represents an example of concerted, and at least to some degree effective, action by the environmental community to place environmental issues on the international trade agenda. Moreover, the NAFTA experience has potentially wider applicability than merely in the North American context. At a minimum, of course, the approach will certainly prove important with respect to the question of admitting additional parties to the agreement. It is virtually impossible to imagine the terms of accession for such parties   not including environmental provisions similar to those in the NAFTA and its side agreement on the environment. The NAFTA approach may, however, have even wider precedential value owing to the nature of the parties   involved. NAFTA is a North-South trade agreement very unlike those concluded in the past. Previous trade agreements between developed and developing countries have involved largely nonreciprocal trade concessions from developed countries toward developing states; in sum, they were typically regarded as a form of development assistance. The NAFTA, however, provides an example of an arrangement that was bargained for on a reciprocal basis, with both North and South making concessions. Indeed, it could be argued strongly that it was the developing state that made the bulk of the concessions.

The possible interest in the NAFTA approach as a precedent may prove especially high in respect of the environment. The concerns that were reflected with regard to the environment in the NAFTA negotiations are not unique to the North American experience. More and more they permeate the trade agenda, both among developed states and between developed and developing blocs. They cut to the heart of issues such as how one balances development and environmental objectives, and how one reconciles traditional international legal concepts of sovereignty with the need to establish supranational environmental norms. While this chapter focuses on the North American experience, therefore, it may nevertheless have broader implications.

This chapter begins with a brief description of the background to the environmental provisions of the NAFTA, focusing on the growing interest, especially on the part of environmentalists, in trade-environment issues. It then gives a brief overview of some of the major environmental provisions of the NAFTA; the NAFTA does make at least some modest contributions toward "greening" international trade law. Arguably, however, the greater contribution in the long run to resolving trade-environment problems (or, for that matter, environmental problems alone) is found in the side agreement on environmental cooperation. Accordingly, it is this agreement, rather than the NAFTA as such, to which the chapter turns for the bulk of the discussion. Finally, some brief comments are offered on the broader implications of the NAFTA experience for the future of environment/trade relations.

BACKGROUND

The past five years have seen the growth of a voluminous body of legal literature on issues relating to the intersection of trade and the environment (see, for example, Buckley, 1993; Charnovitz, 1993a; Jackson, 1992b; Petersmann, 1993; Thomas and Tereposky, 1993a). The increased (and, in a sense, renewed[1]) interest in trade and environment reflects both multilateral and regional factors. As to the former, the interest in the GATT and the environment is due partly to a number of environment-related trade disputes that have arisen before the GATT in recent years[2] and partly to the realization that the Uruguay Round of the GATT did not seem to be addressing environmental concerns effectively.[3]

Regionally, although the interest in the environment-trade nexus was not a major focus of the Canada-United States Free Trade Agreement (FTA)—either in the negotiation of the agreement or in the substance of the text finally negotiated—the FTA did act as the catalyst, at least in Canada, for discussing a number of environment-related issues. The particular emphasis on environmental issues in Canada was initiated not only by environmental groups, but also by a strong, and to a significant extent overlapping, nationalist constituency that was opposed to the agreement for a number of reasons. In the case of the FTA, this coalition of environmentalists and nationalists (together with other groups such as organized labor) found common cause in the issue of whether or not Canada had effectively surrendered its sovereignty with respect to management of its natural resources—and in particular its energy resources (Hudec and Quinn, 1989; Saunders, 1990a) and water resources (de Mestral and Leith, 1989).

Against this backdrop, it was not surprising that environmentalists in both Canada and the United States should concentrate their attention on the NAFTA negotiations. On the one hand, many American environmentalists were clearly frustrated with the treatment of environmental issues by the GATT, and especially the treatment of such issues in the *Tuna Dolphin* case (*United States Restrictions on the Imports of Tuna*, 1991). This frustration reflected a wider suspicion of the willingness of trade institutions generally to give full credit to environmental concerns. On the other hand, for Canadian environmentalists, the NAFTA negotiations were seen as an opportunity to redress some of the unresolved concerns flowing out of the FTA, or at least as a challenge to prevent further "losses." In addition to these background issues, a new dimension was introduced by the inclusion of Mexico.

The possible addition of Mexico to a free trade area raised directly the problem of dealing with the trade consequences of environmental policies, owing to a widespread assumption that enforcement of environmental laws in Mexico was substantially more relaxed than in either Canada or the United States.[4] In the view of many environmental and labor groups in Canada and the United States, this held at least three important implications for both trade and investment flows in North America. First, Mexican products would enjoy an "unfair" competitive advantage because of the lower costs of environmental compliance in Mexico. Secondly, the existence of such an advantage would inevitably draw investment—again "unfairly"—away from the other two partners to seek a pollution haven in Mexico. Finally, there would inevitably be downward pressure on domestic environmental standards in both Canada and the United States as businesses demanded relaxation of these standards in order to remain internationally competitive.

This was not the first time that these considerations had been raised in the context of North American free trade. Indeed, all of these factors had been advanced previously in Canada—but vis-à-vis the United States, and focusing particularly on certain southern states—as reasons for rejecting the FTA. However, they had special appeal in the case of the NAFTA because of the much greater gulf in effective (as opposed to de jure) environmental protection among the parties . The following section addresses briefly some of the major provisions of the NAFTA designed to deal with these environmental issues. As will be discussed, these provisions ultimately were not enough to satisfy political sentiment in the United States; however, they represented the first part of an environmental package that was eventually completed with the conclusion of a separate side agreement on the environment.

THE NAFTA AND THE ENVIRONMENT: AN OVERVIEW

As with the FTA, the NAFTA is preeminently a trade agreement. While it does have significant environmental provisions, and indeed goes well beyond previous trade agreements in this respect, the fundamental character of the NAFTA as a treaty on trade must underlie any analysis of its implications for the environment. Since the focus of this chapter is not the NAFTA per se, but rather the separate agreement on environmental cooperation, the discussion below will merely outline the major environmental aspects of the NAFTA.[5] Three of these are of particular interest: (1) the relationship between the NAFTA and international environmental obligations, (2) the implications of the NAFTA standards chapter with respect to setting environmental standards, and (3) the NAFTA provision dealing with the issue of pollution havens for investment.

International Environmental Obligations

With respect to international environmental obligations, the NAFTA attempts to address the fundamental concern of many environmentalists that trade obligations should be made to give way to international environmental obligations. This was an issue raised in the wake of the *Tuna Dolphin* decision[6] although that case did not itself involve an instance of a state in violation of its international environmental commitments. The NAFTA does not resolve entirely the question of the possible inconsistency of international trade and environmental commitments. However, it does take one step in this direction by spelling out the consequences of such inconsistency for certain specified agreements. For such agreements, the environmental obligations "shall prevail to the extent of the inconsistency, provided that where a Party has a choice among equally effective and reasonably available means of complying with such obligations, the Party chooses *the alternative that is the least inconsistent with the other provisions of [the NAFTA]."*[7]

Even accepting the "least inconsistent" test (which some environmentalists would resist), there remains of course the question of the possible conflict between the NAFTA and other international agreements not included under this provision. To an extent, some of the potential problems in this respect can be dealt with by established rules of treaty interpretation. However, these will not always provide satisfactory or even clear answers. Moreover, such rules would not address the even more vexing question of the conflict between the NAFTA and possible rules of customary international environmental law. However, the challenge faced by the NAFTA in this respect is not unique. Similar problems exist with respect to the GATT and the new World Trade Organization, where indeed they are more serious given their large and diverse membership.[8] In summary, while the NAFTA has not resolved this problem, it certainly represents a first useful step beyond the status quo.

Standards

With respect to the issue of environmental standards, the NAFTA deals separately with sanitary and phytosanitary (SPS) measures[9] and other standards-related measures (SRMs).[10] In negotiating these sections of the NAFTA, the negotiators were heavily influenced by the work that had already been accomplished in preliminary drafts emerging from the Uruguay Round of the GATT negotiations. Accordingly, although the NAFTA predates the final text of the Uruguay Round, many of its provisions are strikingly similar to those found in the latter (*Agreement on the Application of Sanitary and Phytosanitary Measures*, 1994; *Agreement on Technical Barriers to Trade*, 1994).

As to SPS measures, the NAFTA establishes the right of each party to take such measures, even if they are more stringent than international standards (Art. 712:1); concomitantly, it is the right of each party to establish the level of protection that it deems appropriate (Art. 712:2). However, this right is subject to constraints. The measure shall be based on "scientific principles" (Art. 712:3(a)) and "based on a risk assessment, as appropriate to the circumstances" (Art. 712:3(c)). Furthermore, there are prohibitions on nondiscriminatory treatment with respect to the goods of all parties (Art. 712:4), on the creation of unnecessary obstacles (Art. 712:5), and on the creation of disguised restrictions on trade (Art. 712:6). Despite the affirmation of sovereignty with regard to SPS measures, the NAFTA nevertheless encourages the reliance on international standards "as a basis for such measures" (Art. 713) and commits the parties "to the greatest extent practicable . . . [to] pursue equivalence of their respective sanitary and phytosanitary measures" (Art. 714). More generally, there are a number of provisions—largely based on the Uruguay Round negotiations—designed to increase the transparency of SPS provisions and to further cooperation between the parties.[11]

Regarding SRMs, including environmental measures, there is again established a general right to take such measures, including a right in each party to establish the level of protection it deems appropriate in the pursuance of "its legitimate objectives of safety or the protection of safety or the protection of human, animal or plant life or health, *the environment* or consumers" (Art. 904:2, emphasis added); a legitimate objective "does not include the protection of domestic production" (Art. 915:1). Again also, these rights are coupled with duties to provide non-discriminatory treatment (Art. 904:3) and to ensure that unnecessary obstacles to trade are not created (Art. 904:4). There is also a requirement on each party to use international standards as a basis for its SRMs, "except where [they] would be an ineffective means to fulfill its legitimate objectives" (Art. 905:1) and to work toward compatibility and equivalence in SRMs (Art. 906). In line with the chapter on SPS measures (and following the Uruguay Round of the GATT), there are additional provisions designed to emphasize the scientific basis of standards and to promote transparency and cooperation with respect to SRMs.

In summary, the environmental provisions of the NAFTA relating to standards are strongly influenced by the negotiations in the Uruguay Round of the GATT. As such, they emphasize the sovereign rights of each party to set its own standards (even though they may be more stringent than international standards), but at the same time attempt to ensure that such standards are scientifically based and do not merely serve to act as disguised protectionism.

Environment and Investment

Where the NAFTA does depart in a significant way from the GATT is in its provision concerning environment and investment. This provision is directed primarily at the earlier-noted concern on the part of the United States and Canada that the NAFTA could give rise to pollution havens.[12] In this respect the NAFTA parties "*recognize* that it is inappropriate to encourage investment by relaxing domestic health, safety or environmental measures" and agree that "a Party *should not* derogate from . . . such measures as an encouragement for . . . investment" (Art. 1114:2, emphasis added). Clearly, this provision is not worded as strongly as it might be; moreover, the only remedy provided where one Party feels that another is indeed offering such encouragement is consultations. However, given the reluctance of the GATT until recently to even deal with investment measures, this provision represented at least a modest step forward.

Conclusion

In summary, the NAFTA does address some important environmental issues, although the response will not be far-reaching enough to satisfy many environmentalists. While many of the provisions with respect to standards are modeled on the negotiations of the Uruguay Round of the GATT, there are also provisions where the NAFTA moves unambiguously—albeit modestly—beyond existing trade treaties. These include especially the provisions relating to the treatment of conflicts between the NAFTA and certain international environmental agreements and the provision relating to environment and investment.

Precisely because these provisions were somewhat modest, especially with respect to the binding character of the obligations, it was clear from an early point in the NAFTA debate (and became even clearer with the election of President Clinton) that separate provisions would have to be negotiated outside the NAFTA to meet environmental concerns not addressed in the NAFTA itself. The most serious of these concerns, especially for the United States, was the question of enforcement of environmental law. It is this concern that is at the heart of the separate agreement negotiated on environmental cooperation.

THE NORTH AMERICAN AGREEMENT ON ENVIRONMENTAL COOPERATION (AEC)

Introduction

The AEC (final draft, September 13, 1993 was, in effect, one of the prices[13] Mexico paid for admission to a North American free trade zone. Although it does not constitute a part of the NAFTA as such, it must nevertheless be viewed as part of the NAFTA package. However, the AEC differs from the NAFTA in approach in a fundamental respect. If the NAFTA can be characterized as a trade agreement with some environmental provisions, then the AEC can be characterized as an environmental agreement with some trade implications.

Examination of the AEC begins with an overview of the agreement's objectives and obligations. As will be evident, many of the obligations are what at best might be called "soft law." The discussion then turns to the institutions established under the AEC, the success of which will ultimately determine the real value of the agreement. Finally, there is a discussion of the agreement's provisions on dispute resolution; while politically these were crucial to the salability of the agreement, it will be suggested that in practice they may prove less interesting than other aspects of the AEC.

AEC: An Overview of Objectives and Obligations

Objectives

The degree to which the AEC is an agreement about environment rather than trade is reflected in its first article, which sets out the objectives of the agreement. Of the ten objectives listed, all but one are explicitly related to the promotion of environmental goals. These include references to sustainable development (Art. 1(b) and by implication 1(a)); increased cooperation for environmental protection and conservation (Art. 1 (c), (d), (f)); enhanced compliance with and enforcement of environmental requirements (Art. 1(f)); the promotion of transparency and public participation in developing environmental norms (Art. 1(h)); and the promotion of pollution prevention policies and practices (Art. 1(j)). The only explicit reference to trade obligations is in the objective to "avoid creating trade distortions or new trade barriers" (Art. 1(e)).[14] Some oblique reference to trade obligations may also be found in the objectives to "support the environmental goals and objectives of NAFTA" (Art. 1(d)) and to "promote economically efficient and effective environmental measures" (Art. 1(i)).

Obligations

This environmental thrust is similarly reflected in the obligations undertaken by the parties. The basic obligations under the AEC are of essentially two types—the first relating to domestic environmental law (Arts. 2–7, which constitute the bulk of the obligations), and the second relating to international cooperation (Arts. 20–21). Of these the former is by far the most important source of obligations.

The basic obligations with respect to domestic environmental law are in the main directed not at the heart of environmental laws and policy—that is, the level of environmental protection that is afforded by each Party. Rather the emphasis is on secondary, albeit extremely important, issues relating primarily to procedure and enforcement. The obligations include those of a general nature, such as the broad commitments by each party under Article 2 to take certain steps regarding environmental law and policy with respect to its territory,[15] to "consider implementing" as law a recommendation of the council under Article 10(5)(b) (discussed below), and to "consider" the prohibition of toxic or pesticide exports where the substance is prohibited in that party's own territory. There are also more specific commitments directed at the issues of transparency,[16] government enforcement action.[17] effective private access to remedies (Art. 6), and procedural guarantees.[18]

While most of the obligations set out above are directed procedural and enforcement concerns, with the level of protection treated as a matter reserved to the sovereign discretion of each party, Article 3 does speak directly to the latter issue:

Recognizing the right of each Party to establish its own levels of domestic environmental protection and environmental development policies and priorities . . . each Party shall ensure that its laws and regulations provide for high levels of environmental protection and shall strive to continue to improve those laws and regulations.

At first blush, this balancing of sovereign rights and environmental protection might seem to reflect the compromise that was achieved both in the *Stockholm Declaration on the Human Environment* (1972), Principle 21, and, more recently, in Principle 2 of the *Rio Declaration on Environment and Development* (1992)[19]; as such it would be disappointing to environmentalists, who have sought a stronger sense of obligation in respect of environmental protection. On closer examination, however, the AEC principle goes beyond either of these declarations insofar as it strikes a balance between sovereign rights and environmental protection in the context of purely domestic environmental law. That is, the obligations in Article 3 obtain even in the absence of transboundary environmental harm, whereas for both *Rio* and *Stockholm* the implicit assumption is that a duty to the international community is triggered only where there are transboundary effects.[20] As such, despite its relatively weak formulation, Article 3 represents a step forward in the articulation of binding international environmental norms.

Apart from the AEC obligations with respect to domestic environmental protection, there are also obligations with respect to cooperation and provision of information. These obligations include not only a general obligation to "endeavor to agree" on the application of the agreement, and to cooperate and consult in resolving matters affecting its operation (Art. 20(1)), but also to provide notification to "any other Party with an interest in the matter" of an environmental measure, actual or proposed, that "might materially affect the operation of [the] agreement or otherwise substantially affect that other party's interests under [the] Agreement" (Art. 20(2)). There is also a requirement to provide information on such measures when requested (Art. 20(3)) and, most interestingly, a right in any party to bring to the attention of another party possible violations of its environmental law (Art. 20(4)). There is a separate obligation to provide information to the Council and Secretariat set up under the agreement, subject to requirements of reasonableness (Art. 21).

The obligations regarding cooperation and provision of information have their genesis in a number of international law documents, although in some important respects they go beyond what might be considered emerging customary norms of international environmental law. For example, there are numerous illustrations now in international law of the principles of cooperation (Experts Group on Environmental Law, 1987, Art. 14; *Rio Declaration*, 1992, Principle 7; *Stockholm Declaration*, 1972, Principle 24), consultation (Experts Group, 1987, Art. 17; *Rio Declaration*, 1992, Principle 19), and notification to other states (Experts Group, 1987, Arts. 16, 19; *Rio Declaration*, 1992, Principles 18, 19) concerning activities having possible environmental impacts. (Earlier illustrations of such principles can be found in other international instruments—for example, those relating to international water law.) However, the thrust of such international obligations to date is, again, that they are predicated on extraterritorial environmental effects (usually phrased in terms of transboundary harm, although one could probably phrase a broader duty extending to effects on the global commons). Principle 19 of the *Rio Declaration* is typical in this respect: "States shall provide prior and timely notification and relevant information to potentially affected States on activities that may have *a significant adverse transboundary environmental effect* and shall consult with those States at an early stage and in good faith." (Emphasis added.)

The duties imposed on parties under the AEC would seem to go beyond those arising merely in the context of actual or potential transboundary harm, although admittedly the language of the agreement could be more helpful in this respect. Presumably, however, the reference to a Party with "an interest" in an environmental measure is not intended to refer only to those instances where the party is suffering direct environmental harm, especially since the article goes on to speak more generally of the party's interests under the agreement (Art. 20(2)). Read broadly, then, this interest could extend to virtually any environmental measure, insofar as the rights under the AEC include the right to demand that the obligations with respect to "high levels of environmental protection" under Article 3 be complied with.

In summary, the obligations under the AEC have much of their genesis in international environmental law, and similarly reflect an attempt to both give effect to the principle of state sovereignty with respect to domestic environmental law and to recognize the interests of all states in environmental protection. The AEC goes beyond general international environmental law in articulating an interest by all parties, not only in environmental policies that may affect them through transboundary impacts, but also in what would normally be considered the purely domestic environmental issues of another state. While the substantive commitment to "high levels of environmental protection" is not onerous, the obligations with respect to openness, transparency, and effectiveness of environmental law may prove particularly useful when considered against the backdrop of the institutional arrangements established under the agreement.

Institutional Arrangements: The Commission for Environmental Cooperation

While the obligations contained in the AEC arguably represent some modest advances on existing international environmental law, in many respects the greatest potential for innovative approaches to improving cooperative action on the environment is found in the institutional provisions of the agreement, which establish the Commission for Environmental Cooperation. The commission is based in Montreal, and comprises three bodies, each of which exercises distinctly different functions. These are the Council, the Secretariat, and the Joint Public Advisory Committee (JPAC) of the Commission for Environmental Cooperation. The first two of these are typical of intergovernmental organizations; the last, however, is atypical and is one of the most interesting aspects of the AEC, both in terms of its role in the functioning of the agreement and in terms of its potential as a model for other international agreements, especially those concerned with the environment.

The Council

The Council is the governing body of the Commission (Art. 10) and, as is typical of international organizations, comprises, in effect, the political masters ultimately responsible for the agreement; accordingly it is composed of "cabinet-level or equivalent" representatives or their designees (Art. 9(1)). The council will meet at least once a year in regular session (Art. 9(3)(a)) and shall meet in special session at the request of any of the parties (Art. 9(3)(b)). With some important exceptions (noted *infra*), council decisions will normally be taken by consensus (Art. 9(6)). Again as is typical of international organizations, much of the work of the council may be delegated to committees, working groups or expert groups (Art. 9(5)(a)), and it is anticipated that the council will seek the advice of non-governmental experts, including nongovernmental organizations (Art. 9(5)(b)).

As the governing body of the commission, the council approves the Commission's annual program and budget (Art. 10(1)(e)); oversees the operations of the secretariat (Art. 10(1)(c)); and exercises broad policy functions, including the consideration and development of recommendations on a wide range of environmental issues.[21] It is also charged with "strengthen[ing] cooperation on the development and . . . improvement of environmental laws and regulations" (Art.

10(3)), and "encourag[ing]" enforcement and compliance with environmental laws and regulations, and technical cooperation between parties (Art. 10(4)).

The Council also serves as the link between the Commission for Environmental Cooperation and the Free Trade Commission established under the NAFTA. In this respect, it is noteworthy that the Council is charged with the duty to "cooperate with the NAFTA Free Trade Commission *to achieve the environmental goals and objectives of the NAFTA"* (Art. 6, emphasis added). The essentially subordinate place of the Council vis-à-vis the Free Trade Commission is emphasized in the specification of the Council's functions. For example, it is to "provid[e] assistance in consultations under Article 1114 of the NAFTA" (Art. 10(6)(b)).[22] Similarly, with regard to preventing or resolving "environment-related trade disputes,"[23] it is to make recommendations to the Free Trade Commission only with respect to avoiding disputes (Art. 10(6)(c)(ii)) and identifying appropriate experts to assist NAFTA bodies (Art. 10(6)(c)(iii)). Finally, it is charged with "otherwise *assisting* the Free Trade Commission in environment-related matters" (Art. 10(6)(e), emphasis added).[24]

The Secretariat

The Secretariat is, in effect, the day-to-day operating arm of the Commission: it "shall provide technical, administrative and operational support to the Council... and such other support as the Council may direct" (Art. 11(5)). It is headed by an executive director, appointed by the council for a three-year term (renewable for one additional term, with the position rotating among nationals of the different parties: Art. 11(1)). Staffing of the Secretariat is then the responsibility of the executive director, subject to general standards established by the Council (Art. 11(2)); the Council has the power to reject appointments that fail to meet such standards.[25] While there is therefore room for political considerations intruding at the initial appointment stage (especially for the executive director, where any party could effectively exercise a veto), the intention is that, once appointed, the director and staff should be free of political influence.[26]

The Secretariat has three major specific functions assigned to it under the agreement: preparation of the annual report of the Commission (Art. 12), preparation of reports on other matters (Art. 13), and certain duties relating to submissions on enforcement matters (Arts. 14–15). Of potentially most interest is its role with respect to the annual report are the Secretariat's power to undertake reports on its own initiative. Such reports are of two types. First, the Secretariat has the right to prepare a report for the Council "on any matter within the scope of the annual program" (Art. 13). Depending upon how broadly one interprets this language this alone could amount to a substantial power of investigation. Second the Secretariat may prepare a report on "any other matter related to the cooperative functions of this Agreement" provided that it notifies council of its intention and provided that there is not a Council objection (based on a two-thirds vote) within thirty days of notification.[27] The agreement is therefore tilted in favor of such reports going forward, rather than requiring the granting of permission from the Council.

It might of course be objected that the right to report is not a right to decide, and as such the actual powers of the Secretariat are less than impressive. However, given that this is an international forum, it would be unrealistic to expect that governments would allow final decision-making powers on significant questions of policy to pass out of the hands of political masters (and indeed, one could argue that such an approach would be questionable as a matter of democratic responsibility). As a practical matter, however, the political weight of such independent reports may be very significant, especially given that during the course of the information gathering the Secretariat may draw upon the widest array of sources, including the JPAC (Art. 13(2)(c)) and "public consultations, such as conferences, seminars and symposia" (Art. 13(2)(e)). Moreover, the report is to be made public within sixty days of its submission to the Council unless the latter decides by consensus to the contrary (Art. 13(3)), effectively preventing any one party from "vetoing" its release. In summary, this power of the Secretariat to report on matters on its own initiative may well be an effective tool for raising the international visibility of environmental issues. Obviously, however, much will depend in this respect on the willingness of the Secretariat, and especially its executive director, to exercise a strong and independent voice. The Secretariat could also be hampered significantly in exercising a strong voice by financial constraints, given that ultimately its budget must be approved by the Council.

Apart from its reporting functions under Articles 12 and 13, the Secretariat also has separate functions with respect to the issue of effective enforcement of environmental law. In this regard, the Secretariat acts as the Commission's initial point of contact for complaints, from either NGOs or private individuals, that a party is failing to effectively enforce its environmental law. Assuming such a complaint meets some minimum threshold criteria of acceptability (Art. 14(1)).[28] the Secretariat determines "whether the submission merits a response from the Party" (Art. 14(2)). Again, in making this decision, the Secretariat is to be guided by specified criteria.[29]

In the event that the Secretariat decides to request a response from a party, the latter is given thirty days (in exceptional cases sixty days) to reply (Art. 14(3)). The party may respond in two ways. First, it may advise the Secretariat that "the matter is the subject of a pending judicial or administrative proceeding," in which case the Secretariat is precluded from taking any further action (Art. 14(3)(a)). Alternatively, it may submit other information as it wishes.

In light of the response from the Party, the Secretariat must then make a further decision as to whether or not the submission warrants the development of a "factual record" (Art. 15(1)). If it decides this step is appropriate, it must then approach the Council for permission, which can instruct the Secretariat to take this step by a two-thirds vote (Art. 15(2)). In preparing this record, the Secretariat is required to consider any information provided by any party, and may also consider other information from a variety of sources, including that developed by itself or independent experts (Art. 15(4)). Following the submission of the Secretariat's draft of the factual record to Council, further comments on the accuracy are restricted to parties, who have forty-five days to respond (Art. 15(5)). Following the Secretariat's incorporation of such comments into the draft, the Council by a two-thirds vote "may" make the record publicly available (Art. 15(7)) or available to the Joint Public Advisory Committee (Art. 16(7)). Although there is room at this stage for the Council to withhold release permanently, this would seem highly unlikely in practice, given the expectations raised by the previous public input into the process and given the voting procedure.

The Joint Public Advisory Committee (JPAC)

The JPAC is the most innovative institution established under the AEC. However, its role is only briefly described in the agreement,[30] and its effectiveness will ultimately depend not only on the role it sees for itself, but also the financing allocated to it by the Council.

The JPAC will normally comprise fifteen members, with equal numbers appointed by each party (Art. 16(1)). The JPAC would not appear to have a day-to-day operational existence. This is suggested by the lack of any supporting institutional infrastructure, and by the fact that it is required to meet only once a year (Art. 16(3)). The functions of the JPAC are both generally to provide advice to the Council on virtually any matter related to the agreement (Art. 16(4)) and to provide information to the Secretariat, including information related to the development of a factual record (Art. 16(5)).

The provisions on the JPAC provide cause for both disappointment and optimism. With respect to the former, of the three institutions in the Commission, the JPAC has the least well-defined role. While there also remain details to be fleshed out regarding the interplay of the Council and Secretariat, there is more than a mere fleshing out required for the JPAC. For example, there are lacking even such basic provisions as a fixed term for members (to encourage their independence) or a reference to the qualifications expected of them (to encourage appointments of a high caliber). Nor is there any direction as to the extent to which JPAC members should represent a range of perspectives on the environment; indeed, under the wording of the agreement it would be open to a party to appoint nothing but government officials to the JPAC, although that has not been the case to date.[31] Presumably these are issues that will be worked out by the ministers responsible for the agreement. More problematically though—as perhaps reflected in the shortcomings noted above—it is not clear that the parties to the AEC have clearly thought out the role of a body such as the JPAC. As it stands, the JPAC would seem to be a largely reactive body, providing input to the Council and Secretariat largely on an ad hoc basis as required. The JPAC is not given an explicit role with respect to undertaking on its own initiative its own work agenda—a role that is given to the Secretariat. One could imagine a number of roles for a body such a the JPAC, including actively fostering transborder ties amongst environmental NGOs, but there is little direction provided in this regard in the AEC.

It is possible of course that, with the right membership, the JPAC could assert a strong activist presence. For example, the provision that the JPAC "may provide advice to the Council on any matter within the scope of [the AEC]" (Art. 16(4)) could be read as granting a mandate to give unsolicited as well as solicited advice.

Again, however, as with the Secretariat, the ability of the JPAC to pursue this course may be largely determined by the budget allocated to it by the Council.

Conclusions

In summary, the institutional provisions of the AEC are a blend of features characteristic of international organizations and features that are new to this agreement. While the potential of these institutions has yet to be realized, there are at least three aspects of the AEC that hold particular promise. First, the ability of the secretariat to exercise an independent role in the issuance of reports on a wide range of environmental issues suggests that the commission may prove more than a captive of its political masters. Secondly, the procedure for the development of a factual record at the initiation of nongovernmental bodies is an interesting and innovative means of allowing citizens and NGOs a role as watchdogs on government in an international forum. Finally, while one would have hoped for more than the skeletal provisions on the JPAC, the concept is in principle encouraging and the role as defined in the agreement could allow for the development of an activist committee capable of forging and encouraging ties across borders among environmental NGOs.

It is true, of course, that the powers of the secretariat and the JPAC are largely recommendatory, with ultimate decision-making power in the hands of the council. However, there is much to suggest in the evolution of domestic environmental law and policy that the power to air environmental issues openly and publicly in an institutionalized forum may prove to be highly effective if properly utilized.

Dispute Resolution

A crucial aspect of the commission in terms of its acceptability to all parties was the regime for dispute resolution. Indeed, agreement on a regime with some teeth was critical to the larger issue of the "selling" of the NAFTA in the U.S. Congress. By contrast, the Canadian government made it clear that if these teeth included trade sanctions, this would be a "deal breaker" for Canada.[32] The regime ultimately agreed upon reflects both these concerns, and procedurally would appear to be heavily influenced by the dispute resolution mechanisms found in the NAFTA. The approach, typical of international agreements, is a graduated series of steps, beginning with consultations, moving on to other attempts to resolve the dispute, then to arbitration, implementation of the arbitrative report, and, as a last resort, penalties for noncompliance. If practice under the GATT (where one finds a sequence that is in some respects similar) is instructive, it is likely that most disputes will never reach the stage of arbitration.

The most notable aspect of the AEC's dispute resolution procedures is their highly limited scope, a scope that reflected the most serious concern on the part of the United States in negotiating the AEC. Rather than provide for the settlement of a broad range of environmental disputes, the AEC restricts application of the mechanism to cases where there is alleged a "persistent pattern of failure" by a party "to effectively enforce its environmental law." This is critical in that the AEC mechanism does not provide a forum to address other shortcomings under the agreement—perhaps most notably, each party's commitment in Art. 3 to "ensure that its laws and regulations provide for high levels of environmental protection."

A second important restriction on the dispute resolution mechanism is that it is available only to parties to the agreement. While this is typical of international agreements, it does stand in contrast to the earlier-discussed provisions allowing significant room for actions initiated by individuals and NGOs.

Consultations

One example of the influence of the NAFTA approach to dispute resolution is found in the provisions on consultation, which are very similar to those provided in Article 2006 of the NAFTA. Consultations are, of course, the first step in dispute resolution typically provided for in international agreements generally. Under the AEC, any party may request consultations "regarding whether there has been a persistent pattern of failure of [another] Party to effectively enforce its environmental law" (Art. 22(1)). It is anticipated that a third party that "considers it has a substantial interest in the matter" will also be entitled to participate in the consultations (Art. 22(3)).[33]

Initiation of Procedures

Failing the resolution of the matter through consultations, a consulting party may request a special session of the council (Art. 23(1).[34] The council may then use its good offices, conciliation, mediation, or other procedures in an attempt to assist in the resolution of the dispute (Art. 23(4)(b)). It may also make recommendations that, at the council's option, may be made public (Art. 23(4)(c)).

Arbitrative Panels

If the dispute is still unresolved within sixty days of the council convening under Art. 23, a party may request the convening of an arbitrative panel to consider the matter. However, the ambit of the dispute resolution mechanism is narrowed significantly at this point: such panels can be convened only where the pattern of failure to enforce environmental law

relates to a situation involving workplaces, firms, companies or sectors that produce goods or provide services:

(a) traded between the territories of the Parties; or
(b) that compete, in the territory of the Party complained against, with goods or services produced or provided by persons of another Party. (Art. 24(1))

This provision again emphasizes the degree to which the agreement is driven by trade considerations. Although it is certainly true that a wide range of environmental issues will be open for consideration at a number of points in the agreement, when it comes to the issue of binding arbitration, only those environmental issues with a trade nexus can trigger action.

The process for selecting the arbitrative panel is similarly modeled on the process established under the NAFTA, but with some differences reflecting the need for appropriate expertise given the environmental nature of the agreement. The council is required to establish a roster of qualified individuals (Art. 25(1)) with expertise in either environmental law, international dispute resolution, or other relevant experience (Art. 25(2)(a)). The professional and independent nature of the roster is emphasized, with an explicit prohibition on a member maintaining an affiliation with, or receiving instructions from, any party, the secretariat, or the JPAC (Art. 25(2)(c)). In the event of a dispute going to arbitration, a panel of five members is selected, with the disputing parties   jointly choosing a chair (Art. 27 (1)(b)) and each selecting two panelists who are citizens of the other party (Art. 27(1)(c)); where there are more than two disputing parties, the selection of the panel proceeds on a similar path (Art. 27(2)(b),(c)). Panelists will normally be selected from the roster, although nonroster individuals may also be nominated, subject to a peremptory challenge from another disputing party (Art. 27(3)).

After submissions and arguments by the parties, and possibly also by a third party that wishes to be heard (under Art. 29), and after receiving any relevant expert advice, the panel is then required to present an initial report to the disputing parties. The report must contain findings of fact, a determination as required in the terms of reference and, in the event of an affirmative finding, recommendations for resolution of the dispute (Art. 31(2)). After receiving any comments by disputing parties on the initial report, the panel shall then present a final report to these parties, who shall transmit it to the council together with any comments a disputing party wishes to append. Five days later the report is to be published (Art. 32).

In implementing the recommendations consequent on an affirmative finding by an arbitration panel, the disputing parties themselves may agree on a satisfactory action plan to remedy the "persistent pattern of failure" (Art. 33). Alternatively, if there is a failure to agree either to an action plan or to whether a party is fully implementing an action plan, the council shall reconvene the panel upon the request of a disputing Party (Art. 34(1); there are time limits attached to these various stages).

Once reconvened, in cases where there is nonagreement on an action plan, the panel may approve the plan proposed by the party complained against or establish an appropriate plan (Art. 34(4)(a)), and also impose a monetary penalty "where warranted" (Art. 34(4)(b)).[35] This assessment is to be paid into a commission fund "and shall be expended at the direction of the Council to improve or enhance the environment or environmental law enforcement in the Party complained against, consistent with its law" (Annex 34(3)). In those cases where the panel is reconvened to consider whether there is indeed full implementation of an action plan, the panel, in the event of an affirmative finding, is *required* to impose a monetary penalty (Art. 34(5)). Continued failure to fully implement the action plan may result in a reconvening of the panel by the council at the request of a complaining party (Art. 35).

As a final resort, in the event of continuing noncompliance either with respect to paying an assessed penalty or with respect to implementing an action plan, a complaining Party may suspend the NAFTA benefits against the offending party (Art. 36)[36] unless that party is Canada. While enforcement through the removal of NAFTA benefits is not allowed vis-à-vis Canada (Annex 36A(3)), panel determinations that could otherwise result in such trade sanctions may be filed by the commission in a Canadian court, where for enforcement purposes they will be treated as court orders, not subject to review or appeal (Annex 36A(2)). The commission may then have the order enforced by way of summary proceedings (Annex 36A (2)(d),(e)).

In summary, the AEC does indeed provide the teeth that were promised to the environmental community. However, given the steps that must be taken to arrive at this point, it is unlikely that the teeth—at least with respect to the imposition of trade sanctions—will be often employed. This does not detract entirely from the importance of the arbitrative provisions, of course; the very fact that they exist should act as a strong inducement toward compliance. However, the scope of the disputes that can be reached by arbitration—and by the dispute resolution mechanism more generally—is such that many significant environmental issues will not fall within it. This points once again to the importance of relying on those provisions in the AEC that are built on cooperation.

CONCLUSIONS

Although the NAFTA has a number of innovative provisions dealing with the environment, it remains preeminently a trade agreement. As such, it is unlikely that any version of the NAFTA concluded by trade negotiators would meet with the full approval of the environmental community in North America. Some environmentalists, indeed, would assert that the very concept of an international trade system works against the ideal of local sustainability and is therefore bad in itself. A broader range of environmentalists, while not opposed to international trade as such, would nevertheless contend that international trade institutions are inevitably biased in favor of open trade, even at the expense of legitimate environmental concerns. It is to this segment of the environmental community that the compromises in the NAFTA are directed. That the NAFTA does not go far enough in this direction is evidenced by the political demands that led to the North American Agreement on Environmental Cooperation.

The AEC, like the NAFTA itself, represents inevitably a series of compromises. The major compromise negotiated in the AEC is between two primary interests. On the one hand there was a demand (especially on the part of the United States) for an environmental agreement, with teeth, that would address concerns regarding the use of lower environmental standards to gain trade advantages and to attract investment. On the other hand was a concern (especially on the part of Mexico) that trade indeed be free and that environmental standards not be used as a justification either for protectionism or for interference with state sovereignty in purely domestic affairs. Canadian interests, somewhat quixotically, lay in both camps: while there was popular concern in Canada regarding the loss of jobs due to lower environmental standards elsewhere, there was also concern, on the basis of experience with natural resources protectionism in the United States, that an agreement that allowed for trade sanctions as a means of enforcing environmental obligations would see unfair attacks (especially by U.S. interests) on Canadian industry.

The compromise achieved in the AEC speaks to both these concerns. There are indeed teeth in this agreement, with the ultimate possibility of significant penalties, whether in the loss of trade sanctions or a court-enforced monetary penalty. However, the teeth are those of an international arbitrative body, not those of a domestic trade tribunal that may be suspected of playing to more parochial concerns. Moreover, the ultimate penalty most probably will never or rarely be imposed, given the likelihood of agreement or compliance with panel findings before this stage is reached. Finally, and most importantly, the very scope of the dispute resolution mechanism is highly limited, especially for those disputes that go to arbitration.

What implications does the AEC hold for environmental policy as we move into the twenty-first century? Arguably the agreement reflects and supports at least three trends in international environmental policy. The first is the growing integration of environmental and other socioeconomic policies. Of course, environmentalists have always paid at least lip service to the notion that environmental concerns are inevitably linked to the broader questions of how we organize ourselves as a society. The recognition of the relationship between trade and environment in the NAFTA and the AEC is only one aspect of this integration (witness also the growing links between environmentalism and other forces such as feminism and human rights), but given the pivotal role of trade in shaping international economic relationships today, it is an extremely important one. Moreover the paths taken in the NAFTA and the AEC may well prove influential in a broader multilateral setting, in the context of both an expanded NAFTA and a new round of multilateral trade negotiations under the auspices of the World Trade Organization.

A second important trend reflected in the NAFTA and the AEC is the changing nature of relations between developing and developed countries (even assuming the crude distinction between developed and developing is still useful). As noted in this chapter, the NAFTA breaks dramatically with the traditional approach to North-South trade agreements insofar as it represents a true bargaining process; it does not reflect the traditional paternalistic approach to such relationships, which assumed that concessions would inevitably flow in one direction. Similarly, the AEC casts equivalent environmental duties on all parties, although the costs of such obligations are likely to fall most heavily, at least in the initial years, on Mexico. While many environmentalists would suggest that these obligations are not as onerous as would be ideal, they nevertheless represent a welcome change in direction from the unilateralist tendencies reflected in such controversies as the *Tuna Dolphin* case, which have raised the specter of ecoprotectionism or ecoimperialism.[37] It should be stressed, however, that to serve as such a model, the

AEC must first demonstrate its effectiveness as a forum for cooperation, rather than as a body focused primarily on disciplining its members.

Finally, there is discernible now in the environmental community a growing sense of the need for international cooperation at the level of NGOs to address environmental concerns, including environmental concerns related to international trade; this goes beyond merely acting through international NGOs and involves direct contact between domestic NGOs in different countries. In this respect, the AEC holds the potential for encouraging much greater transborder cooperation between environmental groups in North America, both because of the transnational focus that the commission will bring to bear on environmental problems, and because of institutional structures such as the JPAC, which will involve joint cooperation at a personal level of representatives from different national environmental constituencies. This is, however, the optimistic view; it follows, of course, that without sufficient funding and high-quality appointments, the commission could be reduced to little more than a shell. Again, this would be a missed opportunity not just for the parties to the agreement, but also to the development of North-South environmental relations more generally.

NOTES

I would like to thank Lee Lau and KayLynn Litton-Goelzer, law students at the University of Victoria and the University of Calgary, respectively, who served as Research Assistants at the Institute and provided assistance with this chapter. An earlier version was published as "NAFTA and the North American Agreement on Environmental Cooperation: A New Model for International Collaboration on Trade and the Environment," in (1994) *Colorado Journal of International Environmental Law & Policy* (1994), 5(2), 273–304.

1. There was considerable interest in trade-environment issues in the 1970s on the part of trade theorists, especially economists. The early work in this area, beginning in the 1970s and continuing through the 1980s, was centered especially in the Organization for Economic Cooperation and Development, focusing particularly on pollution-related issues (most notably the so-called Polluter Pays Principle). However, the interest of lawyers and environmentalists in such issues is of much more recent vintage. The history of the evolving interest in trade-environment issues is discussed in Saunders, 1990b.

2. Some of these disputes have been the subject of the GATT panels—most notably, the highly visible dispute over the incidental killing of dolphins associated with tuna fishing: *General Agreement on Tariffs and Trade: Dispute Settlement Panel Report on United States—Restrictions on Imports of Tuna*, GATT Dispute Settlement Panel Report, submitted to the parties 16 August 1991, reproduced in 30 International Legal Materials 1594 (1991). Others, such as the dispute between the United States and the European Union regarding the use of hormones in the production of beef, while not going to a GATT panel, have nevertheless proved to be serious irritants in international trade relations. See Jackson, 1992a.

3. The general unhappiness on this score has led to proposals for a new "green round" of multilateral trade negotiations to address environmental issues: see De Vries, 1992.

4. It seems generally conceded that it is enforcement rather than the substance of Mexican environmental laws that is the real problem to be addressed, although the latter has also caused concern; see Charnovitz, 1994, at 279–280.

5. For more detail on the environmental provisions of the NAFTA, see: Charnovitz, 1993b; Thomas and Tereposky, 1993b; and Condon, 1993. While the aspects discussed below are the most important ones, they are by no means the only provisions with possible implications for the environment. For example, NAFTA Art. 2101:1 usefully clarified the interpretation of GATT Art. XX(b) and XX(c), the so-called "environmental exceptions," to remove any doubt that these provisions (at least for the NAFTA parties) included, respectively, environmental measures to protect human, animal or plant life or health and measures relating to the conservation of living and non-living natural exhaustible resources.

6. The case involved, among other things, the question of whether U.S. legislation designed to protect the incidental killing of dolphins associated with purse-seine tuna fishing in the Eastern Tropical Pacific, and which had the effect of prohibiting imports of Mexican tuna into the United States, placed the United States in violation of its GATT obligations. The GATT panel decided in favor of Mexico on the major points (although finding in favor of the United States with respect to a separate issue of labeling requirements). In rejecting the U.S. attempts to rely on two GATT exceptions relating to protection of animal health (Art. XX(b)) and conservation (Art. XX(g)), the panel held that these exceptions were aimed at production or consumption within the jurisdiction of the importing country. It rejected the notion that the United States had the right to "unilaterally determine" the health protection or conservation policies of other states. The ruling, while never adopted because of a political settlement of the dispute between the United States and Mexico, infuriated many environmentalists in the United States. Interestingly, however, there was no serious contention that Mexico had violated international fisheries laws by its practices. Rather, the case represented a situation where a nation (the United States), unhappy with the state of international law attempted to apply its domestic law, in such a way as to influence fishing practices beyond its own borders. For a discussion of the U.S. legislative initiatives in this respect, and their intersection with GATT norms, see McDorman, 1991. A reaction to the case typical of the U.S. environmental community can be found in Housman and Zaelke, 1992. For a more general argument that unilateralism (and U.S. unilateralism specifically) has worked to the benefit of the environment, see Charnovitz, 1992, at 206–208; for a perspective less sympathetic to the use of unilateral measures, see Saunders, 1992.

7. Art. 104:1. Emphasis added. Art. 104 includes specifically as such agreements, the *Convention on International Trade in Endangered Species of Wild Fauna and Flora* (1973) [CITES]; the *Montreal protocol on Substances that Deplete the Ozone Layer* (1987); the *Basel Convention on the Control of Transboundary Movements of Hazardous Wastes and Their Disposal* (1989) [on its entry into force for all three parties]; as well as any agreements included in Annex 104.1 (two bilateral agreements were included at the time of negotiation), which may (pursuant to Art. 104:2) be added to by agreement of the parties.

8. Moreover, it should be noted that such conflicts may prove more theoretical than actual. For example, no GATT panel (nor any panel established under the FTA or the NAFTA) has yet held that international environmental treaty obligations would have to yield to obligations under international trade law, and, as a practical matter, a state making such a claim might well face intense political pressures (not to mention embarrassment).

9. In Chapter 7 (Agriculture and Sanitary and Phytosanitary Measures), Section B. Sanitary and phytosanitary measures refer to those measures designed to protect human, animal, or plant life from risks related to additives, contaminants, pests, or disease (for a definition—which follows the text of the Uruguay Round—see Art. 724).

10. Chapter 9, including specifically environmental protection (Art 904:1). For a detailed discussion of the NAFTA's treatment of SRMs, see McConnell (1993).

11. See, for example, Art. 717 ("Control, Inspection and Approval Procedures"), Art. 718 ("Notification, Publication and Provision of Information"), Art. 719 ("Inquiry Points"),

Art. 720 ("Technical Cooperation"), and Art. 722 ("Committee on Sanitary and Phytosanitary Measures").

12. Although some writers have questioned whether investment flows are heavily influenced by the level of environmental standards imposed by a country. For different perspectives on this question, see Low, 1992.

13. See also (concluded by the parties at the same time) the *North American Agreement on Labor Cooperation* and the *Understanding Between the parties to the North American Free Trade Agreement Concerning Chapter Eight—Emergency Action*, September 13, 1993.

14. Interestingly the language would seem to be entirely prospective here; that is, there is no explicit goal under this agreement of eliminating or even reducing *existing* trade distortions or barriers.

15. These include (under Art. 2(1)) commitments to:

(a) periodically prepare and make publicly available reports on the state of the environment;
(b) develop and review environmental emergency preparedness measures;
(c) promote education in environmental matters, including environmental law;
(d) further scientific research and technology development in respect to environmental matters;
(e) assess, as appropriate, environmental impacts; and
(f) promote the use of economic instruments for the efficient achievement of environmental goals.

16. Art. 4 requires prompt publication of "laws, regulations, procedures and administrative rulings of general application" and, to the extent possible, advance publication of proposed measures and the provision of an opportunity to interested persons and parties to comment on them.

17. Art. 5(1) requires that "each Party shall effectively enforce its environmental laws and regulations through appropriate government action" and then lists a number of illustrative actions that might be taken toward this end. It also addresses the issue of judicial and quasi-judicial or administrative enforcement proceedings (Art. 5(2)) and speaks to the appropriateness of sanctions and remedies (Art. 5(3)).

18. Art. 7 speaks to issues such as the openness and fairness of hearings, the timeliness of proceedings, the desirability of written reasons, and the availability of judicial review. In essence the procedures contemplated in Art. 7 are of the sort that would typically be expected of judicial or quasi-judicial tribunals under either Canadian or U.S. law.

19. The *Rio Declaration* (1992) provides in Principle 2:

States have, in accordance with the Charter of the United Nations and the principles of international law, the sovereign right to exploit their own resources pursuant to their own environmental and developmental policies, and the responsibility to ensure that activities within their jurisdiction or control do not cause damage to the environment of other States or of areas beyond the limits of national jurisdiction.

This is an almost verbatim restatement of Principle 21 of the *Stockholm Declaration*.

20. Admittedly, the *Rio Declaration* also provides for a more general obligation, not dependent on transboundary harm, in Principle 11:

States shall enact effective environmental legislation. Environmental standards, management objectives and priorities should reflect the environmental and developmental context to which they apply. Standards applied by some countries may be inappropriate and of unwarranted economic and social cost to other countries, in particular developing countries.

Obviously, however, this does not speak directly to the *level* of environmental protection that should be enacted in such legislation.

21. Art. 10(2). The article lists eighteen specific topics that touch on most areas of environmental law and policy, and then adds (Art. 10(2)(s)) "other matters as it may decide." Additional recommendatory powers are found in Art. 10(5), with respect to public access to information and decision making, and to appropriate limits for specific pollutants; in Art. 10(7) with respect to environmental impact assessment of projects with potential "significant adverse transboundary effects"; and in Art. 10(9) with respect to reciprocal access of persons to rights and remedies in the event of harm caused by pollution originating in another party.

22. This refers to the NAFTA's provisions on environmental measures relating to investment, discussed earlier.

23. The very language is revealing; the disputes here are phrased as trade-related with environmental aspects, rather than environmental disputes with a trade aspect.

24. The council is also charged with "considering on an ongoing basis the environmental effects of the NAFTA." However, it would appear to have no power to exercise any significant powers on the basis of its considerations.

25. Only a two-thirds vote is required for such decisions, in contrast to the consensus that is required for the appointment of the executive director. In making appointments to the secretariat, the executive director is further required to take into account lists of possible candidates prepared not only by the parties themselves, but also by the JPAC (Art. 11(2)(b)). Additionally, "due regard shall be paid to the importance of recruiting an equitable proportion of the professional staff from among the nationals of each Party" (Art. 11(2)(c)).

26. Thus Art. 11(4) provides that the executive director and staff "shall not seek or receive instructions from any government or any other authority external to the Council. Each Party shall respect the international character of the responsibilities of the Executive Director and the staff and shall not seek to influence them in the discharge of their responsibilities."

27. There is one significant constraint on what the secretariat can report on under this provision: Art. 13(1) excludes "issues related to whether a party has failed to enforce its environmental laws and regulations." The secretariat's role in this respect is dealt with separately in the agreement (in Arts. 14–15). The commission has already acted under Art. 13 to investigate the death of waterfowl at the Silva agricultural reservoir near León, Mexico, at the request of three environmental NGOs.

28. These criteria relate primarily to clarity, certain procedural regularities, and a finding that the submission "appears to be aimed at promoting enforcement rather than at harassing industry" (Art. 14 (1)(d)). One can see some obvious difficulties in assessing this last requirement, especially, for example, if an NGO complainant is an industry association.

29. These include (Art. 14(2)) whether:

(a) the submission alleges harm to the person or organization making the submission;
(b) the submission, alone or in combination with other submissions, raises matters whose further study in this process would advance the goals of this Agreement;
(c) private remedies available under the Party's law have been pursued; and
(d) the submission is drawn exclusively from mass media reports.

Unfortunately, this provision gives no indication of how these criteria should be weighted. To take only one problem, what is the significance of the reference to "harm" to the complainant as a factor guiding the secretariat's response? Narrowly read, this could raise obstacles that have confronted plaintiffs in domestic courts with respect to standing in environmental cases (albeit the criterion here is formally directed at the remedy rather than the issue of standing).

30. The JPAC is established in one Article, Art. 16, under Part Three, Section C ("Advisory Committees"). There are two other types of committees provided for in this section. The others, however—national advisory committees and governmental committees—may be set up at the discretion of each party to advise it on the implementation and elaboration of the agreement. Since they have no formal role at the international level, they will not be discussed here. Indeed, other than for hortatory purposes, it is not clear why they are referred to in the agreement, since presumably a Party could establish such committees without authorization under the AEC.

31. The initial appointment of fifteen members to the JPAC (five from each of the parties) comprises a blend of representatives from the private sector, foundations, aboriginal and environmental groups, academia, and regional/local government. The initial work of the JPAC has focused on gathering recommendations for possible procedures for citizens to make submissions on enforcement matters under Art. 14 and 15 of the AEC. The JPAC report in this respect was given to the council in August 1995.

32. The Canadian insistence on the avoidance of trade sanctions as a means of inducing compliance was rooted in a long-standing distrust of the U.S. willingness to use trade sanctions for protectionist ends, especially in the natural resources sector. For a discussion of the background to these fears, see Yoder, 1987.

33. The council may, however, provide otherwise in setting the rules and procedures for the commission. This provision mirrors the third-party rights established in the NAFTA, Art. 2006(3).

34. This mirrors, though with some differences, the NAFTA Art. 2007.

35. The penalty, referred to as a "monetary enforcement assessment," is specified in greater detail in Annex 34, which both places limits on such a penalty and provides factors to consider in the determination of the assessment.

36. The suspension in benefits is limited, however, pursuant to Annex 36B. In the event of a request on the part of the party complained against, the panel may be reconvened by the council to consider whether that party has since fully complied with the action plan or has paid the monetary assessment; given an affirmative finding, the suspension of benefits will be terminated: Art. 36(3). The panel may be similarly reconvened to consider whether the suspension of benefits is "manifestly excessive": Art. 36(5).

37. The concerns of developing countries in this respect were reflected in Principle 12 of the *Rio Declaration*, supra, note 62, which provides:

States should cooperate to promote a supportive and open international economic system that would lead to economic growth and sustainable development in all countries, to better address the problems of environmental degradation. *Trade policy measures for environmental purposes should not constitute a means of arbitrary or unjustifiable discrimination or a disguised restriction on international trade. Unilateral actions to deal with environmental challenges outside the jurisdiction of the importing country should be avoided.* Environmental measures addressing transboundary or global environmental problems should, as far as possible, be based on an international consensus. (Emphasis added.)

REFERENCES

Agreement on the Application of Phytosanitary Measures, GATT Doc. MTN/FA/Corr.5-Annex 1A (March 11, 1994).

Agreement on Technical Barriers to Trade, GATT Doc. MTN/FA/Corr.5-Annex 1A (March 11, 1994).

Basel Convention on the Control of Transboundary Movements of Hazardous Wastes and Their Disposal (March 20–22, 1989) 28 *International Legal Materials* 657.

Buckley, Ralf. (1993). International Trade, Investment and Environmental Regulation. *Journal of World Trade* 27(4): 101–148.

Canada-United States Free Trade Agreement, December 10, 1987, *entered into force* January 1, 1989 (implemented in Canada by the Canada-United States Free Trade Agreement Implementation Act, ch. 65, 1988 S.C. 1999 (Can.), and in the United States by the United States-Canada Free Trade Agreement Implementation Act of 1988, Pub.L.No. 100–449, 102 Stat. 26 (1988).

Charnovitz, Steve. (1992). GATT and the Environment, Examining the Issues. *International Environmental Affairs* 4: 203–233.

Charnovitz, Steve. (1993a). Environmentalism Confronts GATT Rules; Recent Developments and New Opportunities. *Journal of World Trade* 27(2): 37–53.

Charnovitz, Steve. (1993b). NAFTA: An Analysis of Its Environmental Provisions. *Environmental Law Review* 23: 10067–10073.

Charnovitz, Steve. (1994). The NAFTA Environmental Side Agreement: Implications for Environmental Cooperation, Trade Policy and American Treatymaking. *Temple International & Comparative Law Journal* 8: 257–314.

Condon, Bradly. (1993). *Making Environmental Protection Trade Friendly under the North American Free Trade Agreement*. Unpublished Masters Thesis, Faculty of Law, The University of Calgary, Calgary, Alberta, Canada.

Convention on International Trade in Endangered Species of Wild Fauna and Flora, March 3, 1973, 993 U.N.T.S. 243 (amended June 22, 1979, T.I.A.S. 11079).

de Mestral, A.L.C., and D. M. Leith, eds. (1989). *Canadian Water Exports and Free Trade, Rawson Academy Occasional Paper No. 2*. Ottawa: Rawson Academy of Aquatic Science.

De Vries, Gijs M. (1992, April 30). How to Banish Eco-Imperialism. *Journal of Commerce* 8A.

Experts Group on Environmental Law of the World Commission on Environment and Development. (1987). *Environmental Protection and Sustainable Development, Legal Principles and Recommendations*. London: Graham & Trotman/Martinus, Nijhoff Publishers.

General Agreement on Tariffs and Trade (*opened for signature* January 1, 1948), T.I.A.S. No. 1700, 55 U.N.T.S. 194, *as amended*.

Housman, Robert F., and Durwood J. Zaelke. (1992). The Collision of Environment and Trade: The GATT Tuna/Dolphin Decision. *Environmental Law Review* 22: 10268–10278.

Hudec, A., and J. Quinn. (1989). Energy Aspects of the Canada-United States Free Trade Agreement. *Canadian Petroleum Tax Journal* 2: 1–40.

Jackson, John H. (1992a). Dolphins and Hormones: GATT and the Legal Environment for International Trade After the Uruguay Round. *University of Arkansas Little Rock Law Journal* 14: 429–454.

Jackson, John H. (1992b). World Trade Rules and Environmental Policies: Congruence or Conflict? *Washington & Lee Law Review* 49: 1227–1278.

Low, Patrick, ed. (1992). *International Trade and Development*. World Bank Discussion Paper No. 159. Washington, DC: World Bank.

McConnell, Irene. (1993). *Treatment of Standards under the North American Free Trade Agreement: Integrating Trade and the Environment.* Unpublished Masters Thesis, Faculty of Law, The University of Calgary, Calgary, Alberta, Canada.

McDorman, Ted L. (1991). The GATT Consistency of U.S. Fish Import Embargoes to Stop Driftnet Fishing and Save Whales, Dolphins and Turtles. *George Washington Journal of International Law & Economics* 24: 477–525.

Montreal Protocol on Substances That Deplete the Ozone Layer, September 16, 1987, 28 *International Legal Materials* 657 (*amended* June 29, 1990).

North American Agreement on Environmental Cooperation Between the Government of the United States of America, the Government of Canada, and the Government of the United Mexican States (September 13, 1993) 28 *International Legal Materials* 1480 (*entered into force* January 1, 1994).

North American Agreement on Labor Cooperation (September 9, 1993) 32 *International Legal Materials* 1499.

North American Free Trade Agreement between the Government of Canada, the Government of the United Mexican States and the Government of the United States of America (December 17, 1992). (*Entered into force* January 1, 1994).

North America Free Trade Agreement Concerning Chapter Eight Emergency Action (September 14, 1993) 32 *International Legal Materials* 1519.

Petersmann, Ernst-Ulrich. (1993). International Trade Law and International Environmental Law, Prevention and Settlement of International Environmental Disputes in GATT. *Journal of World Trade* 27(1): 43–81.

Rio Declaration on Environment and Development, United Nations Conference on Environment and Development, U.N. Doc. A/CONF 151/5/Rev.1 (1992) 31 *International Legal Materials* 874.

Saunders, J. Owen. (1990a). Energy, Natural Resources and the Canada-United States Free Trade Agreement. *Journal of Energy and Natural Resources Law* (U.K.), 8: 3–19.

Saunders, J. Owen. (1990b). Legal Aspects of Trade and Sustainable Development, in J. Owen Saunders, ed., *The Legal Challenge of Sustainable Development.* Calgary: Canadian Institute of Resources Law.

Saunders, J. Owen. (1992). Trade and Environment: The Fine Line Between Environmental Protection and Environmental Protectionism. *International Journal* 47: 723–750.

Stockholm Declaration on the Human Environment.(1972). U.N. Doc. A/CONF.48/14, 11 *International Legal Materials* 1416.

Thomas, Christopher, and Greg A. Tereposky. (1993a). The Evolving Relationship between Trade and Environmental Regulation. *Journal of World Trade* 27(4): 23–45.   •

Thomas, Christopher, and Greg A. Tereposky. (1993b). The NAFTA and the Side Agreement on Environmental Co-operation. *Journal of World Trade* 27(6): 5–34.

United States Restrictions on Imports of Tuna, GATT Doc. DS21/R (August 16, 1991) 30 *International Legal Materials* 1594.

Vienna Convention on the Law of Treaties, May 23, 1969, S. Exec. Doc. L., 92nd Cong., 1st Sess., 1155 U.N.T.S. 331 (*entered into force* January 27, 1980).

World Commission on Environment and Development. (1987). *Our Common Future.* Oxford: Oxford University Press.

Yoder, Christian. (1987). United States Countervailing Duty Law and Canadian Natural Resources: The Evolution of Resources Protectionism in the United States, in J. Owen Saunders ed., *Trading Canada's Natural Resources.* Calgary: Canadian Institute of Resources Law.

5

WORLD TRADE, THE GATT, AND THE ENVIRONMENT

Kerry Krutilla

The emergence of a worldwide environmental movement in the early 1960s followed and thereafter accompanied an international expansion of economic activity and applied technology. The principal medium through which this expansion progressed was trade. In 1947, following World War II, a series of international agreements were negotiated to regularize international relations in finance, monetary policies, and trade. The General Agreement on Tariffs and Trade (GATT) was negotiated without anticipation of an international environmental movement and new policies at the national level that did not reflect, and might be inconsistent with, economic values. Conflict between policies for freedom of trade and environmental protection did not immediately emerge. But with the adoption of numerous environmental protection measures in the United States and many other countries after 1969, the incompatibility of some trade and environmental policies became political issues. Trade policies are not confined to economic changes. They also frequently involve technological issues, as in the Mexican Tuna Controversy, discussed in this chapter. The policy issue developing around the GATT and environmental protection are complex. To understand them requires the type of analysis that follows in this chapter.

On January 1, 1995, after seven years of negotiations, the World Trade Organization (WTO) came into existence as a coherent international organization, absorbing the GATT, which was basically a provisional treaty serviced by an ad hoc secretariat. Although the WTO continues the functions of the GATT, its scope and membership are broader. But many of the issues and problems discussed in this chapter will continue. The GATT provides the only experience that nations have had thus far with reconciling conflicts between environmental protection and world trade.

During the past five years, the environmental impact of international trade policy has emerged as a significant public policy issue. Many environmentalists believe that international trade has adverse environmental consequences, and that the existing, and evolving, rule structure that regulates international trade hinders the ability of countries to implement policies needed for sustainable development. Proponents of this view want to modify the objectives and rules of international trade law to reduce the risk of conflict with environmental policy objectives, and to allow the use of trade policy instruments to actively support the implementation of sustainable development policies (Arden-Clarke, 1991).

Although superseded institutionally since 1995 by the WTO, the GATT rules and issues remain in effect until changes occur under the WTO regime. This chapter will, therefore, treat the GATT agreements and controversies as contemporary. The GATT has provided the legal framework for international trade regulation. Established in 1947 along with such Bretton Woods institutions as the International Monetary Fund (IMF) and World Bank, the GATT was a multilateral agreement that now encompasses 116 member nations accounting for more than 90 percent of the world's merchandise trade. The GATT undertook to promote international economic cooperation, expand global trade, and foster economic development in developing third-world countries. These objectives have been accomplished by establishing and enforcing an agreed-upon set of international trade rules; employing a dispute resolution process to settle trade policy conflicts; and conducting periodic negotiating rounds among GATT members to lower tariff, and other, trade barriers. In 1994 GATT members concluded the seventh trade round negotiation, known as the Uruguay Round, the most ambitious attempt in history to reduce trade barriers and expand global trade, and proposed the WTO.

In the United States, a ruling by a GATT dispute resolution panel in late 1991 was largely responsible for elevating the profile of trade and environmental policy conflict to its present status as a major public policy concern.[1] The United States precipitated the ruling by embargoing Mexican tuna imports. This action was justified under the U.S. Marine Mammals Protection Act, which mandated the restrictions whenever tuna exporters failed to comply with U.S. dolphin kill standards. Mexico challenged the U.S. action. A GATT dispute resolution panel upheld the Mexican claim, arguing that trade policy could not be used to unilaterally impose domestic environmental standards beyond territorial jurisdictions without violating fundamental GATT principles.

The GATT ruling angered many environmentalists, and raised the possibility that other environmental policies could be subject to future GATT rulings (Christensen 1991). A number of multilateral environmental agreements employ trade measures to enforce treaty provisions, including the Montreal Protocol. Using the reasoning employed in the tuna dispute, these treaties appear to violate GATT rules and could be subject to future challenge (Arden-Clarke 1991; Whathen, 1992).[2]

The objective of this chapter is to evaluate critically the public policy issues that have arisen in the debate over the perceived conflict between environmental policy goals and the pursuit of more open multilateral trade under the evolving

GATT framework.[3] I argue that improving the international trade conditions and the state of the natural environment are both desirable, and reconcilable, public policy aims. I offer a conceptual framework to support this position, and set forth a relatively limited set of policy reforms for the GATT which, if adopted, would facilitate both more open international trade and the attainment of domestic, and multilateral, environmental policy objectives.

The balance of the chapter is structured as follows. Section 2 provides a brief overview of the different reality orientations that underlie the dichotomous positions espoused by many environmentalists and economists on free trade and the GATT, and, with this as background, stakes out the conceptual orientation that guides the rest of the chapter. Section 3 describes the GATT rules and rule-making procedures in more detail, and discusses some illustrative cases that provide insight into the GATT's orientation with respect to trade and environmental policy disputes. In section 4, the most likely areas for future conflict between GATT rules and environmental policy objectives are identified, and recommended policy reforms for the next negotiating round of the GATT are put forth. Section 5 offers a brief conclusion.

TRADE AND ENVIRONMENTAL POLICY PERSPECTIVES

The political debate surrounding the potential conflict between international trade law, as embodied in the GATT, and environmental policy objectives, as embodied in a variety of domestic statutes and international agreements, reflects divergent perspectives in two fundamental areas: (a) the benefits of free trade (b) the degree to which trade and environmental policies should be integrated or, to the extent possible, conducted independently. The following provides a brief orientation of the positions held by environmentalists and economists with respect to the value of open trade and appropriate degree of linkage between trade and environmental policy formulation, in the multilateral trade context.

The Environmentalist's Position

Value of Trade

One side of the debate is represented by policymakers, and many environmentalist,[4] who tend to doubt the benefits of free trade and policies designed to promote it.[5] This group sees trade as a vehicle that accelerates environmental degradation and resource depletion—costs not borne in market transactions. The tropical timber trade could be cited as a supporting example. Industrial logging for export and wood-based manufacturing have played a significant role in deforesting the rich dipterocarpe forests of the Philippines, Malaysia, and Indonesia.

Environmentalists also fear that open trade can vitiate domestic environmental policy by reducing the competitiveness of industries that comply with stringent domestic standards, and/or, by inducing industries facing such standards to relocate to other countries to evade them (Arden-Clarke, 1991). Foreign countries may also deliberately keep their environmental standards low as a strategic incentive to attract polluting industries from high standard countries (Whathen, 1992). Open trade can also undermine the effectiveness of multilateral environmental agreements, if the number of participants is less than 100 percent. Without trade restrictions in the Montreal Protocol, for example, industries in the participating countries could simply relocate production facilities to the nonparticipating countries and reexport ozone-depleting materials back to home markets (Krutilla, 1991a).

Trade Policy Perspective

To address these problems, many environmentalists have argued that the GATT should be reformed to allow more integration between trade and environmental policymaking. Such a reformation would conform the orientation of international trade rules more closely to the policy proposals resulting from the U.N.-sponsored conference on Environment and Development held in Rio de Janeiro in June of 1992—which call for a greater degree of integration of environmental and economic policymaking.[6]

One policy reform proposal was to amend the GATT rules to allow for the implementation of import tariffs to offset the competitive disadvantage experienced by import-competing industries facing more stringent domestic environmental standards than their foreign competitors (Arden-Clarke, 1991). Under this view, the lack of environmental regulation in foreign countries confers a de facto subsidy. Countervailing duty provisions in existing trade law allow for the levy of compensatory tariffs to offset the impact of foreign subsidies which demonstrably reduce the competitiveness of domestic industries (see section 3). The proposal, therefore, would entail defining low levels of environmental regulation as a de jure subsidy under existing international trade law.

GATT rules could also be changed to unequivocally enable domestic subsidies for environmental protection, and to allow subsidies to assist export industries to penetrate foreign markets whose producers have a competitive advantage due to low environmental standards (Whathen, 1992). Many GATT reformists have supported the use of export bans to conserve natural resources, such as tropical timber and Old Growth Forest in the Pacific Northwest. Yet another area where environmentalists support the activist use of trade measures, as mentioned, is to enhance the effectiveness of multilateral environmental agreements. Finally, environmentalists would like trade policy to be used to influence the domestic environmental policies of trading partners, as in the Tuna Dolphin Case (Christensen, 1991). A similar example would be the requirement that imports of tropical hardwoods to developed nations be made contingent upon sustainable forest management techniques.

The Position of Free Trade Proponents

Value of Open Trade

The other side of the debate is represented by most economists and many free trade-oriented policymakers who believe that the GATT objective to expand world trade is desirable, all else constant. In making an argument for open trade, free trade proponents might cite the example of domestic trade within the United States, which is constitutionally protected. The interstate commerce clause of the U.S. Constitution prohibits states from restricting or regulating trade within the domestic United States.[7] Free trade advocates would argue that the constitutional framers were wise to protect free interstate trade, because aggregate economic wealth, environmental technology development, and environmental protection are now significantly higher in the United States than they would have been under a restricted trade regime. Since the principles of economics do not change when economic activity crosses political jurisdictions, including international borders, the same factors that boost wealth within freely trading regions, or between freely trading states, also increases wealth among nations that trade internationally.[8]

The theory of comparative advantage based on exploiting international differences in tastes, technology, and factor endowments in a competitive market environment provides the classic free trade justification. In the past decade, however, a "new trade theory" has risen that models international trade as the outcome of strategic interactions between oligopolistic firms operating in an imperfectly competitive market environment, for example, Markusen (1986). This theory implies a different conclusion for trade policy than comparative advantage theory. Specifically, the new trade models show that strategic, and carefully crafted, trade intervention can theoretically improve national welfare, *under some conditions*, by shifting oligopolistic rents to the domestic economy (Krugman, 1990).[9] However, the developers of this theory, in the main, do not support the strategic use of trade policy, because they do not believe governments have the information and incentives to implement it effectively. Further, most economists believe that the activist use of trade policy carries a high price that outweighs any conceivable benefit (see the following section).

Turning specifically to the points raised in the environmental critique of open trade, many economists acknowledge that environmental standards implemented in an open trade environment would reduce the competitiveness of regulated industries—holding everything else constant. However, a constellation of competitiveness-diminishing factors often are correlated with low environmental standards, including unskilled labor, poor infrastructure, poor access to markets, and, in the international context, political instability (GATT, 1992). These factors may override the environmental regulation in terms of competitiveness and plant location decisions. In the domestic context, states such as Louisiana, Mississippi,

Alabama, and West Virginia have relatively low environmental standards when compared to California, Oregon, and Colorado, yet, industries in the high standard states are not relatively less competitive, and capital and labor is not migrating to the low standard states.[10] There is limited empirical support for the proposition that environmental standards have been a major factor in influencing international competitiveness or international capital movements (Tobey, 1990; Walter, 1982).[11] Even if differential environmental standards affected international competitiveness, free-trade proponents would argue that there is no conceptual justification for singling out environmental standards for special concern and policy action from the welter of other factors that also affect competitiveness (GATT, 1992).

Open trade can also provide incentives for higher environmental standards. The U.S. auto industry was able to delay the implementation of stringent environmental standards for a number of years on the claim that meeting the standards was technically impossible. However, the force of this argument was significantly undermined when the Japanese started producing cars that met the same environmental standards (Cobb and Cobb, 1991).

Trade Policy Perspective

Free trade proponents agree with the environmentalist's critique that trade, like any economic activity, can lead to resource depletion and environmental degradation (Anderson, 1992a). For this reason, there is no debate about the need for policies to address the environmental side effects of trade liberalization.[12]

However, free trade proponents believe that trade policy instruments, such as tariffs and quotas, are not the appropriate policy instruments to achieve environmental policy objectives related to trade, or other economic activity. Instead, free trade proponents believe that environmental policy instruments should generally be used to address environmental policy problems, whatever their cause. This view, which perhaps defines the most significant policy difference between environmentalists and free trade proponents, is held for two reasons: (a) Trade policy instruments are an inherently inefficient means of attaining environmental policy goals; and (b) a "trade policy" externality, a negative side effect, is associated with actively using trade policy instruments.

Efficiency of Policy Instruments

Trade policy instruments are not usually the most efficient means with which to accomplish environmental policy, or other nontrade-related policy objectives (Corden, 1974; Runge, 1991; Krutilla, 1991b; Lloyd, 1992). This point can be illustrated by simple a example. Suppose a polluting utility produces electricity that is sold in the domestic market and exported. The regulatory authority now decides that the utility needs to reduce sulfur oxide emissions by X percent. There are a variety of policy options with which this objective could be accomplished:

1. the utility could be required to reduce electricity production by X percent;
2. an export tax or quota could be levied to induce the firm to reduce output by X percent;[13]

3. the X percent reduction could be achieved by using such environmental policy instruments as performance standards and pollution taxes.

Using environmental policy instruments is generally the least-cost means of attaining the pollution reduction target (Baumol and Oates 1988).[14] If the firm faces a performance standard to reduce pollution by X PERCENT, the firm can choose whatever abatement option is cheapest to meet the standard. This flexibility minimizes the trade-off between the pollution control objective and the economic performance objective. With the cost savings attained by employing environmental policy instruments, additional resources could be made available, for example, to fund environmental protection and promote sustainable development.

However, the trade-off between environmental policy and economic growth objectives is one-to-one if the pollution control target is achieved by reducing trade, or, equivalently in this context, by implementing output restrictions.[15] Pollution control by trade restrictions reduces the resources which are available to promote sustainable development. Economists would argue then that the proposal for a more integrated trade/ environmental policy, in the sense of using tariffs and quotas as environmental policy instruments, subverts the sustainability objective which motivates the proposal in the first place.[16]

Trade Policy Externality

Perhaps the most important objection to using trade policy instruments for environmental policy purposes is the fear of unraveling the GATT rule system negotiated over the past forty years to keep trading relationships peaceful and encourage more open trade. If Country A was allowed to implement unilaterally a trade tax to protect domestic industries who face foreign competitors with lower environmental standards, then foreign industries subjected to such a tax would likely argue for the implementation of their own trade restrictions to offset what they regard as competitive inequities. Perhaps developing countries subject to a environmental policy-motivated import tariff would retaliate with an import tax against all U.S. manufactured products, because U.S. employers have an unfair competitive advantage in having access to a skilled labor pool whose education is largely subsidized through a public university system. Even if it were possible to conceptually justify a special exemption from the GATT for the activist use of trade instruments specifically for environmental policy purposes, this exemption would guarantee that a host of protectionist interests would adopt the environmental banner to plead their special cause.[17] Rent-seeking behavior of special interests attempting to lobby for protective trade legislation also wastes resources that could be devoted to other purposes (Krueger, 1974), including the promotion of sustainable development policy.

Premises Adopted in This Chapter

Concerning the issues raised, we adopt the following basic premises as a default orientation to guide the subsequent policy analysis:

1. As a default, global trade expansion is a desirable policy objective;
2. As a default, sustainable development is a desirable objective;
   These premises further imply some restrictions and rules for the use of trade policy and environmental policy instruments:
3. As a default, trade instruments should not be used to implement environmental policies.[18] This follows from taking 1 as a premise, since the use of trade restrictions to support environmental policy undermine global trade expansion.
4. As a default, environmental policy instruments should not be trade restricting. This again follows from taking 1 as a premise.
5. As a default, trade law should not interfere with the conduct of environmental policy. This follows from taking 2 as a premise.

Although these are the default premises, special circumstances may justify qualified exceptions. Transboundary pollution that harms another nation can arguably justify trade retaliation against the country causing the problem if the country refuses to participate in an environmental agreement to address the problem. Here, jurisdictional constraints hinder the use of environmental policy instruments (Snape, 1992). We return to this issue in section 4.

Real-world complexities also muddy the distinction between policy instruments. If the transactions costs of environmental policy instruments are so high that they are for all practical purposes infeasible, other policy instruments have to be employed (Deacon 1992). It may also be unclear whether policies ostensively motivated on environmental ground are in reality being used as de facto trade policy instruments. Particularly in the area of health and sanitary regulation, the difference between domestic environmental policy and disguised protectionism may be virtually impossible to distinguish.

Even in a qualified sense noted, however, the basic premises imply a conceptual orientation toward evaluating the policy issues surrounding the trade/ environmental policy debate. Specifically, the objective is to evaluate the GATT to see if it is sufficiently flexible to allow the full use of environmental policy instruments to address environmental problems, whatever their origin, rather than to suggest reforms for the GATT that would allow trade policy, as a general matter, to be more actively used to achieve environmental policy aims. Furthermore, the basic premises imply a particular kind of evaluative stance toward trade/ environmental policy conflict. Specifically, whether trade and environmental policy conflicts are "inherent"—that is, unavoidable regardless of which policy instruments are selected—or merely technical, in the sense that the choice of a different trade policy or environmental policy instrument would reduce the conflict without fundamentally trading off either policy objective. In the latter case, the problem is instrument design rather than competing policy aims.

Before we turn to these issues in detail, we take a closer look at the GATT.

A CLOSER LOOK AT THE GATT EXPERIENCE

General Background

First and foremost the GATT was a multilateral agreement under which contracting parties were bound by international law to certain obligations (Jackson, 1989). Under the tariff obligations, nations agreed to cap their tariffs at an established level and work toward further tariff reductions through periodic multilateral negotiations, called trade rounds. Under the Most Favored Nation Principle, nations agree to extend to all GATT signatories the same preferential tariff treatment extended to the *most favored nation* (MFN) trading partner. An obligation that is closely tied to that of MFN is national treatment. While the MFN principle requires nondiscrimination among nations, the national treatment clause requires non-discrimination between products. It requires that equivalent products, whether produced domestically or by another GATT signatory, be treated identically in domestic markets. The nondiscrimination principle forms an important part of the conceptual orientation that guides GATT evaluations of trade policy disputes.

The notion of reciprocity is closely associated with the nondiscrimination principle. In the narrow sense, reciprocity refers to the benefits of mutual tariff reduction. In a broader sense, however, reciprocity refers to the notion that a nation that offers freer access to its own market will be rewarded with freer access to other markets, and that a nation that agrees to give up the right to use trade policy out of specified rule framework will itself be protected from idiosyncratic trade actions. The benefits of reciprocity provide the essential incentive for GATT participation and continuing compliance with its rules.

Other Rules

The GATT contains many specific rules which clarify the central obligations and lay out a code of conduct for international trade. These range from prohibitions against quantitative trade restrictions[19] to preferred mechanisms for dispute resolution and legal accession into GATT.

The GATT's treatment of subsidies is important from the point of view of the trade/environmental policy debate. Export subsidies are generally prohibited under the GATT.[20] Before the Uruguay Round, domestic production subsidies had generally been permitted with the important qualification that they not materially injure the industries of foreign competitors.[21] In the case where a foreign nation can demonstrate that the subsidy in question was responsible for "material injury" to one of their domestic industries, they have the right under the GATT rules to levy a "countervailing tariff" to offset the subsidy impact.[22]

The Uruguay Round has attempted to provide more clarity about subsidy rules by categorizing subsidies into three types: prohibited; permissible but potentially actionable (under countervailing duty statute); permissible and nonactionable.

The general exceptions contained in Article XX are equally important to the environmental/trade policy debate. This article outlines specific cases in which GATT rules may be conditionally waived. These exceptions are based on particular policy aims rather than the specific trade rule in question. They cover such areas as exceptions for government measures taken to protect national security or public morals and exceptions for international commodity agreements.

Two exceptions within Article XX may be construed as environmental (Charnovitz, 1991). The relevant text reads as follows:

nothing in this agreement shall be construed to prevent the adoption or enforcement by any contracting party of measures...

    (b) necessary to protect human, animal or plant life or health;

    (g) relating to the conservation of exhaustible natural resources if such measures are made effective in conjunction with restrictions on domestic production or consumption.

Article XX(b) allows discriminatory regulation against foreign products that do not conform to domestic sanitary or phytosanitary standards,[23] although exemptions must not be applied "in a manner which would constitute a means of arbitrary or unjustifiable discrimination between countries where the same conditions prevail, or a disguised restriction on international trade." Article XX(g) allows trade restrictions to conserve natural resources, if equivalent restrictions are levied against domestic production, in other words, the nondiscrimination principle is not waived for natural resource conservation.

Environmental Provisions of the Uruguay Round

During the last three years of the Uruguay Round, the trade-environmental policy debate heated up. Indeed, many environmentalists wanted to delay substantially the round to address environmental policy issues as a major agenda item. A compromise was reached; however, most of the major environmental issues were deferred until the subsequent negotiating round. The parties did agree to the broad principles of a preparatory work program to begin developing an agenda in the post-Uruguay period.

The Uruguay Round did produce the following environmental modifications to the GATT:

- sustainable development is now included as one GATT objective;
- textual changes have been made to reduce the risk that increased disciplines in areas of sanitary/phytosanitary and technical barriers to trade will vitiate domestic environmental regulation;
- the dispute resolution procedure has been made more "transparent" and susceptible to input from environmental experts and scientists.[24]
- subsidies offsetting up to 20 percent of cost of adapting existing facilities to stronger environmental regulations cannot be challenged under the GATT subsidy rules.

Not withstanding these changes, the GATT-environmental policy conflicts may arise in a number of areas in the post-Uruguay Round period. We discuss these potential conflicts below, and discuss whether they imply the need for further modification in the GATT rules in the next negotiating round. In fact, the final act of the Uruguay Round established environmental concerns as a priority for the new WTO.

POTENTIAL GATT-ENVIRONMENTAL POLICY CONFLICTS

There appear to be three broad areas where the GATT and environmental policy objectives could conflict in the future (Table 5.1). First, GATT rules may restrict a country's ability to pursue domestic environmental policy objectives within its own territorial jurisdiction. Second, GATT rules might constrain the ability of countries to use trade instruments to influence the domestic policies of other countries. Finally, GATT rules may be in conflict with the trade provisions in a number of already-negotiated international environmental agreements, for example, the Montreal Protocol. We turn to each of these areas below.

Domestic Environmental Policy

Environmental Protection/Resource Conservation Subsidies

Issue. GATT rules may infringe on domestic environmental policy that subsidizes environmental protection or resource conservation, for example, policies that subsidize environmental technology, waste disposal, or reforestation. With the exception of a one-time exemption of 20 percent of the costs of facility improvements, noted above, environmental protection subsidies are actionable under the countervailing duty provisions of the GATT. Countervailing duty statutes do not discriminate between subsidies that are motivated on efficiency grounds, such as environmental protection subsidies, and subsidies that are motivated for equity, or any other reason. The sole criterion for judging

Table 5.1
Actual or Potential Conflict Areas between GATT and Environmental Policy Objectives

I.   Domestic Environmental Policy
      (a) Environmental Protection/Resource Conservation Subsidies
      (b) Trade Measure-Supported Domestic Environmental Policy
      (c) Product Standards and Phytosanitary Standards

II. Trade Measure-Supported Environmental Policy Outside Jurisdictions

III. Trade Measures in Multilateral Environmental Treaties

countervailing duty actions is whether the subsidy can be shown to be responsible for materially injuring a domestic industry.

Two examples illustrate the potential impact of countervailing duty law on environmental policies. In both cases, the United States challenged Canadian environmental subsidies as unfair trade practices. In the first case, the U.S. lumber industry alleged that provincial governments in Canada were subsidizing timber cutting and reforestation. This objection led to a successful U.S. challenge and a countervailing trade action against the Canadians that ultimately culminated in a negotiated solution in which the Canadians imposed an export tax on lumber exports (Boyd and Krutilla, 1988).[25] In the second case, U.S. mining and metal producing interests challenged Canadian programs that subsidize environmental and safety technology in Canadian smelters. This case has not yet been resolved (Shrybman, 1990).

Discussion and Recommendation. GATT rule-making is not conceptually consistent with respect to subsidy policy. The absence of environmental regulation does not constitute a subsidy under the GATT and is exempt from retaliatory trade action under countervailing duty statutes. Yet, environmental protection subsidies are actionable under GATT. Since the absence of environmental regulation confers a cost advantage no less than an explicit environmental protection subsidy, the differential treatment of the two policies reflects a fundamental inconsistency.

In this case, GATT provisions should be changed to allow for the subsidization of environmental protection and resource conservation programs. Subsidies are legitimate environmental policy instruments. Furthermore, Pigouvian-type subsidies reflect a social decision about property rights allocation; namely, that firms have the right to pollute and should be compensated for reducing pollution. Property rights allocation is a social decision upon which trade rules should not impinge.

Furthermore, there is not a trade policy cost to exempting environmental subsidies from the purview of countervailing duty statute—as we have defined trade policy cost. In fact, there is actually a gain. Countervailing duties restrict rather than expand trade. Hence, both the environmental policy and trade policy objectives articulated in premises 1 and 2 would be promoted by exempting environmental subsidies from GATT subsidy disciplines. In this case, open trade and environmental policy are reinforcing, rather than conflicting policy aims. International trade law should accordingly be amended.

Trade Measure-Supported Domestic Environmental Policy

Issue. Many developing countries restrict the export of unprocessed natural resources to encourage domestic resource-based industrialization. Such policies are justified as "adding value" to natural resource products, creating domestic employment, and conserving natural resources.

Indonesia provides a striking example of this kind of resource development policy. The country was the world's largest tropical log exporter in 1978, but between 1980 and 1985 completely phased out log exports and, simultaneously, developed a plywood industry that is now the third largest in the world (Gillis, 1988).

Developed countries also utilize quantitative restrictions for resource conservation. In the United States Federal law prevents exportation of raw logs harvested from federal lands. Similar policies exist in other developed nations.

The present, wide-spread use of trade measures to support resource conservation policies are problematic under GATT rules. Although Article XX(g) permits a possible exemption for natural resource conservation, it also requires that such measures be implemented in conjunction with domestic restrictions. Export restrictions for natural resources, however, are virtually never paired with domestic consumption restrictions. As yet, resource export restrictions have not been formally challenged, but it seems only a matter of time before they are.

Discussion and Recommendation. With the exception of sanitary and phytosanitary standards, the acid test under the GATT of protectionist ulterior motive is whether the nondiscrimination principle is followed. In the case of resource export restrictions, it is clear that conservation is not the only motive, because the domestic use of the resources is not simultaneously restricted. In fact, the principal purpose of such policies is to subsidize local processing industries with artificially cheap inputs. Such policies are not only economically inefficient but in most cases end up accelerating the use of natural resources.[26] Quite apart from the problems with GATT-compatibility, most economists would argue that such policies are bad for domestic economies and bad for resource conservation.[27]

Again in this case, there is not a fundamental trade-off between environmental policy and trade policy objectives. Nondiscriminatory conservation policy could be formulated by auctioning restricted resources to any bidder, whether domestic or international, or, less preferably, by allocating purchase rights between domestic and international buyers in proportion to past consumption shares.

Product Standards and Harmonization

Issue. As successive GATT rounds continue to lower overt tariff barriers, the use of less overt, nontariff trade restrictions, such as technical product standards, have become increasingly prevalent (Runge, 1990). While the GATT recognizes the right of countries to establish domestic product standards based on health, safety, or environmental policy criteria, the Agreement on Technical Barriers to Trade, which was signed and implemented at the end of the Tokyo Round, directs nations to use international standards (where they exist) whenever possible, and "when necessary to deviate from such standards for reasons of safety, health and environment," to use national standards that do not constitute unnecessary obstacles to trade.[28] The agreement also requires signatories to notify other GATT members of products that may be covered by technical regulations differing from international standards. These rules are designed to reduce the propensity of countries to disguise protectionist policies in the form of technical product standards.

In general, technical product standards are fully permitted by GATT if domestic producers are required to meet the same criteria, although the notification requirement for technical regulations presumably puts countries in the position of challenging standards as "unnecessary obstacles to trade." Environmental criteria have been increasingly used to justify technical regulations.[29] And prior to 1995, no challenge overturned an established technical standard justified on environmental policy grounds. A WTO ruling on the discriminatory effect of the U.S. Clean Air Act may be a first case.

Sanitary and phytosanitary regulations pose a more significant risk of conflict with GATT rules than nondiscriminatory technical product standards. Since GATT rules allow discriminatory regulation in this area, the risk of disguised protectionism, is relatively high, as well as the probability of both justified and frivolous challenges against such regulations.[30] To address these problems, there has been a push in recent GATT negotiating rounds to harmonize sanitary and phytosanitary standards to international norms (Robertson, 1991).

The harmonization ideal has created a great deal of controversy. Developing countries are concerned that the harmonized standards would be higher than domestic standards, burdening domestic producers. Environmentalists in developed countries oppose harmonization for the opposite reason; they fear that international standards would be lower than domestic standards. A significant part of the objection voiced by environmentalists to the harmonization proposals is the concern that unelected trade officials would have the power to issue rulings that would undermine domestic regulations determined as the outcome of local democratic processes. That is, environmentalists see the harmonization proposals as threat to the sovereign right of countries to determine their own domestic environmental policy.[31]

Partially to address these fears, the text of the Uruguay Round of GATT contains language that reinforces the right of countries to establish standards that are more stringent than international norms. In essence, the international standards serve as a floor for more advanced economies that have higher standards. Nonetheless, stringent standards must be justified and are subject to challenge.

Discussion and Recommendation. In the area of technical product standards, and even more so for sanitary and phytosanitary regulation, the potential trade-off between trade and environmental policy objectives is inherently difficult to balance. In this area, the policy conflict is more fundamental than technical. Under the premise that trade liberalization is not necessarily good policy unless countries have the flexibility to treat environmental side effects with environmental policy instruments, the rules of international trade should not impede the essential flexibility of countries to conduct legitimate domestic environmental policy. In fact, since sanitary and health standards (and, more generally, environmental standards), can be expected to naturally differ among countries based on differing preferences, income levels, technology, and physical/environmental features, trade policy that reduces the differentiation of domestic policies could create economic inefficiencies that would partially offset trade liberalization gains.

However, allowing the unfettered expression of domestic environmental policy creates the potential for abuse in the form of disguised protectionism. Harmonizing standards reduces the risk of protectionist abuses—at the risk of constraining environmental policy. There obviously is no easy answer to defining the appropriate mix of restraint and flexibility in this area.

As a consequence, the policy aim of further harmonizing technical product standards and regulations in the sanitary and phytosanitary area should be carefully considered in the next negotiating round. The input of environmental scientists, policymakers, and trade experts is needed to assure the appropriate degree of balance in formulating policy in this area.

Trade Measure-Supported Environmental Policy Outside Jurisdictions

Issue. The use of trade policy to influence the environmental process standards of other countries has become a controversial issue of late due to the much publicized and highly debated dispute over the U.S. ban of Mexican tuna-netted dolphins, described before, and political pressure by environmentalists to introduce legislation in the U.S. Congress that would allow the use of trade policy to level crossnational differences in environmental regulation. Such "social tariff" proposals would essentially give countries the unilateral right to "harmonize" international environmental standards to conform to their own by invoking the countervailing duty philosophy in current trade law.

As a general principle, the GATT has remained strongly committed against the use of unilateral action. "In principle, it is not possible under the GATT's rules to make access to one's own market dependent on the domestic environmental policies of practices of the exporting country" (GATT, 1992). In the GATT view, government regulations and policies are considered to be functions of culture, national preferences, and natural endowments. On this basis the stringency of a nation's environmental policies are viewed as constituting a "natural" feature of the economy, rather than an unfair trade advantage.

Discussion and Recommendation. The GATT stance against the use of activist trade policy to influence the domestic environmental process standards of trading partners is justified for four reasons. First, the countervailing duty philosophy of GATT itself contradicts the trade expansion objective. The scope of countervailing duty statute should be narrowed, rather than broadened, to allow another actionable category of subsidy.

Second, as discussed before, leveling differences in international standards would create economic inefficiencies that partially override trade liberalization benefits.

Third, the legitimization of trade policy as a means to influence the domestic environmental practices of trade partners would open up a pandora's box of trade retaliation and warfare, potentially reducing global trade.

Fourth, even if there were no punitive, or strategic retaliation to the levy of social tariffs, the consistent application of the social tariff principle—as distinct from its idiosyncratic implementation by large countries like the United States— would itself lead to a radical reduction in global trade. For example, assume that the stringency of a country's environmental policy is proportional to its per capita income. Hence, the environmental policies of the countries of the world could be rank ordered from most to least stringent on the basis of per capita income. In this case, if the social tariff principle were consistently applied, the highest income country would levy import duties against all trading partners making the import-competing product in question. The next richest country would be subject to a tax on its exports to the richest country, but would levy import taxes on the import-competing exports of all its lower income trading partners. The lowest income country would face tariffs on exports from all of its trading partners. In short, the consistent application of the social tariff principle is a prescription for radically reducing the volume of global trade.

Furthermore, it is obviously not efficient, equitable, or just to use coercive trade measures as a stick to encourage less developed countries to adopt stringent, and expensive, environmental standards. In view of international income disparities, it would be fairer for the developed world to pay for environmental protection in third world countries through subsidy programs and technology transfer than to attempt to force such change through coercive policy action.

Trade Measures in Multilateral Environmental Agreements

Issue. GATT rules do not distinguish between unilateral and multilateral trade actions. International environmental agreements that levy trade restrictions have to meet the same criteria for exception to the national treatment and nondiscrimination principle as domestic environmental policies, as outlined in Article XX.

There were as of 1994 sixteen multilateral environmental agreements with trade provisions. Perhaps the most notable of these are the Montreal Protocol to control ozone-depleting substances, the Basel Convention, which regulates the hazardous waste trade, and the Convention on International Trade in Endangered Species of Wild Fauna and Flora (CITES).

Montreal Protocol. Under the Montreal Protocol all trade of controlled substances with nonsignatories to the agreement is prohibited. Using the GATT tuna ruling as a guide, this provision appears to violate GATT rules on two counts. First, by suspending the trading rights of only the nonsignatory countries, the treaty violates the nondiscrimination principle. Second, in so doing, the agreement attempts to influence environmental policies extra-jurisdictionally, in other words, influence the production and trade of ozone depleting substances of the non-signatory nations.

The Montreal Protocol also contains a provision for additional trade restrictions on products that are produced with ozone-depleting substances. Although this provision has not been evoked, it would violate the GATT rules on national treatment of like products, since the GATT panel decision on tuna determined that process differences do not constitute process differences. Although the Montreal Protocol has not yet been challenged, there have been indications that Korea intends to initiate such an action.[32] A negative GATT ruling would effectively put two international agreements of roughly the same legal standing into direct conflict with one another.

Basel Convention. The Basel Convention is an attempt to establish a framework for the control and monitoring of the international hazardous waste movements (Hilz and Ehrenfeld 1991). Under the agreement, each party has the sovereign right to refuse the shipment of hazardous waste into its own territory. Like the Montreal Protocol, trade with nonparties to the agreement is prohibited. Further, hazardous waste exporters are not allowed to ship hazardous waste to parties unless the parties can dispose of the waste in an "environmentally sound" manner. "Environmentally sound" is not defined in the agreement.

Although the Basel Convention contains a number of discriminatory trade restrictions, most of the provisions are probably justified under Article XX(b), since hazardous waste is indisputably a potential health risk. The one possible exception is the provision that restricts exports to parties unless the receiving parties' disposal standards are "environmentally sound." This provision involves the possible extra-jurisdictional application of environmental standards. Following the GATT Tuna ruling, this export restriction would appear to violate GATT principles.

Convention on International Trade in Endangered Species of Wild Fauna and Flora (CITES). CITES is one of nine international agreements with the principle objective of wildlife conservation and species protection. These agreements employ a variety of trade restrictions or outright bans. Under CITES, for example, ivory imports are banned by the signatory nations, and certain nations among the signatories have banned the imports of other endangered species, for example, whales, migratory birds, and so on (Whathen, 1992). Because, in many instances, the trade restrictions in the agreements are not coupled with similar domestic trade restrictions, a number of wildlife treaties could be found to be GATT incompatible—in the unlikely event that they are challenged.

Discussion and Recommendation. The basic public policy question raised by the potential conflict between GATT rules and multilateral environmental agreements is whether the agreement should be restructured to conform to the GATT, or, on the other hand, be exempted from GATT provisions—either on the basis of general principles established for multilateral environmental agreements, or on a case-by-case basis, through explicit amendment to GATT rules.

It is possible to structure multilateral agreements to be GATT compatible without trading off environmental policy objectives. The wildlife agreements, for example, would be strengthened by provisions that banned the domestic trade of products embargoed in international trade. The Montreal Protocol, without sacrificing the policy goal to reduce CFC consumption, could be made GATT compatible by allowing producers from all countries to bid on CFC production rights, rather than banning imports and restricting CFC production quotas to domestic producers—a policy partially motivated to grant domestic producers monopoly profits during the treaty implementation period (Krutilla, 1991a).[33]

Since trade and environmental policy objectives are not inherently in conflict in such cases, it is tempting to conclude that the treaties in question should be restructured to conform to GATT rules. Beyond the transaction costs of renegotiating major multilateral agreements, however, this course of action may not necessarily be prudent.

In the case of the Montreal Protocol, there is a global commons issue: by continuing their CFC production activities, the no-signatory nations impose environmental damage costs on the signatories. Persuading the nonsignatories to join the protocol is obviously the preferred solution to the problem. However, if negotiations fail, it could be argued that the use of trade restrictions, both as a stick to encourage participation in the agreement and as a policy instrument to reduce domestic environmental damage, is a justifiable action. In such cases, a philosophical question has to be answered: are the negative side effects associated with the activist use of trade policy justified by the environmental damage costs imposed by the nonsignatory nations?

Our position is that this question cannot be answered on general principle, for two reasons: (1) it involves an evaluation that is situation-specific, and (2), enunciating general principles for "multilateral" environmental agreements leads to the possibility that any block of three nations or larger could institute trade actions in transboundary pollution cases. The costs of activist trade policy with relatively large numbers of small trading blocks unilaterally undertaking environmental-policy motivated trade actions would likely be very high.

Hence, in terms of the Montreal Protocol, the rational policy decision would appear to be whether or not the agreement should be specifically exempted from GATT provisions by specific waiver.[34] Reasonable people can obviously differ in their judgment in this case.[35]

In terms of the wildlife agreements, a general exemption from the GATT would probably be appropriate. For these agreements, the economic stakes are low, the conservation objectives are not tainted by protectionist ulterior motives, and the transactions costs of renegotiation are not worth the nicety of exact conformance to GATT principles.

Finally, it would seem reasonable to exempt the regulation of the international hazardous waste trade from GATT protocols by specific waiver, due to the unique environmental and health risk associated with this particular problem.

CONCLUSION AND THE WORLD TRADE ORGANIZATION

Environmental policymaking and the pursuit of more liberal global trade are both important policy objectives. Although the "trade versus environment" debate has become extremely heated in the past several years, a number of perceived conflict areas to do not appear to represent inherent trade-offs between policy objectives. In some cases, policies that are generally perceived to be environmentally motivated are in fact motivated for other reasons and may have negative environmental consequences, for example, natural resource export restrictions. In such cases, trade liberalization and environmental protection are compatible, rather than conflicting, policy aims.

In other cases, conflicts between trade and environmental policy reflect the specific ways in which environmental policies have been formulated. Many multilateral environmental agreements could be restructured to conform to international trade rules without trading off environmental policy objectives. Yet, there are good arguments for specifically exempting such treaties from the purview of GATT, not the least of which is the transactions cost of renegotiating them. Exemptions in trade law for the regulation of such prominent environmental problems as ozone depletion, hazardous waste trading, and endangered species protection would not significantly compromise the free trade ideal.

Other modifications to trade law may be necessary to achieve environmental policy objectives, but can be made without seriously compromising trade policy objectives. The exemption of environmental protection subsidies from countervailing duty statutes, for example, can be made without any cost to essential trade policy goals.

The desirability of differentiating product standards for environmental, health, and safety reasons, on the one hand, while attempting to control the abuse of such standards setting as disguised protectionist measures, on the other, poses perhaps the greatest inherent conflict between trade and environmental policy objectives. But achieving a reasonable balance between the need to maintain flexibility in domestic environmental policymaking, while protecting against protectionist abuses, does not appear to be a policy problem outside the realm of reasonable compromise.

The debate about whether to allow the use of trade restrictions to influence the domestic environmental policies of trading partners appears to represent a significant conflict between free-trade and environmental policy objectives. From the viewpoint of natural economic policymakers, the arguments against modifying trade law to accommodate environmental policy objectives appear to be compelling. However, the political climate affecting trade and environment has been changing.

The GATT was established in 1947 in lieu of an international trade organization which was unable to obtain international agreement. The GATT was consummated a quarter-century before environmental protection became a national and international issue. Objection to the proposed ITO had more to do with issues of national sovereignty and trade advantage. Conservative opinion held that a mix of policy reform and maintenance of the international status quo would be the best approach to addressing world trade policy. As the environmental movement became increasingly international during the 1970s and 1980s many economists and politicians saw no compelling argument for radically restructuring the objectives and rules of international trade to accommodate environmental concerns.

By the time of the final act of the Uruguay Round of trade negotiations under the GATT, it had become widely apparent that status quo ad hoc approaches were no longer adequate to address the multifaceted aspects of expanding world trade. Concluding the Uruguay Round negotiations, the Ministerial Decision on Trade and Environment taken at Marrakesh, Morocco on April 14, 1994 stated that "the linkages between trade policies, environmental policies and sustainable development will be taken up as a priority of WTO—the WTO General Council will establish a new committee on Trade and Environment."

Consultations on trade and environment had already begun under the GATT in preparation for the 1992 United Nations Conference on Trade and Development. These discussions concluded with the convening of an (interim) Group on Environmental Measures and International Trade. Opposition to the GATT by environmental organizations in various countries, notably in the United States, made the inclusion of environmental concerns and sustainability necessary for ratification of the Marrakesh decisions.

On 1 January 1995 the WTO came into existence, officially replacing the GATT.[36] A period of transition follows as GATT members ratify the WTO and new members are admitted. Committees on Trade and Environment and Trade and Development have been established pursuant to the Declaration of Marrakesh. Experience under the GATT, however, will continue to be relevant as new trade-environment policies are proposed and considered. At the close of the twentieth century there appears to be a real prospect that the division of opinion between economic laissez-faire and guided economy may be closing. It seems probable that the WTO will play an important role in the development of national and international environmental policies in the twenty-first century.

In its first major decision on a trade-environment dispute, a three-judge panel of the WTO ruled against the United States on a charge by Brazil and Venezuela that the U.S. Clean Air Act discriminated against foreign oil refiners and ordered the United States to change its rules on imported gasoline or face trade sanctions. As of this writing, the outcome of this controversy remains to be seen. However, it appeared that the United States was prepared to submit a compliance plan to the WTO.[37]

NOTES

1. Debates over bilateral free trade agreements have also contributed to the current political atmosphere.

2. The political environment appears to be generally favorable for the evolution of conflicts between trade and environmental policymaking. Trade liberalization and environmental policy agendas are becoming increasingly ambitious, raising the prospect of further conflict between objectives. Protectionist sentiment is also on the rise worldwide, and the environmental mantle is increasingly being invoked to justify protectionist policies (*Economist*, 1993).

3. There are number of aspects of the "trade vs. environment" debate that this chapter does not specifically address; for example, the environmental policy issues surrounding the negotiation of bilateral free trade agreements, such as the NAFTA. The focus on the GATT itself is somewhat specific: I do not evaluate the arguments put forward by environmentalists for greater citizens participation in the GATT dispute resolution process, or dwell on the debate about the appropriate procedure and pacing of GATT reform. Instead, the chapter

focuses on the issues surrounding the GATT rule structure and its consequences for environmental policymaking.

4. The terms "environmentalist" and "economist" are used for expositional convenience, notwithstanding the obvious semantic limitation that both groups manifest a diversity of opinion that cannot be neatly labeled.

5. The treatment of the trade/environment debate in this and the following section in relatively brief. In depth analysis may be found in Low (1991) and Anderson and Blackhurst (1992).

6. The term "integration" appears to have several meanings as used by environmentalists in the trade/environment debate. In the context of bilateral free trade agreements, it refers to the need to negotiate environmentally sensitive agreements or negotiate side-agreements to address environmental impacts. In the multilateral context, it encompasses the view that the policy influence of environmentalists should be institutionalized through more active representation in GATT councils. It also encompasses the view that GATT rules should be modified to enable trade policy instruments to be actively used to support environmental policy objectives. It is the last sense in which the term "integration" is used in this chapter.

7. Interestingly, some of the same kinds of trade policy conflicts witnessed on the international scene have also arisen domestically. In the early 1980s, Nebraska attempted to restrict the export of water across state boundaries, as a resource conservation measure. In *Sporhase* v. *Nebraska ex rel. Douglas* [458 U.S. 941 (1982)], the Supreme Court ruled that the restriction was unconstitutional. In 1990, California voted on the so called "Big Green" initiative, which would have imposed a virtual ban on the use of chemicals in agriculture. Agricultural interests argued that such restrictions would place California producers at a competitive disadvantage vis-à-vis producers in other states who did not face such stringent controls (Doering, 1990).

The most recent domestic controversy involves the interstate shipment of solid waste. A number of states restrict interstate waste shipments. In repeated rulings the Supreme Court has held that these restrictions are unconstitutional.

8. A recent study by Grossman and Krueger (1991) is often cited by free trade proponents to bolster the contention that economic expansion of the type encouraged by trade ultimately improves environmental quality. The Grossman and Krueger study shows that SO_2 pollution in cities is correlated with GNP increases up to a per capita GNP level of around $5,000. Thereafter, SO_2 pollution begins to decline as per capita GNP increases. Higher incomes enable the financing of technology innovation which lowers environmental protection costs, and increases the publics willingness to pay for environmental protection.

9. Even under the comparative advantage theory of trade, large countries can strategically use trade policy to increase national welfare (Krutilla 1989). Oligopolistic pricing by OPEC oil cartel, for example, increases the welfare of the OPEC by capturing rents from other countries.

10. In the past decade, the "high standard" states have had higher population growth and investment rates than the "low standard" states.

11. Plant closings in the United States and the rise of the maquiladoras in Mexico appears to offer dramatic evidence of the movement of capital in response to the incentive structure of open trade. It is instructive to note, however, that U.S. investment in all of Mexico in 1989 totaled less than $2 billion, an amount less than 1/5 of 1 percent of total private investment in the United States in that year (Boyd et al., 1993).

12. The net environmental impact of trade liberalization is far from clear, due to manifold market distortions that exist in the economies of trading countries (Antle, 1991; Anderson, 1992b; Runge, 1991; Cruz and Repetto, 1992; Lutz, 1990). As a generalization,

agricultural and resource-intensive industries throughout the world are inefficient, heavily subsidized, and protected by tariff barriers. If these industries are differentially protected and inefficient, then the rigors of international competition—even "imperfect competition"— will place them at competitive disadvantage relative to industries that use resources less intensively. Trade liberalization in such cases will have a net positive impact on resource consumption and the environment.

13. Export restriction would divert exports to the home market, dropping the price of electricity. The price drop would induce the firm to curtail production.

14. This conclusion is premised by the assumption that the transaction costs of implementing environmental policies are not higher than the alternatives. In most cases, it does not seem likely that transaction costs would systematically vary between policy options, particularly when the rent-seeking behavior of political interests associated with all of the options is considered. If, for some reason, the transactions cost of environmental policy were higher than other options, the added efficiency gain to using the environmental policy instruments would have to be weighed against its higher transaction cost.

15. "Equivalently" is used here as defined by Lloyd (1992).

16. The economic woes of Eastern Europe provide interesting insight into what the costs would be of attaining environmental policy objectives by output (or equivalently) trade restrictions. For example, in the Dresden area of Germany, 60 percent of state enterprises have shut down in the last two years, creating a very deep recession. As a result, air quality in the region has substantially improved (Horsch 1991). From the woes of this region it is clear that reducing production as a deliberate policy strategy to attain the realized air quality improvements would not be the first way to attain the pollution reductions, or to motivate sustainable development.

17. The presumption that industries would use environmentalism to argue for trade restrictions, and that such arguments would influence policy, is not fanciful. Trade protection for honey producers is now justified on national security grounds.

18. Less strongly, this premise can be justified on the theory of instrument selection. This justification is "less strong" because, as mentioned, transaction cost issue undermines the a priori instrument rank-ordering that is usually made in the literature.

19. Article XI: "No prohibitions or restrictions other than duties, taxes or other charges, whether made effective through quotas, import or export licenses or other measures shall be instituted or maintained by any contracting party on the impositions of any product or the territory of any other contracting party or on the exportation or sale for export of any product destined for the territory of any other contracting party."

20. There is some leeway in the GATT for export subsidies. Distinction is made between primary and nonprimary products. Export subsidies are in some cases allowable on primary products.

21. Tokyo Round, Agreement on Interpretation and Application of Articles Vi, XVI and XXIII of the General Agreement on Tariffs and Trade Article 8: Subsidies-General Provisions (GATT, 1986).

22. This exemption for the activist use of trade policy under the GATT is opposed by free trade proponents for two reasons: (a) a trade policy externality is associated with the active use of trade policy, as discussed before, and (b) free trade proponents hold the fundamental premise that trade does not have to be fair to be beneficial. This latter view is well expressed in Yeager and Tureck (1976), pp. 131: "it hardly matters that an import is cheap just because it is subsidized by some foreign government. A subsidy, though probably wasteful to the country offering it, is just one of many considerations that may combine to make an import a bargain from the American point of view."

23. This terminology pertains to standards imposed to protect human, animal, and plant life and health, particularly on products destined for consumption."Phytosanitary" standards apply only to plant products.

24. This change was in response to concerns by environmentalists that "GATT technocrats" were in the position to make decisions impinging on local environmental regulations, without sufficient scientific/public participation.

25. Under countervailing duty law, the country rendering the decision is the country of the industries who file the appeal.

26. The Indonesia case offers a good example. The amount of logging significantly increased during the 1980s to meet the input requirements of a dramatically expanding, inefficient domestic plywood industry (Braga, 1991; Gillis, 1988).

27. The "value added" argument, for example, implicitly presumes that the amount of value added is greater than processing costs and resource wastage during processing. In Indonesia, half of a log that enters a plywood mill ends up as sawdust. Ignoring processing costs, plywood would have to sell for at least twice the value of the raw log on a log-equivalent basis for "value added" manufacturing to add, rather than subtract, value from the domestic economy. This necessary condition does not appear to be met in the Indonesian case.

28. Agreement on Technical Barriers to Trade, Article 2. (GATT, 1986).

29. Between 1989 and 1990, 211 notifications were made by the United States of technical regulations based on environmental policy grounds (GATT 1992). Noise standards promulgated by the EPA for motor vehicles, boats, and household appliances are examples.

30. The continuing dispute between the United States and the European Union over growth hormones in beef provides a good example of the kind of conflicts that are apt to arise.

31. Environmentalists have not been conceptually consistent on the sovereignty issue. In arguing for trading restrictions or suspensions to induce foreign competitors to adopt domestic environmental standards, such as in the Tuna Dolphin case, environmentalists are essentially advocating the harmonization of international environmental standards at their own domestic level. If such a harmonization plan were implemented, countries on the receiving end would experience a conceptually analogous sovereignty infringement that environmentalists oppose in connection with GATT harmonization proposals.

32. See Hudson (1991) for this speculation.

33. The transactions costs of monitoring and enforcing an international permit trading system for CFCs might be prohibitively expensive, in which case, the first best environmental policy option would not be feasible. As a second-best environmental policy option, domestic CFC consumption shares could be allocated to domestic producers and international suppliers in proportion to historic production patterns. From an economic efficiency point of view, this option is not necessarily better than trade sanctions. However, it would avoid the trade policy externality.

34. Note that the Montreal Protocol could be exempted under current GATT rules if two-thirds of the contracting members voted to do so. Hence, broadly supported multilateral environmental agreements are not likely to conflict with the GATT. However, "the prevailing view is that waivers are to be granted only exceptionally and for a limited period of time, and they are not a substitute for rules revision." (GATT, 1992)

35. It might be argued that ozone depletion is an environmental calamity that requires drastic action, justifying the use of coercive trade measures to enforce treaty provisions. Yet, the severity of the problem is not an ipso facto argument for the use of coercive policy instruments. The same policy objective might be more effectively accomplished by massive

subsidy payments and technology transfer to the nonparticipant countries. Since the industrialized signatory nations are largely responsible for creating the ozone-depletion problem, and are wealthier than the nonparticipant countries, the noncoercive solution would also be more equitable than the use of coercive policy instruments.

36. On the establishment of the WTO, the Declaration of Marrakesh, and subsequent action on trade, environment, and sustainability see the following: *Focus, GATT Newsletter* No. 107 Special Issue, May, 1994; *GATT-WTO News* December 21, 1994; for difference between GATT and WTO; *World Trade Organization: Trade and the Environment* Press/ TE 002, 8 May, 1994; and WTO *FOCUS* No. 1 (January-February 1995).

37. David E. Sanger, World Trade Group Orders U.S. to Alter Clean Air Act, *New York Times*, 18 January 1996, pp. 1, 5.

REFERENCES

Anderson, K. (1992a). The standards welfare economics of policies affecting trade and the environment, in *The Greening of World Trade Issues*, Anderson and Blackhurst (eds.). Ann Arbor: The University of Michigan Press.

_____ . (1992b). Effects on the environment and welfare of liberalizing world trade: The case of coal and food, in *The Greening of World Trade Issues*. Anderson and Blackhurst, (eds.), Ann Arbor: The University of Michigan Press.

Anderson, K. and R. Blackhurst (eds.). (1992). *The Greening of World Trade Issues*. Ann Arbor: The University of Michigan Press.

Antle, J. M. (1991). Farm policy and the environment, *American Journal of Agricultural Economics* 73(3): 917–921.

Arden-Clarke, C. (1991). The general agreement on tariffs and trade; Environmental protection and sustainable development. WWF International Discussion Paper, November.

Baumol, W. J. and W. E. Oates. (1988). *The Theory of Environmental Policy*, Cambridge: Cambridge University Press.

Boyd, R. and K. Krutilla. (1988). The politics and consequences of protectionism: A case study in the North American lumber market, *Journal of Policy Modeling* 10(4): 601–609.

Boyd, R. G.; K. Krutilla; and J. McKinney. (1993). The impact of tariff liberalization between the United States and Mexico: An empirical analysis, *Applied Economics* 25: 81–89.

Braga, C. (1991). Tropical forests and trade policy; the case of Indonesia and Brazil, in *International Trade and the Environment*, P. Low, (ed.). World Bank Discussion Paper #149, World Bank, Washington, DC.

Charnovitz, S. (1991). Explaining the environmental exceptions in GATT Article XX, *Journal of World Trade* 25(5): 37–55.

Christensen, E. (1991). *GATT nets an environmental disaster: A legal analysis and critique of the GATT panel Ruling on imports of Mexican yellowfin tuna into the United States.* Working Paper, Community Nutrition Institute, Washington, DC.

Cobb, C. W and J. B. Cobb (1991). The cost of free trade, *Christian Century* October 23, 967–969.

Corden, W. M. (1974). *Trade Policy and Economic Welfare*. Oxford: Clarendon Press.

Cruz, W. and R. Repetto. (1992). *The Environmental Effects of Stabilization and Structural Adjustment Programs: The Philippine Case*. World Resources Institute: Washington, D.C.

Deacon, B. (1992). Controlling tropical deforestation: An analysis of alternative policies. Conference Paper, European Association of Environmental and Resource Economists, June, Kraców, Poland.

Doering, O. (1990). The fate of farmers, veggies, and food consumers under Big Green regulation, Symposium on "Big Green," Graduate School of Public Policy, Berkeley, CA, September 5.

Economist. (1993). Trade and the Environment: The greening of protectionism, February 27, 25–28.

GATT. (1986). *The Texts of the Tokyo Round Agreements*, Geneva.

———. (1992). *Trade and the Environment*, Geneva.

Gillis, M. (1988). Indonesia: Public policies, resource management, and the tropical forest, in *Public Policies and the Misuse of Forest Resources*, R. Repetto and M. Gillis (eds.). Cambridge: Cambridge University Press.

Grossman, G. H. and A. B. Krueger. (1991). Environmental impacts of a North American free trade agreement. Conference paper, Princeton University, October.

Hilz, C. and J. R. Ehrenfeld. (1991). Transboundary movements of hazardous wastes: a comparative analysis of policy options to control the international waste trade. *International Environmental Affairs* 3(1): 26–63.

Horsch, G. (1991). Personal Communication; Visiting Fulbright Scholar, School of Public and Environmental Affairs, Bloomington, Ind.

Hudson, S. (1991). Trade, environment, and the pursuit of sustainable development. World Bank Discussion Paper #149, P. Low (ed).Washington, DC.

Jackson, J. H. (1989). *The World Trading System: Law and Policy of International Economic Relations.* Cambridge, Mass: MIT Press..

Krueger, A. (1974). The political economy of the rent-seeking society, *American Economic Review* 65(3): 291–303.

Krugman, P. R. (1990). Is free trade passe?, in *International Economics and International Economic Policy*, P. King (ed.). New York: McGraw-Hill Publishing Co.

Krutilla, K. (1989). Tariff burdens and optimal tariffs under alternative transport costs and market structures, *Economics Letters* 31: 381–386.

———. (1991a). Unilateral environmental policy in the global commons, *Policy Studies Journal* 19(2): 126–139.

———. (1991b). Environmental regulation in an open economy, *Journal of Environmental Economics and Management* 20: 127–142

Lloyd, P. J. (1992). The problem of optimal environmental policy choices, in *The Greening of World Trade Issues*, Anderson and Blackhurst (eds.). Ann Arbor: The University of Michigan Press.

Low, P. (ed.). (1991). International Trade and the Environment. World Bank Discussion Paper #149, World Bank, Washington, DC.

Lutz, E. (1990). Agricultural trade liberalization; Price changes and environmental effects. World Bank Divisional Working Paper No. 1990–16, World Bank, Washington, DC.

Markusen, J. (1986). Explaining the volume of trade, *American Economic Review* 16(5): 1002–1011.

Robertson, D. (1991). Trade and the environment: Harmonization and technical standards. World Bank Discussion Paper #149, P. Low (ed.). World Bank, Washington, DC.

Runge, C. F. (1990). Trade protectionism and environmental regulation: the new nontariff barriers, *Northwestern Journal of International Law and Business* 11: 47–61.

———. (1991). *Environmental effects of trade in the agricultural sector: A case study.* OECD Environmental Directorate, December 1, 1991.

Shrybman, S. (1990). International trade and the environment: An environmental assessment of the General Agreement on Tariffs and Trade, *The Ecologist* 20: 30–44.

Snape, R. H. (1992). The environment, international trade, and competitiveness, in *The Greening of World Trade Issues*, Anderson and Blackhurst (eds.). Ann Arbor: The University of Michigan Press.

Tobey, J. A. (1990). The effects of domestic environmental policies on patterns of world trade: An empirical test, *Kyklos* 43(2): 191–209.

Walter, I (1982). Environmentally-induced industrial relocation to developing countries, in Environment and Trade, S. J. Rubin and T. R. Graham (eds.). London: Frances Pinter.

Whathen, T. (1992). *A Guide to Trade and the Environment*. New York: Environmental Grantmakers Association, Consultive Group on Biological Diversity.

Yeager, L. and D. Tureck. (1976). *Foreign Trade and U.S. Policy: The Case for Free International Trade*. New York: Praeger Publishers.

6

POLICY REGIMES FOR INTERNATIONAL WASTE TRADE

Laura A. Strohm and Roy W. Shin

Among the unforeseen problems of the new industrial age has been the disposal of increasing quantities of wastes—many hazardous and toxic. Industrial chemistry has produced numerous products, that while useful, are alien to nature and resistant to biodegradation or detoxification. Growing public awareness of the possible hazards and risks involved in disposal of the residuals of industrial activities is arousing a popular demand for environmental protection. But this popular awareness depends upon public information and a degree of scientific literacy—conditions that vary widely among nations. An initial consequence has been environmental regulations and restrictions respecting waste disposal in scientifically developed countries, and vulnerability among less developed countries to the export of hazardous wastes from the countries of their origin. A secondary consequence has been the emergence of international waste trade as a national and international multidimensional policy problem.

As the twenty-first century comes upon us, we find that many environmental problems formerly contained within domestic boundaries have spilled over into international domains. Waste disposal is a dramatic case in point. Transboundary movements of wastes, hazardous and otherwise, began in earnest around 1980. The new activity raised serious questions as to whether all "products" were welcome in an increasingly free-trading global economy. The new international dimensions of this waste trade brought new environmental policy challenges: of accountability and liability for operations in the global commons; of changing rights and duties within sovereign jurisdictions; of ethics and equity in the distribution of cost and benefit.

Even as environmental policy encompasses new international dimensions, it also is spilling over beyond traditional diplomatic circles. Governments are no longer the exclusive players on the international stage, but they are joined by growing numbers and types of nonstate actors. In the waste trade politics of the 1980s influential roles were played by unusual participants, such as Greenpeace, scrap metal recyclers, and Nigerian students studying in Italy.

The waste trade also clearly demonstrates the coming era of "leapfrog opportunity," which developing and industrialized countries must seize together. Waste dumping scandals highlighted the woefully inadequate regulatory and physical waste management infrastructures of many less developed countries (LDCs). It is understandable that nonindustrialized countries had little ability to handle toxic wastes properly as they had little need. Yet as these countries develop their need is growing. Rather than the usual follow-the-leader development paradigms, new techniques could be both better and cheaper. Transfer of appropriate waste technologies coupled with adequate training could offer the less developed countries (South) the chance to skip the whole past era of uncontrolled toxic dumping for which the industrialized countries (North) are now paying. In addition, thoughtful technology cooperation would also provide economic opportunity for innovative waste technology entrepreneurs. Newstyle government-industry partnerships may strengthen necessary domestic waste management redesigns in developed countries as well.

Complex intricacies in definition and purposeful misclassification of wastes create difficulties in estimating the true scale of current waste trading activity. Few cases clearly link waste trading to actual consequences of environmental or public health degradation. Nevertheless, waste trading elicits important political, legal, and economic dilemmas for international environmental policy. It triggers surprising North/South interactions. It invites a new look at the old tension between sovereignty and multilateral cooperation. It demonstrates the basic spectrum of options between free markets and government control.

A major concern is hazardous waste disposal and illicit dumping in developing countries. A fundamental question is: when do North-to-South waste imports constitute a sovereign free choice of governments to accept risk in exchange for benefit or adequate compensation? Alternatively, when is the export of environmental hazard an unethical transfer of risk to vulnerable populations?

Opinions about waste trading divide into two main groups that can be called (1) the "comparative advantage" school, and (2) the "environmental risk transfer" school. The former, generally composed of the developed nations, economists, and the waste disposal industry, view an international trade in toxic wastes as a normal and appropriate extension of market forces between consenting nations (Summers, 1991). The latter school, however, including developing nations, environmentalists, and other members of the international community, find transboundary movements of hazardous wastes alarming (Bollag, 1988).

Any successful waste trading policy must reconcile these incompatible views of the issue. The Basel Convention (1989) is making progress toward a workable international public policy by modifications in its Prior Informed Consent (PIC) regime, its trade ban from OECD to non-OECD countries, and the postponement of recycling restrictions until 1997. This study contends that the root causes of waste trading must be addressed by improved clean production processes and waste management practices around the world. Key questions for the next century ask what are the best technologies and how can they be shared?

DESCRIPTION OF THE PROBLEM

No exporting country, importing country, or international treaty adequately regulates or even monitors transboundary waste movements as yet. The majority of cases are most likely movements to so-called "best-technology" facilities—that is, North-to-North trade. However, some are North-to-South trade, or involve the global commons.

The increase in global trade in toxic wastes during the 1980s is attributed to the combination of several factors: growing populations and growing per capita consumption levels are producing more wastes; the Not In My Back Yard (NIMBY) syndrome in developed countries blocks new disposal sites; the regulatory climates for waste management vary considerably among countries; and many countries suffer heavy debt burdens and poverty.

Hazardous waste is a by-product of modern technological development and production. Yet it is a unique commodity different from other by-products because it is regarded as having a negative economic value. Many rules and regulations normally applicable to economic transactions therefore become inoperative. The payment is reversed: waste is not a desired commodity voluntarily purchased for use; parties must be compensated to knowingly accept waste. In addition, the interest of the consignor and consignee in the satisfactory state of the cargo upon arrival may not exist. In other words, no economic agent has personal interest in the fate of the cargo. Thus, a major problem with the transport of hazardous waste is the temptation to arrange for its disappearance en route unless offset by economic return to the disposer (Remond, 1985, p. 211). Externalities are inherent in the waste trade, not due to a lack of competition, but to the fact that producers can ignore the by-product consequences of their operations. The confused legal status of trade, and the inherent negative value waste carries, combine to make controlling transboundary waste movements difficult.

Scale and Types of Waste Trading

Substances that are most costly to dispose of domestically are the first to move internationally: PCBs, heavy metals, plastics, and radioactive wastes. There is no uniform international approach concerning what the properties of a waste should be in order for that waste to be labeled "hazardous" (Wynne, 1987, 46). The dividing line between hazardous products and wastes becomes blurred when chemicals lapse out-of-date, or wastes become feedstocks for recycling.

Uncertainties in definition, and incomplete data, make quantifying waste exports an inexact science, particularly as "hazardous" is inevitably an imprecise term. A great deal of the research and compilation has been done by the media and nongovernmental organizations (NGOs), rather than by properly equipped or designated government institutions (Moyers, 1990).

A 1985 Organization for Economic Cooperation and Development (OECD) estimate calculated that approximately 350 million tons of hazardous waste are generated each year worldwide, 90 percent of which are produced in industrialized countries. Five to 10 percent of the total generated is probably transported across national borders each year (Yakowitz, 1987). At least fifty countries have been involved in proposed shipments. In the period 1986–1990 proposals to ship wastes internationally totaled an estimated 163 million tons (Vallette, 1990, 7). But the majority of these proposals was not consummated.

Many waste movements occur between European Union nations and from Western Europe to Eastern Europe (Aeppel, 1989). Britain has become a major hazardous waste importer in recent years, offering Europe's cheapest disposal prices (Rublack, 1989, 14). Traditional routes and connections are the most likely pathways for the wastes: they are shipped to former colonies, trusteeship territories, and regular trading partners.

Koko, Nigeria, where an Italian firm's mixed wastes were illegally dumped (Brooke, 1988) was not an isolated case. In 1986 the *Khian Sea* ship loaded with municipal incinerator ash from Philadelphia set sail for a two-year odyssey, wandering the oceans looking for dumpsites (Rabe, 1991, 109). Transboundary movements of waste have occurred in the Caribbean, Latin America, and Asia. In 1988 a broker from Global Telesis Corporation, in Walnut Creek, California, offered the government of Papua New Guinea U.S.$60 per metric ton to accept over 600,000 metric tons per month of mixed hazardous waste from the West Coast of the United States (Vallette, 1990, 188). Several U.S. Indian tribes have recently accepted wastes onto their quasi-sovereign reservations from nearby urban areas (Vallette, 1990, 281).

Causes of Waste Trading

A complex interaction of growing waste quantities, shrinking disposal capacities, and new opportunities for profits set the stage for trading. Two apparently paradoxical demands are gaining momentum everywhere in the world: greater consumer demand from increasing populations; and growing desire on the part of citizens for greater environmental protection. In response to the first demand, the chemical industry has provided 5,000 new chemicals and twenty times more chemical products (by weight) since World War II (Underwood, 1988, 29). The petroleum and transportation sectors have increased dramatically and the extractive industries have accelerated production. Levels of per capita energy and materials consumption are higher than ever before in most countries.

But, on the other hand, heightened environmental consciousness and stricter regulations have put pressure on the old ways of disposing of waste. Many emissions and effluents previously discharged to air and water are now concentrated and packaged for specialized disposal (Wynne, 1987, 46). A burgeoning environmental cleanup industry collects considerable quantities of wastes and contaminated soils that require special treatment, ironically adding to the burden on commercial waste disposal facilities.

Waste treatment and disposal facilities are limited, and unlikely to keep up with the growing demand. Most municipal and commercial landfills are nearing capacity, and many in the United States were closed when it was discovered that they were polluting groundwater. Well publicized illegal dumps and old landfills, such as Love Canal, which caused tragic health and environmental disasters in the 1970s (Levine, 1982), strengthened neighborhood opposition to any new treatment and disposal facilities. The NIMBY syndrome has successfully blocked unpopular proposals by waste facility developers in most industrial countries. Marine incineration and ocean dumping, once considered viable alternatives to land disposal, have also been severely curtailed by recent international agreements (Ditz, 1989).

As a result, hazardous waste generators are experiencing a steady incremental rise in capital, operating, and administrative costs required to handle their wastes, including higher insurance costs to cover growing liability potential. Facing these increasing waste disposal costs and public opposition to new waste storage and disposal facilities, companies began a search for alternatives. This "push," spurred by domestic disposal constraints from behind, met the "pull" of potential profits to create an active international waste trade. Supply and demand dynamics increased disposal costs in the United States from about $15/ton in 1980 to about $250/ton by 1988 for typical landfill disposal; incineration can cost as high as $2,000/ton, depending on materials and methods (Lief, 1988, 54). Some incinerator facilities have a scheduling backlog, requiring appointments two years in advance.

In contrast, dumping fees in developing countries are much lower, ranging from U.S.$4/metric ton to U.S.$40/metric ton, if they are paid at all, without any question of delays. International transportation costs, especially by bulk tanker, have plunged over recent years. Waste export schemes once considered ridiculous have become economically viable. One U.S. firm proposed sending garbage to China for less than it cost to bury it in New Jersey! (Lief, 1988, 56). Thus, the predictable market response to the pressure on domestic waste disposal options has been some export of hazardous wastes to other nations.

TWO SCHOOLS OF THOUGHT

Policy regimes for international trade in toxic wastes traverse a spectrum between two polarities. On one end is the "comparative advantage" school, opposed on the other end by the "environmental risk transfer" school. Most individuals and nations locate themselves somewhere along this continuum of opinion, not at the extremes. Any successful international waste trade policy will address the concerns of both camps, synthesizing solutions in the middle range.

The "Comparative Advantage" School

The classical law of comparative advantage states that overall market efficiency, and thereby the greatest good for the greatest number, is best achieved if each country produces the raw materials, goods, and services that it can make most proficiently, trading for the rest of its needs. Specialization in a niche derived from some national comparative advantage leads to success in the international marketplace.

Supporters of the comparative advantage school argue that "the environmental factor" ought to be included in the calculation of national strengths offered in the international marketplace. Just as mineral resources and lower labor wage rates are turned to trade advantage, environmental factors can be considered. Political and cultural valuation of environmental quality, usually thought to correlate with income levels (Leonard, 1988, 68), is also a component of the environmental factor in comparative trade advantage. Four main themes underlie this position:

1. Assimilative Capacity as Geographic Advantage. Untapped environmental assimilative capacity—nature's ability to absorb wastes and neutralize toxicity—can be perceived as a saleable commodity. As industrialized countries progressively consume the assimilative capacity of their own waters, soils, and atmosphere, the relative purity of certain Third World environmental conditions becomes attractive. Waste trading markets can be seen from an inverted point of view as environmental quality markets. The "comparative advantage" school advocates this international commoditization of environmental quality as a valid source of foreign currency for developing nations.

Some sites are clearly superior over others for waste disposal. Geographic advantages for landfill or incinerator construction may exist in certain clay soils, low water tables, aridity, high dispersal winds, easy access to fill locations, or lack of population. Some nations (or private firms) may own specialized high technology waste treatment facilities unavailable elsewhere, such as Britain's high temperature polychlorinated byphenols (PCBs) incinerators. A multinational firm may wish to treat all of its troublesome waste at one facility, and therefore export wastes to or from its subsidiaries.

2. The Pollution Haven Hypothesis. This hypothesis states that relatively weaker environmental regulations will be used to comparative advantage in the international competition for foreign investment by developing countries. Industrial flight will occur away from those countries that demand stringent environmental standards.

The United States began to regulate environmental pollutants to air, water, soil, and in the workplace by the early 1970s (Brickman et al., 1985; Vogel, 1986). Industries were required to pay for changes in their operating procedures: installing pollution control equipment, redirecting waste streams, and protecting workers. In response, they voiced concerns that the costs and logistics of compliance with the new wave of environmental regulations would impair their competitiveness abroad.

To overcome these fears, some Western leaders proposed at several iternational forums globally uniform environmental standards. The Third World ⁄as not interested in pursuing this option, and even industrialized nations found armonization of their environmental regulations easier said than done. National riorities, government institutions, and cultures proved too disparate to standardize n an operational level. In addition, the relationship between environmental tandards and costs was complex, as identical standards did not necessarily yield qual pollution control costs among the nations, nor equalized competition.

Some scholars thus speculated about the possible influence on international rade of different pollution control regulations among countries. The U.N. Industry nd Development Organization (UNIDO) suggested that developing countries ntentionally integrate lenient environmental regulations into their industrial evelopment strategies in order to attract manufacturing away from those countries hat preferred more environmental quality (UNIDO, 1980, 94). Conscious design s not necessary in order to become a pollution haven, only a lack of conscious lefense may lead to that condition through inept negotiation, poor planning, lax nforcement of laws, corruption, and other political factors.

The comparative advantage camp is quick to point out that by the early 1980s mpirical studies (Pearson, 1987; Leonard, 1988) on trade and investment effects ⁀f the new strict environmental regulations firmly rejected the pollution haven heory. Analysis showed that environmental factors did not eclipse traditional ndustry considerations such as labor costs, political stability, and financial ncentives. "Dirty" industries did not move in any disproportionate way compared ⁀o other industries or previous trends during the 1970s and early 1980s. These indings suggest that waste movements might not follow a pollution haven pattern ⁀ither.

3. Sovereign Risk Assessment. No matter where the limits of responsibility are lrawn for company liability, or government control over the private sector, nternational cases must always address the issue of sovereignty. The right to make overeign decisions was asserted in the North/South dialogue on environmental ssues: the North insisting it can set standards as high as it wants to, even if this ⁀loses markets to some producers; the South claiming the sovereign right to pollute ⁀f necessary in order to attain economic growth. The Stockholm Declaration in ⁀972 affirmed that each country's unique economic, cultural, and geographic ⁀ondition must dictate its own sovereign calculus of cost-benefit. Principle 21 from he same declaration, however, stated that every nation also has the responsibility ⁀o control any environmental effects from its activities that spill over its borders.

International waste trading is currently operating under the international ⁀egime called "Prior Informed Consent" (PIC), which is based on a respect for ⁀overeignty. Under the PIC regime, government authorities of importing countries nust be provided with adequate and timely information about a proposed ⁀azardous shipment, and they must give their consent before it arrives. Thus PIC ⁀atisfies the "rules" of sovereignty, where each nation has the responsibility to ⁀rotect its own citizens (Waldo, 1985, 4).

4. Government Failures. The comparative advantage school also expresses concern about potential government failures in any attempt to control the market which are often magnified at the international level. Typical government failures can include: inefficiency, jurisdictional confusion, administrative incompetence inconsistency of enforcement, undue political influences, and lack of accountability. Clearly every jurisdiction makes a trade-off between ease of administration (discretionary freedom) and technical detail (precise mandate), trying to provide the best protection at reasonable cost, balancing comprehensiveness, and specificity. Tighter regulations can be an illusion, and do not necessarily provide better control.

Lack of accountability is a special problem at the international level (Horberry and LeMarcant, 1991). Oversight functions normally performed by sovereign governments do not occur. No supranational waste management agency, nor any global environmental protection agency with overarching regulatory powers exists.

In the current global wave of support for free trade, it should come as no surprise that this comparative advantage school in support of waste trading has many adherents. The concepts of the environmental factor in international trade are intriguing, and the urgent need of the poor adds weight to this argument.

The "Environmental Risk Transfer" School

At the opposite end of the opinion spectrum are those who label international waste trading an unethical transfer of environmental risk from rich to poor countries. This school of thought construes the waste trade as a forced choice between "poverty or poison" and just one more example of "imperialistic exploitation" of the Third World by the Western World.

The "environmental risk transfer" school cites the distressing realities of the trading system when they contradict the free traders' theoretical arguments about comparative advantages, sovereignty, and government deficiencies. Evidence on waste trading cases shows persistent patterns of deception, illegal connections confusion, and improper disposal. They claim that only concerted national governmental actions, in harmony with international guidelines, can prevent a devastating black market in toxic wastes. This approach is conditioned by the following factors:

1. Realities of the Waste Trading System. Potential consequences of improper toxic waste disposal include significant adverse health effects, ecosystem degradation, economic burdens, and unpredictable political repercussions. These consequences may be delayed over time, and borne by people other than the original waste contractors.

Third World nations are particularly vulnerable, unequal participants in the waste trading system. In the face of poverty and debt burdens, governments are naturally attracted to any contract that offers foreign exchange. This apparent opportunity to mitigate their fundamental economic problems places them in the compromising position of opting for short-term economic benefits at the potential expense of hidden environmental costs (Hilz and Ehrenfeld, 1991, 33). Public participation in government decisionmaking is weak, and often not tolerated by authoritarian regimes. Most developing countries possess neither the technology nor the administrative capacity to ensure the safe handling of hazardous waste.

The players in the international waste trading system are generators, brokers, transporters, and disposers. Generators often hire brokers at a negotiated price to take their wastes, rather than deal with disposal themselves. The brokers then arrange for collection, hire transporters, re-sell whatever possible to recyclers, and contract for treatment, storage, and disposal as necessary. High potential profits are attracting many newcomers to this "open access" profession, where no special training nor start-up costs are required. Little monitoring or accountability occurs.

2. Waste Havens and Sacrifice Zones. Global waste disposal ideas reveal a universal attraction to the easy solution of adding toxic wastes to places already surrendered to pollution by historical happenstance, such as existing dumps, weapons disposal facilities, previous accident locations, or abandoned mines. If such a zone is not conveniently located, fresh sites have been suggested in deserts or barren high mountains, space or deep ocean, unpopulated areas, or areas inhabited by poor rural people who cannot make effective complaint.

Wastes move much easier than whole factories. Intentional invitation of waste contracts is not necessary, as a lack of conscious defense can allow waste shipments. Contracts can be quietly agreed upon without government participation. Thus waste havens could happen much easier than pollution havens. A logical extension of the waste haven hypothesis is the concept of sacrifice zones." These are disaster areas abandoned entirely for human use. No cleanup or reclamation efforts are contemplated by anyone. Recent nuclear and ecodisasters have introduced this concept to the modern world.

3. Implementation: Failure of Prior Informed Consent. Careful investigation has revealed serious inadequacies in the PIC regime. In reality, notices rarely reach beyond embassies to environmental protection offices or local areas where wastes are dumped. Notification discharges all obligations for exporters and provides a kind of official rubber stamp (Roelants du Vivier, 1989, 3). Currently, Third World nations must rely on industrial countries for information, regulatory judgments, and help in controlling trade in hazardous materials.

A U.S. EPA employee in charge of sending such notifications about chemicals followed her official notices to Africa, curious about their fate. The case she chose to study was the emergency suspension from sale or use of Ethylene Dibromide (EDB), a rare and serious step for EPA, taken only on the basis of convincing evidence of serious potential harm. She found no nation in effective possession of her notices, none that understood the implications, none that reached offices that would have done something if they had known (Halter, 1987). Notification and consent becomes another opportunity for bribery. Nobody wants the responsibility of giving permission, and it takes too long. More fundamentally, information alone is no guarantee that a hazard will be adequately evaluated.

4. Market Failures. Although adequate markets and entrepreneurial skills often serve the public most efficiently, this school argues that fundamental

Environmental Policy

distortions of the free market are inherent in the waste trading case. For Adam Smith's invisible hand to function properly, economists have assumed equality and full information among players, and ignored distribution questions and environmental costs. The waste haven dynamic is possible only because of market failures, rather than as a result of natural market efficiency.

Whether or not waste havens actually develop, opponents denounce waste trading as a classic case of market failure. The social and private costs and discount rates diverge in this case; private costs are lower because the public takes the risk. Limited time horizons, hegemony, and monopoly also distort the waste trade free market. Waste trading exhibits three broad categories of market failure: externalities (unaccounted costs over the long run); unequal participants (asymmetrical information and capacity); and maldistribution (costs and benefits unfairly allocated).

Waste exports lower disposal costs, thereby depressing incentives for domestic waste minimization and management research. The waste export loophole postpones the search for better alternatives, preventing the emergence of innovative backstop technologies. Thus waste exports deprive the domestic waste management industry of business, causing economic and employment losses.

The market also fails in this case because the waste trade is rarely concluded among equals, but rather one party dominates the exchange. Incomes of waste exporters and importers can diverge by orders of magnitude. Sophisticated international waste brokers often approach fledgling environmental ministries for contract approvals. This imbalance is accentuated by an information gap between industrialized and developing worlds about hazardous waste management. The independent, informed judgments required of each party in order to maximize their own utility are absent in waste trading.

Beyond externalities and unequal participants, markets fail to address equity questions about who benefits and who pays over time, which for waste trading is very uneven. The risks and benefits of an industrial economy are not fairly spread over geographic regions, socioeconomic groups, or between generations.

In summary, the environmental risk transfer school is clearly outraged by international waste trading and their arguments rest fundamentally on ethical and equity principles. Environmental quality should not become a luxury commodity, but must remain a human right available to all. The serious potential consequences of waste trading, added to the special Third World vulnerability to such practices, clearly shows that the trade takes advantage, not of a market niche, but of disadvantaged groups. The reality of current waste trading systems, which use unlicensed brokers and deceptive methods, invites the creation of waste havens or sacrifice zones.

The PIC regime has failed miserably to counteract the information gap in waste trading. The market failures of unaccounted external costs, unequal participants, and distributional neglect clearly justify governmental intervention. At the international level, that means multinational cooperation, which began with the signing of the Basel Convention in March of 1989.

In contrast, the comparative advantage school welcomes toxic wastes to the global marketplace, seeing no justification to limiting the trade. The environmental factor in comparative trade advantage ought to be exploited to the fullest in international competition. The pollution haven hypothesis (that weak environmental regulations would attract the dirtiest industries to poor countries) has been discounted. Waste trading simply makes efficient use of global assimilative capacity for pollutants, and differences in valuation and preferences.

The governments of many developing nations welcome the opportunity to earn hard currency, and possibly even obtain modern waste management technology and services. The PIC regime gives any nation a chance to refuse waste shipments if they are not desired. Indeed, every nation must make its own sovereign choice based on its own risk assessment profiles. Government regulation is traditionally fraught with a variety of failures, which are avoided by letting the market take its course.

Bridging these two schools of thought on the matter is important, otherwise no progress will be made. Upon what points can they, if not agree, at least find compromise that might serve everyone's interests? And how might these points of agreement or compromise lead to specific waste trade prescriptions?

Synthesis in the Middle Range of the Opinion Spectrum

The first major zone of compromise or even integration between the comparative advantage school and the environmental risk transfer school of thought about the international waste trade lies in the popular concept of sustainable development. Economics and environmental concerns come together in mutually reinforcing ways, with government establishing a successful policy base for market operations (Panayotou, 1993). The series of *government failures* criticized by waste free trade supporters includes: inefficiency, jurisdictional confusion, administrative incompetence, inconsistency of enforcement, and undue political influences. The series of *market failures* criticized by anti-waste trade advocates includes: extensive externalities, especially over the long run; unequal participants (hegemony and information gaps); and maldistribution of costs and benefits that raised equity concerns. But the market and government can counterbalance one another, correcting some of the failures of the other.

The waste management industry has acknowledged its need for government partnership both domestically and internationally. In the United States, it seeks assistance from the federal government on facility siting in order to overcome the NIMBY syndrome. Internationally, responsible elements in the industry desire government assistance in contract enforcement. Government regulations can create significant new market opportunities in technologies and services. Predictability in expected standards, license requirements, and liability regimes benefit industry. As governments learn to eliminate or reduce policy distortions that favor environmentally unsound practices (certain subsidies, for instance), they can at the same time improve economic efficiency.

In the reverse direction, governments around the world are discovering that the use of market tools, such as carefully structured taxes as incentives to encourage environmentally sound behavior, are much cheaper and more effective than old style command-and-control regulation. No nation nor any international secretariat can hope to stem waste trading by decree alone if the root economic causes are not addressed. Thus cooperation of these two systems in domestic waste management redesign, and international cooperation on waste trading has wide scope to produce mutually beneficial compromise.

Other dimensions that stretch between our two extreme schools of thought attempt to bridge the classic tension between national sovereignty and multilateral cooperation. National autonomy and self-rule, or the sovereign right of nation states to control activities within their own borders, is a legal reality that endures. Perceived breaches of sovereignty in the waste trading regime abound, and have been met with strong resistance especially by newly independent nations. Yet multinational cooperation also has strong appeal and practical utility. Participation in international forums imparts status and legitimacy to parties at home. More importantly, multilateral cooperation sometimes serves best to protect a nation from events it would otherwise be unable to defend against; or to provide resources it would not otherwise obtain. Thus the Basel Convention and other international efforts have attracted considerable cooperation from both developing and industrialized nations. In addition, efforts have begun to harmonize guidelines on domestic waste management redesign.

The North/South divide on the waste trade issue can find common ground as well. Negative and angry rhetoric from Third World leaders showed an unusual symbolic value to the waste trade: that it signaled a potential new dimension to international environmental affairs; that the South would become the dumping grounds of the North, which amplified their perception of risk from international waste movements. Yet the best information shows that in fact most of the waste trade is between industrialized countries, and the "tip of the iceberg" theory about illegal dumping in poor nations has not been verified (Montgomery, 1995). The Basel Convention, Bamako Convention, and E.U. directives have all attempted to protect developing countries from any wholesale transfer of environmental risk in the form of toxic wastes.

The following waste trade prescriptions are grounded in these zones of compromise or mutual benefit, which begin to bridge the classic tensions between the market and government; sovereignty and multilateral cooperation; and North and South.

WASTE TRADE PRESCRIPTIONS

We believe a combination of national regulation, international agreements, and private sector efforts can work together to allow minimal waste trading in clearly justified cases, yet prevent abusive transfer of environmental risk. The two schools of thought on waste trading, the comparative advantage school, and the environmental risk transfer school will never completely melt away in any grand compromise, but they can work together on the following framework to make progress.

Domestic Waste Management Redesign

In order to reduce the pressure to export, most industrialized nations must fundamentally redesign their domestic waste management systems. A prioritized series of preferred actions can be established that match wastes with the best alternatives. This strategic matching will vary with geography, type of industry, available facilities, and feasibility of proposed changes.

The best technical option to the hazardous waste problem is, of course, prevention. Reduction of waste generation at the source, through modification of production processes, product (input) substitution, packaging reduction, and consumer education, is the first goal. Governments should require waste audits and waste reduction plans as a precondition for any permit issuance. Economic incentives to minimize waste, such as taxation on throughput or energy use, or subsidized waste reduction research, are components of a good waste management policy. Companies themselves are discovering considerable cost savings in waste reduction planning.

Recycling is the next priority, when conditions permit. Refundable deposits, community effort, and industry willingness to consider recycling, should be incorporated into the new waste management strategies. New markets for recycled materials and new competition among contractors are improving performance in this arena. Recovery and reprocessing of recycled materials can be quite hazardous to worker and public health and the surrounding environment, for instance, as it is with lead recovery from old batteries, or the transformation of old tires. These industries must themselves be subject to high quality environmental audits and standards.

After source reduction and recycling, new disposal technologies are important. New incinerator prototypes are promising, among them combustion with microwaves, or electric vitrification. New pre-treatment technologies of a biological, chemical, and/or physical nature are providing exciting options.

Among management options, Brian Wynne suggests the public utility model for waste disposal, such as the United States uses for power and water supply (Wynne, 1989, 144). An accountable public/private consortium, a utility is essentially a heavily regulated and assisted private industry providing a public service. A clearinghouse could direct particular wastes to certain treatments, reducing uncertainties in hazardous waste life-cycles. Classifications must not be assigned to wastes by the shipper or generator, as that carries an inherent conflict of interest.

Waste exports to best-technology facilities, with adequate justification, might be permitted if consistent with international agreements. The U.S. EPA and similar agencies in other nations should evaluate and oversee waste exports, and be given the clear mandate and resources necessary to do that. Environmental Impact

Reports (EIRs), public hearings, and baseline health surveys should be required. Formal licensing of waste brokers, with appropriate training and reporting, should be instituted at the national level, consistent with international treaties. National governments can prohibit exports, closing the international avenue for their wastes, or maintain a "white list" of reputable, bonded, and licensed waste disposers permitted to send or receive international waste shipments.

International Efforts

In addition to keeping their own houses in order, industrialized countries have a responsibility to assist developing nations with waste management. Information and technical assistance should include legal and institutional advice, training, and technologies. Industrialized countries also have some emergency preparedness experience to offer the developing world. Expert response teams, methods and equipment, and industry training programs are likely candidates for exchanges.

Two caveats with waste management technology transfer: we must be careful about which technologies are used; and we must ask whose waste will be treated. As with all technology transfer, but especially in waste management, the systems should offer modern leapfrog opportunities that are appropriate to place and culture. The second point, about whose waste, is important in order to weigh whether an unethical transfer of environmental risk underlies the aid.

International organizations can facilitate these technology and personnel exchanges, assist database collections, publicize abuses, develop expertise, encourage appropriate technology transfer, and support education. New resolutions for multilateral action include a two-tiered system for hazardous waste trading consisting of an export ban to the developing world, but a notification and consent procedure for industrialized nations, where appropriate (Shaikh, 1990). The use of an international financial security bond sufficient to overcome the negative economic value of waste and deter dumping has been suggested (Smets, 1985, 185–196).

The 1989 Basel Convention on the Control of Transboundary Movements of Hazardous Wastes and Their Disposal encourages waste minimization as the ultimate goal and establishes conditions (PIC regime) on transfrontier shipments but does not prohibit the trade altogether. Although the convention finally entered into force on May 5, 1992, there remain major unresolved issues. They include the role of its new secretariat, enforcement procedures, trade with nonparties, liability, reimportation clauses, and definition of "environmentally sound manner." However, subsequent meetings of the parties are working on these, and on a North-to-South waste trade ban.

The environmental risk transfer school claimed that the convention only validated and legitimized a trade that should be banned and does not even provide for adequate data collection. Other observers viewed it as a first step in multilateral cooperation on the issue, which is flexible and open to improvement in future negotiations. Establishing a fund along the model of the Montreal Ozone Fund would go some distance in assisting countries to meet their international obligations with Basel. The most important work in the coming decade, however, will be redesigning production and consumption patterns in industrialized countries so that less toxic waste is generated in the first place.

CONCLUSION

The waste trade market has not really been driven by the "environmental factor" as a geographic comparative advantage. Natural environmental assimilative capacity is an extremely complex and unmeasured quality in the Third World. Rather, the waste trade has flowed to countries with weaker environmental regulations. Those who can afford to insulate themselves from environmental degradation can buy some time, but in the long run nature's whole systems will hold us all accountable. The waste trade is a crisis of equity and ethics that we must confront together through negotiation, institutional reform, information and technology transfer, and national transparency.

Future policy directions into the twenty-first century will split and struggle against each other. On the one hand, domestic waste management in industrialized countries will grow more sophisticated, emphasizing prevention and source reduction. Facilities and practices in developing countries will also improve. This reduced "push" for waste trading, when combined with a progressively tightening Basel Convention and increasing transparency, will minimize international waste movements.

On the other hand, even though trade in recycling materials is scheduled to stop in 1997 according to Basel, the politics of the North/South positions on this is changing. Indeed some developing nations, once outraged by the waste trade, are now claiming that current bans are plots to deprive them of income. China's development strategy is counting on affordable raw materials obtained through its participation in major international recycling markets in scrap metals and the like.

The transboundary movements of radioactive waste materials have not yet been addressed in any international agreement as of this writing. The International Atomic Energy Agency (IAEA) has been promising to develop a plan on this critical issue since before Basel was signed in 1989, and perhaps it will do so soon.

The international and bilateral assistance available for LDC waste management efforts seems to be increasing, although many projects include some dimension of waste trading. Whether the world will track, minimize and properly handle wastes moving among countries—or whether uncontrolled dumping and trading continue despite agreements—will depend upon how well nations address the underlying causes of waste trading: polluting and wasteful production processes; inadequate domestic waste management regimes; and lagging economic development in poor countries.

Many practical lessons can be derived from the waste trade that are useful for other international environmental policy negotiations. (1) *Increasing complexity*, of an international, interdisciplinary, and science-based nature, mixed with many political participants, will strain even the brightest and best-educated negotiators.

(2) *Leapfrog opportunities* may overcome vested interests in some cases, if multilateral or bilateral funds support the best "green" technologies. (3) *International standards* on broad environmental objectives and principles can provide guidelines for national regulation, if not detailed harmonization at the operational level. In this regard, national governments can be cast as the best level for implementing international environmental agreements (Sand, 1990, 42). (4) Future *environmental conventions will need flexibility* in order to adapt quickly to new information and conditions. Jessica Mathews described such a framework design as "a rolling process of intermediate or self-adjusting agreements" (Mathews, 1989, 175); and (5) *Innovative partnerships between government and industry* hold promise for solutions to international environmental problems. Each system contains within it the strengths that counteract the weaknesses or failures of the other, and linkages should be carefully explored.

REFERENCES

Aeppel, Timothy. (1989). West Pays Price for Dumping on East. *The Christian Science Monitor*, February 10, p. 4.

Bollag, Burton. (1988). Developing Countries Win Support for Curbs on Toxic Dumping. *New York Times*, 22 November, p. C4.

Brickman, Ronald, Sheila Jasanoff, and Thomas Ilgen. (1985). *Controlling Chemicals: The Politics of Regulation in Europe and the United States*. Ithaca, NY: Cornell University Press.

Brooke, James. (1988). Waste Dumpers Turning to West Africa. *New York Times*, 17 July, pp. 1 and 10.

Ditz, D. W. (1989). The Phase Out of North Sea Incineration. *International Environmental Affairs*, 1(3): 175–202.

Halter, Faith. (1987). Regulating Information Exchange and International Trade in Pesticides and Other Toxic Substances to Meet the Needs of Developing Countries. *Columbia Journal of Environmental Law*, 12(1): 1–39.

Hilz, Christoph. (1992). *The International Toxic Waste Trade*. New York: Van Nostrand Reinhold.

Hilz, Christoph, and John R. Ehrenfeld. (1991). Transboundary Movements of Hazardous Wastes. *International Environmental Affairs*, 3(1): 26–28.

Horberry, John, and M. LeMarchant. (1991). The Role of Institutional Strengthening in International Environmental Consulting. *Public Administration and Development*, 11(4): 38–42.

Insight (1989, 23 October). Soviet Union Proposes Green Cross to U.N., p. 26.

Leonard, H. Jeffrey. (1988). *Pollution and the Struggle for the World Product: Multinational Corporations, Environment, and International Comparative Advantage*. The Conservation Foundation. Cambridge, U.K.: Cambridge University Press.

Levine, Adeline Gordon. (1982). *Love Canal: Science, Politics, and People*. New York: Lexington Books.

Lief, Louise. (1988). Dirty Job, Sweet Profits. *U.S. News and World Report*, 21 November, pp. 54–56.

Mathews, Jessica Tuchman. (1989). Redefining Security. *Foreign Affairs*, 68(2): 175.

Montgomery, Mark A. (1995). Reassessing the Waste Trade Crisis: What Do We Really Know? *The Journal of Environment and Development*, 3:1 (Winter): 1–28.

Monroy, Miguel Zoroaster. (1988). An Overview of the International Aspects of Hazardous Waste Laws and the Transfrontier Movement of Hazardous Waste. Environmental Science and Engineering Dept., UCLA. Unpublished.

Moyers, Bill. (1990). *Global Dumping Ground: The International Traffic in Hazardous Wastes*. Cabin John, MD: Seven Locks Press.

Panayotou, Theodore. (1993). *Green Markets: The Economics of Sustainable Development*. San Francisco: Institute for Contemporary Studies.

Pearson, Charles S. (1987). *Multinational Corporations, Environment, and the Third World: Business Matters*. Durham: Duke University Press.

Rabe, Barry G. (1991). Exporting Hazardous Waste in North America. *International Environmental Affairs*, 3(2): 109.

Remond, Martine. (1985). The Carriage of Hazardous Waste and the Liability Question. *Transfrontier Movements of Hazardous Wastes*. Paris: OECD.

Roelants du Vivier, François. (1988). *Les Vaisseaux du Poison, La Route des Dechets Toxiques*. Paris: Editions Sang de la Terre.

_____. (1989). The South Mustn't Be the Rubbish Tip of the North. *The Courier* (ACP-EEC), 113: 2–5

Rublack, Susanne. (1989). Controlling Movement of Hazardous Waste. *The Fletcher Forum of World Affairs*, 13(1): 113–125.

Sand, Peter H. (1990). Innovations in International Environmental Governance. *Environment*, 32(9): 16.

Shaikh, Rashid. (1990). Presentation to the Fletcher School of Law and Diplomacy, Boston, 6 February.

Smets, Henri. (1985). Financial Security as a Means to Improve Control of Transfrontier Movements of Hazardous Wastes. *Transfrontier Movements of Hazardous Wastes*, Paris: OECD.

Summers, Larry. (1991). World Bank Internal Memo of December 12, 1991, excerpted in part by Michael Weisskopf, in *The Washington Post*, February 10, 1992, A9.

Underwood, Joanna D. (1988). Managing Hazardous Wastes Is Not Enough. *UNEP Industry and Environment*, 11(1): 29–31.

Uni, Jun. (1989). Pollution Export. In *Environmental Policy in Japan*, Shigeto Tsuru and Helmut Weidner, eds. Berlin, Germany: WZB.

UNIDO. (1980). *Mineral Processing in Developing Countries*. New York: United Nations.

Vallette, Jim. (1990). *The International Trade in Toxic Wastes: A Greenpeace Inventory, Fifth Edition*. Washington, DC: Greenpeace.

Vogel, David. (1986). *National Styles of Regulation: Environmental Policy in Great Britain and the United States*. Ithaca, NY: Cornell University Press.

Waldo, Andrew B. (1985). A Review of U.S. and International Restrictions on Exports of Hazardous Substances. In *The Export of Hazard*, Jane Ives, ed. Boston: Routledge and Kegan Paul.

Wynne, Brian. (1987). *Risk Management and Hazardous Waste: Implementation and the Dialectics of Credibility*. Berlin and New York: Springer Verlag.

_____. (1989). The Toxic Waste Trade: International Regulatory Issues and Options. *Third World Quarterly*, 11(3): 120–146.

Yakowitz, Harvey. (1987). *Waste Management Activities in Selected Industrialized Countries*. Environment Directorate, Paris: OECD.

7

BOUNDARY ISSUES AND CANADIAN ENVIRONMENTAL LEGISLATION

Steven Kennett

Students of comparative environmental policy should find an interesting subject of inquiry in the analysis and assessment of environmental policy regimes in Australia, Canada, New Zealand, and the United States. All four countries have a common basis in English law, yet all have developed distinctly different structures and procedures for the enactment and implementation of environmental policy. Such comparisons have not been the objectives of this book. Yet some comparisons are implicit in chapters dealing with environmental legal procedures in the governments of Canada, the United States, and New Zealand. In all of the afore-named countries, authority and responsibility for environmental policies are divided between national and subnational jurisdictions. Among these, Canadian federal arrangements appear to be characterized by the greater informality and ambiguity. As in all federal systems today, jurisdictional boundaries were determined by historical events and practices pre-dating ecosystems and watersheds as organizational concepts. In both Canada and the United States the practical meaning of environmental law is most realistically defined in practice. Neither the Canadian Environmental Protection Act (CEPA) nor the Canadian Environmental Assessment Act (CEAA) can be understood by a reading of the acts without information regarding how they are in fact applied. This, of course, is equally true of the environmental legislation in the United States. The discussion that follows illustrates the difficulty of fitting a new objective of public policy into a structure of government pre-dating environmental concepts and concerns. A place is being made for environmental policy within the conventional structures of government. But it is plausible to suspect that its present situation relative to traditional functions of government will not be its ultimate position.

Boundaries created to impose structure on the political world are often arbitrary from an ecological perspective. As a result, they can constitute significant impediments to effective environmental law and policy. In Canada, boundary issues give rise to particular difficulties for environmental management in three areas. The first concerns the boundary—and often the extent of overlap—between federal and provincial regulatory authority.[1] Second, ecosystem management has proven difficult where ecosystems straddle interprovincial and provincial-territorial boundaries. Finally, Canadian legislation and policy are adapting to emerging international environmental law that is driven by transboundary and global issues.

An integrated response to these boundary issues can be achieved in two ways in federal systems: centralization of authority, or coordination of law and policy among the constituent parts of the federation (Rehbinder and Stewart, 1985, 371). Environmental management in the United States has generally followed a centralized model (Huffman and Coggins, 1985:, 59). In Canada, where a relatively decentralized version of federalism is practiced, a cooperative approach to boundary issues is the preferred option.

This chapter examines the approach taken in Canada's federal environmental legislation to issues raised by jurisdictional, interprovincial, and international boundaries. It begins with an outline of the constitutional division of powers as it relates to the environment. An overview of boundary issues is then presented. The next two sections focus on the Canadian Environmental Protection Act[2] (CEPA) and the Canadian Environmental Assessment Act[3] (CEAA), the two principal environmental statutes at the federal level. Finally, some comments are offered on the likely determinants and direction of Canada's response to boundary issues in the coming years.

THE CONSTITUTIONAL CONTEXT

The environment is not referred to directly in Canada's Constitution. Instead, legislative authority regarding environmental matters is a function of the operating divisions of government—federal and provincial. While both levels of government have jurisdiction in this area, the predominant role of the provinces results in considerable decentralization of power.

Provincial environmental jurisdiction has two foundations. First, the Constitution allocates broad legislative authority to the provinces regarding property rights, commercial activities, legal relationships among individuals, local and provincial works and undertakings, and the management of natural resources.[4] These powers enable the provinces to regulate most activities affecting the environment in Canada. Second, the provinces own all public land and resources within their boundaries, except for limited federal holdings.[5] These property rights are complemented by legislative power over "the management and sale of public lands belonging to the province and of the timber and wood thereon."[6]

Although the provinces enjoy the preponderance of environmental authority under the Constitution, federal activity can be based on property rights, a number of fairly narrow sources of power that touch on environmental matters, and two broad federal powers. First, federal proprietary rights associated with ownership of certain land within the provinces (and much larger land holdings in the northern territories) provide a basis for environmental authority. For example, national parks and Indian reserves are federal property, subject to federal environmental regulation.

Second, environmental aspects of certain activities may be regulated under specific heads of federal power. These powers concern such matters as sea coast and inland fisheries, interprovincial or international works and undertakings, and navigation and shipping.[7] For example, industrial effluent can be regulated under federal legislation that protects fish and fish habitat. The federal criminal law power can also support environmental controls in the form of criminal sanctions intended to protect public health.[8]

Substantive regulation (e.g., standard-setting for effluent) can be complemented by procedural requirements in areas where federal activities and decision making have environmental consequences. For example, environmental assessment (EA) jurisdiction is auxiliary to federal decision-making powers since, as recognized by the Supreme Court of Canada, EA is "an integral component of sound decision-making" (*Friends of the Oldman River Society* v. *Canada (Minister of Transport)* [hereinafter *Oldman*], 1992, 71). The Court was careful to point out, however, that federal EA jurisdiction cannot serve as "a constitutional Trojan horse enabling the federal government, on the pretext of some narrow ground of federal jurisdiction, to conduct a far ranging inquiry into matters that are exclusively within provincial jurisdiction" (*Oldman*, 1992, 71–72). Although the federal government may conduct an EA with respect to any decision that it makes, the factors that it can legitimately consider are a function of the source of power that supports decision-making authority (*Oldman*, 1992: 67–68).

If the subject matter of a decision is explicitly designated in the Constitution as a federal matter, all environmental effects may be examined. However, if the basis of federal authority is the effects of an otherwise provincial activity on areas of federal authority (e.g, the effect of a dam on fisheries), then the federal EA of the project must be restricted to these effects if it is not to constitute an intrusion on provincial authority (Kennett, 1993a, 189–193). Federal EA jurisdiction is thus limited in order to protect provincial authority. While this limitation is fully consistent with Canada's decentralized view of federalism, it raises an interesting boundary problem for EA methodology. A federal EA may be restricted to a partial analysis of a given project, making it difficult to assess the overall costs and benefits (Kennett, 1992, 96).

Finally, federal environmental legislation may be based on two broadly worded powers. The most important of these is the "national concern" statement of Parliament's power to legislate for the "peace, order, and good government" of Canada (generally referred to as POGG).[10] In applying this potentially all-encompassing power, the courts have been conscious of the risk to provincial jurisdiction of an expansive interpretation. This concern is reflected in the Supreme Court of Canada's statements in *R.* v. *Crown Zellerbach* (1988; hereinafter *Crown Zellerbach*] that a matter of national concern "must have a singleness, distinctiveness and indivisibility that clearly distinguishes it from matters of provincial concern and a scale of impact on provincial jurisdiction that is reconcilable with the fundamental distribution of legislative power under the Constitution" (*Crown Zellerbach*, 1988, 432). In other words, POGG supports legislation on distinctive matters requiring federal action, but cannot be used to alter fundamentally the division of powers.

Despite this limitation, the national concern branch is a potentially important source of federal environmental jurisdiction, particularly in dealing with boundary problems. The majority judgment in *Crown Zellerbach* stated that, in identifying a matter of national concern, "it is relevant to consider what would be the effect on extra-provincial interests of a provincial failure to deal effectively with the control or regulation of the intra-provincial aspects of the matter" (*Crown Zellerbach*, 1988, 432). Evidence of "provincial inability"—in this instance an inability to regulate a transboundary matter effectively at the provincial level—is at the very least an indication that a matter is of national concern. More specifically, judicial interpretation of POGG has affirmed federal authority with respect to transboundary water and air pollution (*Crown Zellerbach*, 1988; *Interprovincial Cooperatives Ltd.* v. *The Queen*, 1976; *Re Canada Metal Co. Ltd. and the Queen*, 1982). The limits of Parliament's ability to regulate directly the intraprovincial sources of transboundary pollution under this power have not, however, been tested either politically or through constitutional litigation.

The federal "trade and commerce" power is another general basis for environmental regulation.[10] Like the national concern branch of POGG, however, this power has been interpreted by the courts with a view to limiting intrusion on provincial jurisdiction (Hogg, 1992, 201). It has yet to be judicially tested in the environmental area, although it might be relied on to regulate environmentally harmful articles of trade (Lucas, 1990, 29).

The division of powers regarding the incorporation of international obligations into domestic law warrants a special note. In Canada, legislation is required to implement international obligations that alter internal law (Hogg, 1992, 285–286). The only constitutional provision dealing explicitly with this topic grants Parliament authority to implement "Empire" treaties (i.e., treaties entered into by Britain on behalf of Canada).[11] This section provides the basis for federal legislation implementing the International Boundary Waters Treaty, 1909, and the Migratory Birds Treaty, 1916, both signed with the United States before Canada assumed full responsibility for its international relations in 1926 (Hogg, 1992, 290).

This provision does not, however, apply to treaties entered into directly by Canada. The Privy Council held in the 1937 *Labor Conventions* case that the implementation of those treaties is subject to the normal division of powers (*A.G. Canada* v. *A.G. Ontario*, 1937 [hereinafter *Labor Conventions*]). Although there have been indications that the Supreme Court of Canada might reconsider the *Labor Conventions* doctrine, the federal government has refrained from mounting a jurisdictional challenge (Saunders, 1985, 270). The currently accepted position is that provincial legislation is required to implement treaty obligations outside of areas of federal jurisdiction (Hogg, 1992, 293–297; Saunders, 1985, 268–271). This situation can be contrasted with both the United States and Australia. In the United States, treaties become part of "the supreme law of the land" and take precedence over inconsistent state laws.[12] In Australia, judicial interpretation of the federal "external affairs" power gives the federal Parliament authority to implement treaty obligations, even if the subject would normally be a matter of exclusive state jurisdiction (Hogg, 1992, 288–289).

In Canada in addition to the specific allocation of powers, three principles of constitutional interpretation have important implications for boundary issues. First, each province's jurisdiction is restricted to its own territory, as indicated by the words "in the province" that are found in many provincial sources of authority.[13] As a result, provinces cannot regulate extraprovincial sources of transboundary pollution (*Interprovincial Cooperatives Ltd.* v. *The Queen*, 1976; Kennett, 1991, 103–160). Canada also lacks a clearly defined federal common law that would provide a basis for recourse through the courts in cases of transboundary environmental effects (Saunders, 1988, 120–126).

Second, although powers are formally exclusive to one level of government or the other, the "double aspect" doctrine allows legislation to be characterized as having both provincial and federal aspects (Hogg, 1992, 381–383). For example, pollution control measures may be enacted under provincial powers to regulate commercial activity and under the federal fisheries power. Considerable "functional concurrency" therefore exists in practice (Gibson, 1983, 127).

The third general principle is federal paramountcy. Where constitutionally valid federal and provincial laws conflict, federal legislation prevails (Hogg, 1992, 417–434). This principle only applies, however, where there is an express contradiction between legislation (i.e., when both laws cannot be complied with simultaneously). For example, there is no express contradiction if both federal and provincial pollution control laws can be satisfied by compliance with the strictest standard. Similarly, the requirement that a project be evaluated through separate federal and provincial EA processes does not oust the provincial process.

In addition to these legal rules, Canada's federal system operates according to what one commentator has termed the "political constitution" (Lucas, 1985, 34). The result is that provincial sensitivities operate as a very real constraint on federal authority. Even in areas where Parliament has a strong legal basis for environmental regulation, it has frequently been reluctant to assert this jurisdiction (Lucas, 1985, 34–35).

The constitutional picture in relation to the environment, then, is one of broad provincial jurisdiction with important opportunities for federal action in certain areas. Federal environmental authority, however, is based either on relatively discrete legislative powers or proprietary rights, or on more general powers that the courts have explicitly interpreted in an attempt to limit intrusion on provincial jurisdiction. Constitutional and political factors combine to produce considerable decentralization in environmental management, a situation that differs significantly from that prevailing in Australia (Cullen, 1990) and the United States (Rabe, 1989, 261–262).

The contrast with the United States is particularly striking. Canadian provinces have far greater authority with respect to the environment and natural resources than do American states (Rabe, 1989, 262). From the federal government's perspective, there is nothing in the Canadian Constitution, analogous to the combined effect of the Commerce Clause[14] and Property Clause[15] in the United States, that could provide a vehicle for significant centralization in this area (Huffman and Coggins, 1985, 56, 60–61; Hogg, 1992, 109). Furthermore, except in the Yukon and Northwest Territories, Canada's federal government does not have the extensive public land holdings that confer considerable environmental authority on its American counterpart, particularly in the Western United States and Alaska (Huffman and Coggins, 1985, 53–55). Finally, in contrast to the direct incorporation of international obligations into domestic law in the United States (Huffman and Coggins, 1985, 56), legislation enacted in accordance with the normal division of powers is required to implement these obligations in Canada. These differences explain Canada's distinctive approach to boundary issues in environmental management.

OVERVIEW OF BOUNDARY ISSUES IN CANADA

Boundary issues are increasingly important in Canadian environmental management. In the jurisdictional context, the growth of environmental regulation has increased the scope for overlap and duplication (Dwivedi and Woodrow, 1989). Provincial concerns with perceived federal intrusion on matters of natural resources management have increased, and streamlining environmental regulation has become a priority for both government and the private sector. EA has attracted particular attention, given the costs and delays associated with subjecting a project to both federal and provincial processes (Kennett, 1993b). Inconsistency in federal and provincial monitoring and regulatory requirements are also of concern (Environment Canada, 1993a, 19–21). Harmonization of federal and provincial environmental regulation is aimed at defining the boundaries of each government's regulatory activities in a way that eliminates unnecessary duplication and produces cost savings to the private sector and to government itself (CCME, 1993).

Attention to interprovincial and provincial-territorial transboundary issues within Canada reflects the recognition of ecosystems as the logical units for many aspects of environmental management (Walters, 1991). The importance of this approach is illustrated in the Mackenzie River Basin, where dam construction in British Columbia and the operation of pulp and paper mills in Alberta have raised considerable concerns in downstream jurisdictions (Barton, 1985, 243–247). The experience with persistent toxic substances leaves no doubt that actions in one Canadian province may have significant environmental consequences in another (Lindgren, 1990, 41).

International developments relating to transboundary and global issues also have increasing significance for environmental law and policy in Canada (Tingley, 1990, 12–19). The House of Commons Standing Committee on Environment and Sustainable Development (hereinafter Standing Committee", in its 1995 review of CEPA (hereinafter CEPA review", devoted a chapter of its report to the implementation of Canada's international commitments. It began by noting that (Standing Committee, 1995, 141):

> The Brundtland Commission in 1987 and *Agenda 21* in 1992 recognized the need to have an internationally integrated set of environmental, economic and social development policy objectives. This need is characterized by a growing awareness that ecosystems and environmental effects seldom respect national boundaries and that global economic interdependence continues to spread. Regional transboundary issues being addressed within global and regional environmental protection regimes now include acid rain, smog, air contaminants and hazardous waste. Global issues being addressed include world climate, stratospheric ozone, oceans, biodiversity and Antarctica.

The result of Canada's decentralized system is that the negotiations and legislation relating to international environmental agreements become matters of federal-provincial as well as international diplomacy.

In confronting these jurisdictional, interprovincial and international boundary issues, legislative and policy responses bear the mark of Canada's decentralized federal system. There is much less scope for comprehensive federal environmental legislation in Canada than exists in the United States (Northey, 1989, 130). The preferred Canadian approach has been to use techniques of "cooperative federalism" to overcome jurisdictional and geographic boundaries. These techniques include formal intergovernmental agreements, intergovernmental bodies (e.g., ministerial councils or basin management boards), informal working arrangements, mirror legislation, and administrative interdelegation (Lucas, 1985, 46–50). In this way, Canadian governments have endeavored to sort out jurisdictional responsibilities and address interprovincial issues (e.g., watershed management). The cooperative model is also used in the realm of international environmental obligations, where provincial involvement has extended from the development of negotiating positions to legislative implementation.

Federal leadership has been evident in establishing the procedural and substantive framework for cooperative arrangements. As will be illustrated below, this role can include providing a legislative basis for the coordination or delegation of environmental management functions and setting standards to be met by provincial regimes.

Finally, the federal government has asserted jurisdiction to regulate some boundary matters unilaterally. Such provisions, however, are often coupled with cooperative mechanisms or are triggered by a failure of provinces to agree to satisfactory arrangements. Even where federal intervention is clearly authorized on constitutional and legislative grounds, there has generally been a reluctance to intervene unilaterally on boundary issues.

The following sections examine how boundary issues are addressed in the the CEPA and the CEAA. Both statutes involve federal assertions of environmental jurisdiction, including federal standard setting and the possibility of unilateral action. In both cases, however, specific provision is made for a cooperative approach, aimed at minimizing federal intrusion into traditional areas of provincial jurisdiction.

THE CANADIAN ENVIRONMENTAL PROTECTION ACT

CEPA is Canada's broadest environmental legislation at the federal level. Enacted in 1988, it replaced, amended, or incorporated parts of six other federal statutes.[16] Although the preamble and the prescribed duties of the government of Canada in administering the act (s. 2) suggest a comprehensive approach to environmental regulation, CEPA in fact addresses a series of relatively distinct topics. The substantive provisions are contained in Parts I–VII of the Act.

Part I deals with research, monitoring, and the establishment of nonmandatory guidelines, objectives, and codes of practice. Initiatives have included an eco-labeling program, designed to identify environmentally preferable products and services, and reports on the state of Canada's environment (Standing Committee, 1995, 24).

Part II of CEPA creates a life-cycle regulatory regime for toxic substances. It establishes a process to gather information and evaluate potentially toxic substances and to designate those substances requiring regulation. Once a substance is found to be toxic, its manufacture, labeling, distribution, storage, use, release, and disposal may all be regulated (s. 34). Part II also deals with the export and import of toxic substances and hazardous wastes.

Despite the broad scope of Part II, regulatory activities in the seven years following CEPA's enactment has been relatively modest (Standing Committee, 1995, 31–34). Twenty-five substances have been declared to be toxic, but only a small number of these have been regulated. Regulations are in place to ban the use of lead in most motor fuels, to ensure safe storage of Polychlorinated byphenols (PCBs), and to ban or progressively eliminate ozone-depleting substances pursuant to the terms of the Montreal Protocol. Chlorinated dioxins and furans in effluent from the pulp and paper industry have been controlled, and notification requirements established for new chemicals and polymers. Notwithstanding these measures, the CEPA review concluded that: "One of the central challenges faced by the Committee has been to find ways to improve the effectiveness and efficiency of identifying and preventing the generation and use of toxic substances" (Standing Committee, 1995, 33).

Part III permits the regulation of nutrients in cleaning agents and water conditioners for the purpose of preventing the eutrophication of lakes and rivers. As of 1995, only phosphorous concentration in laundry detergents had been regulated (Standing Committee, 1995, 25).

Part IV differs from the rest of CEPA in that it applies only to federal departments, agencies, and Crown corporations and to federal works, undertakings, and lands. The intent is to fill regulatory gaps with environmental regulations and guidelines. Little regulatory activity has occurred under this part, and the 1995 CEPA review criticized the federal government for "failing to put its own house in order" (Standing Committee, 1995, 169).

Part V of CEPA permits the Minister of the Environment to regulate international air pollution produced by sources within Canada. Consultation with provincial governments is provided for, and no federal action is permitted unless provincial cooperation cannot be achieved. As of 1995, no regulations had been issued under Part V (Standing Committee, 1995, 26).

Part VI regulates ocean dumping, establishing a permitting process and conditions under which disposal at sea may be justified. Methods and sites for disposal are also regulated. Environment Canada conducts an active regulatory program under this part of CEPA (Environment Canada, 1994, 31–35).

Finally, Part VII includes provisions relating to CEPA's operation. Matters addressed include the review process where an objection to a decision under the act is filed, federal-provincial administrative agreements, inspection procedures, enforcement, offenses, and remedies. Enforcement mechanisms include administrative orders, ticketing for minor offenses, and a range of criminal sanctions.

The constitutional basis for CEPA is a combination of the POGG, criminal, and trade and commerce powers (Lucas, 1990, 29). The most important of these powers, particularly for the regulation of toxic substances, is the national concern statement in POGG. The Preamble to CEPA states that "the presence of toxic substances in the environment is a matter of national concern" and notes that "toxic substances, once introduced into the environment, cannot always be contained within geographic boundaries." The potential transboundary movement of persistent toxic substances, combined with their threat to human health (as well as to environmental processes), provide the basis for federal authority (Lucas, 1989, 366). In addition, the ocean dumping provisions were upheld under POGG by the Supreme Court of Canada in the *Crown Zellerbach* case.

CEPA raises jurisdictional, interprovincial, and international boundary issues. The jurisdictional issues concern the potential for overlapping federal and provincial environmental regulation and provincial hostility to perceived federal intrusion into areas traditionally within their authority (Environment Canada, 1993b, 99). To address these issues, CEPA provides for three mechanisms for federal-provincial cooperation: an intergovernmental advisory committee, equivalency agreements, and administrative agreements.

The Federal-Provincial Advisory Committee (FPAC) is established by s. 6(1) of CEPA to create a framework for national action, facilitate intergovernmental cooperation on environmental matters, and avoid conflict between, and duplication in, federal and provincial regulatory activity. FPAC includes representatives from Environment Canada, Health Canada, and each of the provinces and territories.

Through its working groups, it has addressed issues including ozone-depleting substances, air quality, and selection of candidate substances for review under the toxic substances provisions. It has also commented on draft regulations and resolved issues relating to equivalency agreements. The 1995 CEPA review endorsed FPAC as the principal consultative mechanism under CEPA, but suggested that consideration be given to including representatives from aboriginal peoples (Standing Committee, 1995, 262). This recommendation raises the pervasive issue of how to accommodate First Nations within the intergovernmental arrangements that are central to Canadian federalism.

The second mechanism for addressing jurisdictional boundary issues in CEPA is the provision for equivalency agreements (s. 34(5), (6)). These agreements have a "work-limiting" function in that a CEPA regulation ceases to apply in a province when an equivalent (or more stringent) provincial provision has been formally recognized (Standing Committee, 1995, 263). The equivalency provisions were included in CEPA in response to provincial concerns about perceived jurisdictional encroachment (Lucas, 1990, 32). To permit flexibility in provincial regulatory regimes, the federal government requires equivalency of results, rather than identical provisions. More specifically, the criteria that have been used for establishing equivalency include (Environment Canada, 1992, 15):

- equal level of control as sanctioned by law;
- comparable compliance measurement techniques;
- comparable penalties;
- comparable enforcement policies and procedures; and
- comparable rights of individuals, resident in Canada, to request investigation of a suspected offense and to receive a report of the findings.

The last of these criteria reflects the statutory requirement contained in s. 34(6)(b) of CEPA.

As of 1995, only one equivalency agreement has been signed. The limited use of this mechanism may be explained by several factors. Although introduced in response to provincial concerns, there has been resistance to the equivalency criteria, particularly the requirement that individuals have the legal right to have their complaints investigated (Standing Committee, 1995, 264–265).[17] Other impediments include difficulties in establishing the meaning of equivalency, the costs of negotiating and implementing these agreements (including costs of compliance with federal enforcement policies), and the slow pace of regulation making under CEPA (Environment Canada, 1993b, 102–103). Provincial hesitancy to negotiate these agreements may also stem from an unwillingness to modify provincial regulatory regimes, a skepticism about the ability of the federal government to regulate unilaterally (given limited resources), and a reluctance to conclude agreements that tacitly recognize the legitimacy of federal standard setting in this area (Environment Canada, 1993b, 102–103; Lucas, 1990, 32).

Despite these obstacles, the federal and Alberta governments signed an equivalency agreement on June 1, 1994. This agreement and the associated order[18] provide that four CEPA regulation[19] do not apply in Alberta in light of equivalent provisions under provincial legislation. The agreement also provides for the sharing of information between governments.

The third intergovernmental mechanism in CEPA is the provision for administrative agreements (s. 98). These agreements are designed to share responsibilities, eliminate overlap and duplication, and provide a "one-window" approach to regulation (Environment Canada, 1993b, 104). As of 1995, administrative agreements have been signed with the provinces of British Columbia, Quebec, and Saskatchewan and with the Yukon Territory.

Topics addressed in these agreements include inspection, enforcement, monitoring, reporting, and information sharing. Unlike equivalency agreements, administrative agreements are not subject to statutory standards. Nonetheless, provisions may be included to permit federal monitoring of provincial enforcement activities, and the federal government retains the right to intervene in the event that its enforcement and compliance policies are not met (Standing Committee, 1995, 265–266). In addition, there is a statutory requirement that these agreements be made public and that the Minister of the Environment report annually on their implementation (s. 98(3)).

The role of administrative agreements is illustrated by the Canada-Saskatchewan Administrative Agreement for the Canadian Environmental Protection Act (15 September 1994). This agreement contains general principles of cooperation, including a commitment to "timely notification and appropriate consultation" where one party's legislation, regulations, policies, programs or projects affect the other party's jurisdiction (s. 4.0). In addition, the parties undertake "to cooperate in the management of environmental issues relating to natural resources which traverse jurisdictional boundaries within Canada" (s. 4.0). More specifically, subagreements deal with substance releases, compliance promotion and verification, investigations and enforcement, and information sharing. The first of these subagreements, for example, coordinates responses to spills of toxic substances by providing a single telephone number for reporting incidents and establishing mechanisms governing the response by federal and provincial agencies. Provincial staff may be designated as CEPA inspectors, and provision is made for a joint review of response procedures.

The CEPA review strongly endorsed the use of equivalency and administrative agreements, stating that (Standing Committee, 1995, 267): "By reducing duplication and overlap between the federal and provincial governments, they can help reduce the cost of administering regulations, decrease disputes between governments, introduce more certainty into the decision-making process and better define the roles of government in environmental protection." The Standing Committee noted, however, that intergovernmental arrangements such as equivalency and administrative agreements have been criticized for deficiencies in the areas of public input, accountability, transparency, and adherence to federal environmental and enforcement standards (Standing Committee, 1995, 266–270; Gertler, 1993). It therefore recommended greater public and parliamentary scrutiny of the negotiation and implementation of administrative and equivalency agreements (Standing Committee, 1995, 266–269). It also underlined the importance of maintaining federal environmental standards, recommending that the federal government retain the right to prosecute under CEPA administrative agreements in the event that a province or territory fails to enforce federal regulations (Standing Committee, 1995, 268).

By defining the boundaries between federal and provincial roles at the operational level, equivalency and administrative agreements respond to overlapping constitutional authority. Although CEPA represents an assertion of federal authority to regulate toxic substances unilaterally, cooperative mechanisms reflect the inability of the federal government, for legal and political reasons, simply to displace provincial regulation in this area. With equivalency agreements, provinces that agree to follow federal standards preserve their own regulatory regimes and avoid the application of CEPA.

The two other categories of boundary issues, interprovincial and provincial-territorial effects within Canada and international environmental obligations, are both referred to in the Preamble to CEPA. In the substantive provisions of the act, however, they are dealt with in a less systematic fashion than are federal-provincial relations.

CEPA does not specifically address transboundary issues within Canada, except for noting in the Preamble that "toxic substances, once introduced into the environment, cannot always be contained within geographic boundaries." As noted above, this statement is intended to reinforce the national concern branch of POGG as the constitutional basis for federal regulation of toxic substances. CEPA does not, however, provide for federal regulation of interprovincial pollution as a general matter. A regulatory role with respect to water quality in interprovincial watersheds is, however, provided for in s. 11 of the Canada Water Act,[20] a provision that has never been used (Saunders, 1985, 29–30). The CEPA review recommended that the "ecosystem approach" be adopted as a guiding principle for the act (Standing Committee, 1995, 52). It did not, however, propose substantive regulatory provisions to implement ecosystem management at the federal level, nor did it link this concept with transboundary issues. It is therefore unlikely that CEPA will be applied broadly to control interprovincial pollution and improve the management of transboundary ecosystems in Canada.

International boundary issues are also alluded to in the Preamble, which affirms that "Canada must be able to fulfil its international obligations in respect of the environment." To this end, CEPA deals directly with international obligation in several places. The ocean dumping provisions under Part VI reflect Canada's obligations under the London Convention of 1972. CEPA also contains provisions in Part II implementing Canada's obligations relating to the transboundary movement of hazardous waste.[21] In addition, Part II provides a means for implementing international obligations pertaining to substances that meet the CEPA definition of toxic substances. Regulations implementing the Montreal Protocol on Substances that Deplete the Ozone Layer and its 1990 London Amendments have been promulgated under this part.

As noted above, Part V of the Act provides for federal action to address international transboundary air pollution originating in Canada that could result in a violation of an international agreement entered into by the federal government (s. 61(1)). As of 1995, the federal government has apparently been satisfied with intergovernmental cooperation on air quality matters[22] and has refrained from regulatory action under this Part (Standing Committee, 1995, 142; Environment Canada, 1994, 30).

Although Part V carries the threat of unilateral federal action, CEPA does not contain general provisions regarding international environmental obligations or international transboundary issues.[23] The CEPA review recommended amendments to existing regulations relating to transboundary movement of hazardous waste and to the ocean dumping provisions in Part VI of the act in order to reflect current international commitments (Standing Committee, 1995, 145–146). It also recommended that Part V of the act be expanded to authorize federal regulation to prevent transboundary water pollution that could violate international treaty obligations with the United States (Standing Committee, 1995, 144).

It remains to be seen whether the federal government will arm itself with greater statutory authority to act unilaterally on matters of international concern. As with international air pollution, federal-provincial cooperation is likely to be the preferred option. A more assertive federal role in this area will face provincial opposition and constitutional uncertainty regarding the scope of federal authority. For that reason, CEPA's patchwork approach to international environmental issues, both transboundary and global, is likely to continue.

In conclusion, although CEPA constitutes an assertion of federal regulatory authority in significant areas of environmental protection, it exemplifies the Canadian approach to boundary issues by providing for cooperative arrangements in order to minimize federal intrusion on provincial jurisdiction. The concern with provincial sensibilities is best illustrated by the equivalency provisions and the fact that federal action on international air pollution is contingent on a prior failure to achieve cooperation with the provinces.

CEPA's mechanisms for intergovernmental cooperation are intended to define the boundaries of federal and provincial regulatory activities. Although experience to date with equivalency and administrative agreements has been limited, the conclusion of several of these agreements since 1994 suggests that this approach may be gaining acceptance. The pressures for harmonization, emanating both from the private sector (seeking elimination of duplication and overlap) and from within government itself (in the face of significant funding cuts) may lead to serious efforts to rationalize and coordinate federal and provincial regulations.

In response to interprovincial and international boundary issues, CEPA adopts a cautious approach. The federal government has yet to take an active regulatory role in managing transboundary ecosystems within Canada. As to the implementation of international obligations, the approach taken varies according to the jurisdictional basis of federal authority and the state of federal-provincial cooperation.

THE CANADIAN ENVIRONMENTAL ASSESSMENT ACT

CEAA establishes the federal EA process in Canada. It came into effect in early 1995, replacing a nonlegislated EA process that dated back to 1974 (Hanebury, 1991, 969–973). Although CEAA requires the federal government to consider environmental consequences when making decisions regarding projects, the process is purely advisory. Final decisions are made by the responsible federal authorities, the departments or agencies charged with determining whether or not projects should receive federal authorization or support.

CEAA applies to "projects," a defined term in the Act (s. 2(1)). The standard CEAA process is triggered where a federal authority: (a) is the project proponent; (b) provides money or other financial assistance to the project; (c) grants an interest in land to enable the project to be carried out; or (d) exercises a regulatory duty in relation to a project, such as issuing a permit, license or approval, under a statute or regulation included in the CEAA regulations (Law List) (s. 5). The process does not apply to projects carried out in emergencies, and certain types of projects are excluded by regulation (Exclusion List) because they have insignificant environmental effects (s. 7). In addition to the standard process, the Minister of the Environment may order a panel review or mediation of certain projects having transboundary effects or effects on lands of federal interest (ss. 46–53).

Once a project triggers the CEAA process, the appropriate level of EA effort must be determined. Most projects go through an initial screening that is conducted by, or on behalf of, the responsible federal authority (s. 18). A more intensive "comprehensive study" is required for certain projects, specified in the regulations (Comprehensive Study List), that are likely to raise significant environmental concerns (s. 21). If more scrutiny is needed following the screening or comprehensive study, the Minister of the Environment may refer a project to either a panel review or to mediation (s. 28). A referral may be made where the minister is of the opinion that the project may cause significant adverse environmental effects or where public concerns warrant a further review (s. 28).

CEAA specifies the factors that must be considered as part of the screening, comprehensive study, mediation, and panel review processes. The following factors must be considered in all four processes (s. 16(1)):

- the environmental effects of the project, including . . . any cumulative environmental effects;
- the significance of these environmental effects;
- public comments;
- technically and economically feasible measures that would mitigate any significant adverse effects; and
- any other matter relevant to the assessment that the responsible authority may require, such as the need for and alternatives to the project.

In addition to these factors, every comprehensive study, mediation, and panel review is required to consider (s. 16(2)):

- the purpose of the project;
- technically and economically feasible alternative means of carrying out the project as well as the environmental effects of these alternative means;
- the need for and requirements of any follow-up program; and
- the capacity of renewable resources that are likely to be significantly affected by the project to meet present and future needs.

CEAA states that the responsible authority shall determine the scope of a number of these factors (s. 16(3)). In particular, the geographic boundaries and time frames of effects may need to be established.

The federal EA regime raises jurisdictional, interprovincial and international boundary issues. Jurisdictional boundaries are important because of the possibility that a project may trigger both federal and provincial EA processes. In this context, EA should provide a comprehensive review of the project without unnecessary duplication. Geographic boundaries are relevant because projects in one jurisdiction may have effects in another. A significant challenge to EA design is the accommodation within the EA process of the interests of those who may be affected by the transboundary effects of a project. As with CEPA, jurisdictional and geographic boundary issues are referred to in the introductory sections of CEAA and dealt with through various substantive provisions.

CEAA addresses jurisdictional boundaries through provisions for coordination or delegation where more than one EA process applies to a particular project. These provisions reflect one purpose of the act, which is (s. 2(b.1)): "to ensure that responsible authorities carry out their responsibilities in a coordinated manner with a view to eliminating unnecessary duplication in the environmental assessment process." Where another jurisdiction has authority to conduct an EA, the responsible authority may cooperate with that jurisdiction at the screening or comprehensive study stages (s. 12(4)). The term "jurisdiction" is defined to include provincial governments or agencies, EA bodies under land claims agreements, or governing bodies having EA responsibilities under Indian self-government legislation. The responsible authority may also delegate to another jurisdiction all or part of the screening or comprehensive study, the preparation of the screening or comprehensive study report, and the design and implementation of a follow-up program (s. 17(1)). Decisionmaking authority to be exercised following screening or comprehensive study cannot, however, be delegated. Furthermore, decision-making cannot be exercised unless the responsible authority is satisfied that any delegated functions have been carried out in accordance with CEAA and its regulations (s. 17(2)).

CEAA also provides for joint panel review (ss. 40–42). Agreements for joint panels may be negotiated with other jurisdictions that have EA authority over a project (s. 40(2), (3)). In this context, the definition of "jurisdiction" noted above is expanded to include governments or agencies of a foreign state or a subdivision of a foreign state, and international organizations and agencies (s. 40(1)). Any such agreement must be published prior to the commencement of the joint panel review (s. 40(4)). Joint panels are required to consider the factors, noted above, that are specified in the act for panel reviews (ss. 43, 16). In addition, a number of procedural requirements are set out, including: appointment or approval of the panel chairperson (or one co-chairperson) and appointment of at least one panel member by the minister; impartiality and relevant expertise of panel members; terms of reference fixed or approved by the minister; specified powers for the panel; public participation; submission of a report to the minister; and publication of the report (s. 43).

The operation of these provisions will be determined in large measure by bilateral federal-provincial agreements for EA harmonization. The first of these agreements, the Canada-Alberta Agreement for Environmental Assessment Cooperation (6 August 1993), includes a subsidiary agreement on joint review panels. Where both jurisdictions' EA processes have been triggered and both determine that a public review including hearings is required, a single panel review will be held. The joint panel meets the conditions set out in CEAA and will be constituted by the appointment of at least one federal nominee as an acting member of either of the provincial review agencies (the Alberta Energy and Utilities Board or the Natural Resources Conservation Board). A bilateral harmonization agreement has also been signed with Manitoba, and negotiations with other provinces are currently in progress.

CEAA contains specific provisions for projects having interprovincial or international transboundary effects or effects on "lands of federal interest" (ss. 46–53). These provisions reflect the act's purpose (s. 4(c)): "to ensure that projects that are to be carried out in Canada . . . do not cause significant adverse environmental effects outside the jurisdictions in which the projects are carried out." CEAA's specific transboundary provisions do not apply to projects caught by the act's general triggering mechanism (s. 5) or that are subject to a federal regulatory power, duty, or function under another statute or regulation (ss. 46(1), 47(1)). Consequently, they will not apply to all projects having transboundary effects. Furthermore, the minister has complete discretion in determining whether or not to order an EA (in this case a public review) under these provisions.

A project may be referred to mediation or panel review where the minister "is of the opinion that the project may cause significant adverse environmental effects" in another province or outside of Canada (ss. 46(1), 47(1)). Such a referral shall not be made where the federal government and interested provinces have agreed on an EA (meeting certain conditions) to consider transboundary effects (ss. 46(2), 47(2)). In the case of international transboundary effects, the minister must consider whether to order a public review if requested to do so by the provincial government where the project will be carried out or by a foreign government which claims that it may be subject to significant transboundary effects (s. 47(3)). In situations of interprovincial environmental effects, provincial governments and members of the public at risk of transboundary harm may petition the minister for an EA (s. 46(3)). The minister may order that a project not proceed until transboundary effects have been appropriately dealt with (ss. 50, 51).

Transboundary effects may also be addressed through the standard CEAA process. Once an EA is required, its scope may extend to a project's transboundary consequences. However, the standard EA provisions do not explicitly require consideration of transboundary effects, nor are there specific procedural (e.g., notice) requirements tailored to the transboundary context.

It should be noted that Canada has signed the Convention on Environmental Impact Assessment in a Transboundary Context[24] (the Espoo Convention). Canada has not, however, ratified the convention, which has yet to reach the threshold number of ratifications needed to bring it into force. In anticipation of its eventual implementation, international EA obligations are being considered in the context of federal-provincial harmonization. The Canada-Alberta Agreement for Environmental Assessment Cooperation includes a commitment that both parties will adhere to the Espoo Convention.

Boundary issues are thus addressed in several ways in Canada's federal EA legislation. As with CEPA, cooperative mechanisms are established to adapt the EA regime to jurisdictional boundaries. In particular, the delegation of certain EA functions to other jurisdictions and the establishment of joint panels to avoid duplication of public hearing processes are provided for with a view to coordinating EA responsibilities between governments. The Canada-Alberta Agreement suggests that the result may be the predominance of provincial EA processes. Federal EA jurisdiction will likely be restricted in practice to areas of exclusive federal jurisdiction (e.g., projects in national parks, interprovincial and international pipelines, etc.), with federal legislation playing a standard-setting role where there is shared EA authority. In this latter context, the provincial regime, as modified to meet CEAA requirements, would be applied in most cases. More extensive experience with CEAA and harmonization agreements will be required, however, to determine how jurisdictional roles and responsibilities will finally be allocated.

CEAA's provisions dealing with transboundary EA in both the interprovincial and international contexts are highly discretionary. In addition, the federal government's tendency to avoid active involvement in the management of transboundary resources suggests that a strong federal presence in this area may be unlikely (Kennett, 1995). Federal legislation may, however, play a standard-setting role, and the threat of federal intervention may induce provinces to cooperate on transboundary EA. In the international realm, the coming into force of the Espoo Convention could change the dynamic as the federal government would find itself faced with EA obligations vis-à-vis the United States. Provinces may modify their EA regimes to meet the international requirements, as suggested by the commitment in the Canada-Alberta Agreement to adhere to the Espoo Convention, rather than risk federal intervention. In sum, boundary issues in EA seem likely to follow the traditional Canadian pattern of federal-provincial diplomacy. Unilateral federal action, particularly in the case of projects having interprovincial effects, would likely occur only in the context of a high-profile conflict where cooperative options had been exhausted.

CANADIAN ENVIRONMENTAL LEGISLATION
TOWARD THE TURN OF THE CENTURY

As Canadian environmental law and policy near the turn of the century, the approach to boundary issues is far from settled. Three general options are possible: further development of cooperative federal-provincial arrangements, an increasingly assertive federal role, or an ad hoc and uncoordinated response, punctuated with federal-provincial conflict.

One prediction that can be made with some certainty is that boundary issues are unlikely to go away. Jurisdictional overlap in the environmental area is guaranteed by Canada's division of powers. As a result, both levels of government will have an interest in defining the practical boundaries of their respective roles. This interest will undoubtedly be stimulated by pressure from the private sector to eliminate perceived duplication in environmental regulation. Transboundary ecosystems, whether interprovincial or international, will also continue to raise challenges for environmental management. Although legal and institutional arrangements are predictably slow to respond, particularly in the interjurisdictional context, the necessity of an ecosystem approach to environmental issues is slowly gaining general acceptance. Finally, the development of international environmental law gives rise to geographic and jurisdictional boundary issues for Canadian environmental law and policy.

If the determinants of continuing interest in boundary issues are relatively easy to identify, the directions that law and policy will take are far less clear. Three sources of conflicting signals highlight this point: the intergovernmental harmonization initiative, the Standing Committee review of CEPA, and the movement by some governments in Canada toward deregulation and fiscal restraint.

Efforts to establish an overall framework for harmonizing federal and provincial environmental regimes have been under way since this objective was identified as a top priority by the Canadian Council of Ministers of the Environment (CCME) in November 1993. The harmonization initiative, conducted under the aegis of CCME, was directed toward "clarifying federal and provincial roles in environmental protection, eliminating duplication and overlap among programs, and making legislation and regulations more consistent across the country" (CCME, 1994, 2). CCME defined the policy context as follows (CCME, undated: 1):

The elimination of duplication and overlap in federal-provincial/territorial regulatory matters, the harmonization of policies and programs, and the need to re-define working relationships between orders of government, the private sector and the public, have quickly become fundamental issues in the Canadian political context. The reasons for this resurgence in the desire to address these issues stem from concerns over the competitiveness of Canadian industry, serious reductions in government expenditures at all levels, and increased public concern about the public debt issue and government inefficiency.

It is clear from CCME material that rationalization of regulation was part of the explicit harmonization agenda.

Negotiations between federal and provincial representatives produced a draft Environmental Management Framework Agreement (EMFA) in December, 1994. This approach was clearly modelled on the Australian Intergovernmental Agreement on the Environment, a federal-state-municipal umbrella agreement, signed in May 1992 (Gardner, 1994). In contrast to the more fragmented and issue-specific process of bilateral agreements envisaged under CEPA and CEAA, the objective of a comprehensive agreement is to establish general principles for harmonizing environmental regulation and clarifying federal and provincial roles and responsibilities. The EMFA also provided for a series of more specific schedules on matters including: monitoring; environmental assessment; compliance, licensing and approvals; and international agreements. The EMFA package, then, was intended to provide a comprehensive framework for addressing boundary issues in Canadian federalism.

Since the release of the draft EMFA, the harmonization initiative has been stalled, if not completely derailed. At a meeting of ministers in the spring of 1995, the federal Minister of the Environment expressed serious reservations about the direction that the harmonization initiative was taking (Andrews, 1995; CIELAP, 1995). In particular, she indicated her opposition to "a loss of national perspective on environmental issues" and refused provincial demands that CEAA be weakened (Andrews, 1995). Environmental nongovernmental organizations voiced their support for the federal position, arguing that the hidden agenda of harmonization was to undermine the federal government's environmental presence (Andrews, 1995; CIELAP, 1995). Later in the summer of 1995, the federal government officially suspended the harmonization initiative (CCME, 1995).

At the same time that the apparently decentralizing nature of the harmonization initiative was creating controversy, the House of Commons Standing Committee on Environment and Sustainable Development was completing its review of CEPA. The CEPA report, issued in June 1995, summarized its recommendations for the federal role as follows (Standing Committee, 1995, xxi):

This Report is based on the Committee's assertion that effective environmental and human health protection in Canada requires the federal government to play a strong leadership role .... There are three main aspects to the federal role with respect to environmental standard setting. First, the federal government should promulgate national standards for areas under federal jurisdiction and for issues of "national concern", such as toxic substances. Second, it should promote the establishment of national standards in areas requiring inter-jurisdictional cooperation. Third, it should lead cooperative efforts to minimize unnecessary overlap and duplication and to harmonize to the highest possible standard the various provincial, territorial, aboriginal and national environmental management regimes.

Boundary issues figured particularly prominently in the CEPA review's chapter on "The Federal Role in Environmental Protection." Commenting on the constitutional division of powers, the Standing Committee stated its belief "that the growing importance of transboundary environmental issues and the increasing internationalization of trade and environmental issues suggest that the constitutional basis for a strong federal role is, if anything, even greater today than it was when CEPA was first introduced" (Standing Committee, 1995, 4). On the topic of ecosystem management, the report stated that "Where risks to human health or ecosystems cut across administrative borders, . . . these risks are more properly seen as national in scope and lend themselves to federal leadership" (Standing Committee, 1995, 5). The Standing Committee also considered the international dimension of environmental management, stating that "the federal government must continue to take a lead role in participating in international institutions, in negotiating international agreements and protocols, and in ensuring national compliance with such agreements" (Standing Committee, 1995, 14). The stronger federal presence envisaged by the CEPA review stands in sharp contrast to the decentralizing dynamic of the harmonization initiative, with its emphasis on regulatory rationalization and delegation to the provinces.

The third element of the environmental management equation is the significant reduction in resources for environmental protection at both federal and provincial levels. This climate of fiscal restraint, dictated by rapidly accumulating government debt, is complemented by a movement toward deregulation in several Canadian jurisdictions. This movement, in turn, reflects ideological shifts, concerns with international competitiveness, and private sector resistance to the costs of regulation and taxation. At the federal level, the budget of Environment Canada will decline by approximately 32 percent over three years (Standing Committee, 1995, 10). Alberta's environmental budget was reduced by 30 percent in 1994, and the reduction in Ontario was 10 percent (Standing Committee, 1995, 10). Further cuts would appear likely in Ontario following the election in 1995 of a Conservative government committed to a dramatic reduction in the province's deficit.

The significance of these cuts raises serious questions about the capacity of federal and provincial governments to maintain current levels of environmental regulation. While governments and business interests focus attention on harmonization and the elimination of overlap and duplication, some environmentalists are concerned that decreasing financial resources will result in gaps between the boundaries of federal and provincial regulations (Andrews, 1995). Fiscal restraint may call into question the federal government's ability to implement fully and enforce existing regulations under CEPA and other environmental statutes, let alone launch ambitious new initiatives to address transboundary ecosystems. Furthermore, declining resources across the spectrum of governmental activities (e.g., education, health care, social security) may reduce the federal government's willingness to risk a politically charged jurisdictional controversy with the provinces in the areas of environmental and resource management. It may be that jurisdiction "dumping" will replace jurisdiction "grabbing" as a dynamic of federal-provincial relations.

The environmental management puzzle is therefore a complicated one, particularly as it relates to boundary issues. CEPA and CEAA provide for a mix of federal unilateralism, federal leadership in the form of standard setting, and bilateral agreements. Practical experience with these mechanisms, however, is still in its early days. The CCME harmonization initiative proposed a more comprehensive framework agreement covering the full spectrum of environmental management. Concerns with excessive delegation and decentralization, however, have led the federal government to draw back from this process. At the same time, the CEPA review advocated a stronger federal leadership role in environmental protection, particularly in asserting regulatory control over matters of "national concern" and transboundary matters. Finally, the implications of fiscal restraint for environmental management in Canada are not yet clear, and will undoubtedly depend on the political balance between fiscal and environmental priorities that is struck in the coming years.

CONCLUSION

This review of CEPA and CEAA suggests an emerging pattern in federal legislation. Both statutes represent federal assertions of jurisdiction in significant areas of environmental protection and both authorize unilateral federal action on boundary issues. CEPA provides for a federal regulatory regime for toxic substances and certain other pollutants. It also authorizes federal regulation of international transboundary air pollution and reflects international obligations in a number of areas. The general EA regime in CEAA permits federal review of projects that are subject to federal regulatory authority, even though many of these may fall primarily within provincial jurisdiction. In the case of projects that may have significant transboundary effects, a panel review or mediation may be ordered by the federal government without any other basis for involvement.

The assertion of federal authority in both statutes is considerably softened, however, by the provisions for cooperative arrangements that are clearly designed to preserve, to a large degree, provincial authority over environmental matters. In CEPA, equivalency agreements permit the suspension of federal regulations where the provincial regime produces an equivalent environmental effect. In addition, administrative agreements can be used to define and allocate responsibilities for environmental protection, and a federal-provincial committee addresses interjurisdictional issues. Furthermore, in the case of international air pollution, federal action is permitted only if a cooperative approach fails.

CEAA also contains a package of cooperative mechanisms, ranging from the delegation of certain EA functions to the convening of joint panel reviews. These sections will be fleshed out by federal-provincial agreements, which appear likely to accord primacy to the provincial process, so long as the basic federal standards are met. In the area of transboundary EA, whether interprovincial or international, the federal minister is specifically directed not to refer a project to a CEAA review where an alternative EA process has been agreed to with the provinces. Once again, provision is made for a cooperative solution in the place of unilateral federal action.

A significant federal role in addressing boundary issues is possible under CEPA and CEAA. In practice, however, ample opportunities and incentives exist for cooperative arrangements that would confer primary responsibilities on the provinces. Even the provisions for federal leadership, notably the requirement of equivalency under CEPA and the enumeration of conditions for joint panels under CEAA, give considerable latitude to the provinces to establish and administer the overall environmental protection regime.

The range of mechanisms provided for in both CEPA and CEAA gives some hope that boundary issues may not be intractable problems for Canadian environmental law and policy. Nonetheless, the history of federal-provincial cooperation under both statutes is very short. More experience with negotiating and implementing these arrangements will be necessary before their effectiveness in resolving jurisdictional boundary issues and facilitating transboundary environmental management can be assessed. Whatever the outcome of this experience, Canada's decentralized federal system and the contentious nature of environmental issues suggest that boundary issues will remain a major focus of legislative and policy development beyond the turn of the century.

NOTES

1. Jurisdictional issues related to the devolution of authority to Canada's northern territories and the negotiation of land claims and self-government arrangements with first nations are beyond the scope of this chapter, although they too raise important boundary issues for environmental management.

2. S.C. 1988, c. 22.

3. S.C. 1992, c. 37.

4. Constitution Act, 1867, ss. 92(10), (13), (16), and 92A.

5. Constitution Act, 1867, s. 109; Constitution Act, 1930.

6. Constitution Act, 1867, s. 92(5).

7. Constitution Act, 1867, ss. 91(12), 92(10), 91(10).

8. Constitution Act, 1867, s. 91(27).

9. Constitution Act, 1867, s. 91.

10. Constitution Act, 1867, s. 91(2).

11. Constitution Act, 1867, s. 132.

12. U.S. Constitution, Art. VI.

13. See, for example, Constitution Act, 1867, s. 92(13) ("Property and Civil Rights in the Province").

14. U.S. Constitution, Art. I, § 8, cl. 3.

15. U.S. Constitution, Art. IV, § 3, cl. 2.

16. These statutes are: the Access to Information Act, the Canada Water Act, the Clean Air Act, the Department of the Environment Act, the Environmental Contaminants Act, and the Ocean Dumping Control Act.

17. As of 1995, legislation in Alberta, Ontario, Saskatchewan, the Yukon, and the Northwest Territories meets this requirement (Environment Canada, 1993a: 102).

18. Alberta Equivalency Order, SOR/94–752.

19. Secondary Lead Smelter Release Regulations, Pulp and Paper Mill Effluent Chlorinated Dioxins and Furans Regulations, Vinyl Chloride Release Regulations, and Pulp and Paper Mill Defoamer and Wood Chips Regulations (certain sections only).

20. R.S.C. 1985, c. C-11.

21. These obligations are contained in the Basel Convention on the Control of Transboundary Movements of Hazardous Wastes and Their Disposal (1989), the OECD Decision Concerning the Control of Transfrontier Movements of Wastes Destined for Recycling Operations (1992), and the Canada-U.S.A. Agreement Concerning the Transboundary Movement of Hazardous Waste (1986).

22. See, for example, the Comprehensive Air Quality Management Framework for Canada signed by federal, provincial, and territorial governments in November 1993.

23. Some of Canada's international environmental obligations are, of course, dealt with in other statutes, such as the Migratory Birds Convention Act R.S.C. 1985, c. M-7, the International River Improvements Act R.S.C. 1985, c. I-20, and the International Boundary Waters Treaty Act R.S.C. 1985, c. I-17.

24. 30 I.L.M. 800 (1991).

REFERENCES

A.G. Canada v. *A.G. Ontario* [1937] A.C. 326.

Andrews, Bill. (1995). Harmonization Hits Sour Note. *News from West Coast Environmental Law*, 19: 4.

Barton, Barry. (1985). Cooperative Management of Interprovincial Water Resources, in J. Owen Saunders, ed., *Managing Natural Resources in a Federal State*. Toronto: Carswell.

CCME. (1993). CCME Priorities Spelled Out: Harmonization is Job One. *Envirogram* [Newsletter of the Canadian Council of Ministers of the Environment], 2(4): 1.

_____ . (1994). Progress on Harmonization Initiative: Governments to Divide Environmental Protection Work, Reduce Overlap. *Envirogram* [Newsletter of the Canadian Council of Ministers of the Environment] 3(3): 2.

_____ . 1995. Harmonization initiative: Federal government hits the pause button. *Envirogram* [Newsletter of the Canadian Council of Ministers of the Environment] 4(3): 3.

_____ . undated. *Rationalizing the Management Regime for the Environment: Purpose, Objectives and Principles.*

CIELAP. (1995). Harmonization Redux? *CIELAP [Canadian Institute for Environmental Law & Policy] Newsletter* Summer 1995: 1.

Crown Zellerbach, 1988. See, *R. V.* v. *Crown Zellerbach*

Cullen, Richard. (1990). The Encounter between Natural Resources and Federalism in Canada and Australia. *University of British Columbia Law Review*, 24: 275.

Dwivedi, O. P. and R. Brian Woodrow. (1989). Environmental Policy-Making and Administration in a Federal State: The Impact of Overlapping Jurisdiction in Canada, in William M. Chandler and Christian W. Zöllner, eds., *Challenges to Federalism: Policy-Making in Canada and the Federal Republic of Germany*. Kingston, Ontario: Institute of Intergovernmental Relations, Queen's University, p. 265.

Environment Canada. (1992). *Canadian Environmental Protection Act: Enforcement and Compliance Policy*. Ottawa: Environment Canada.

_____ . (1993a). *Environmental Protection Regulatory Review Discussion Document*. Ottawa: Environment Canada.

_____ . (1993b). *Evaluation of the Canadian Environmental Protection Act (CEPA): Final Report*. Ottawa: Environment Canada.

_____ . (1994). *Canadian Environmental Protection Act: Report for the Period April 1993 to March 1994*. Ottawa: Environment Canada.

Friends of the Oldman River Society v. Canada (Minister of Transport) [1992] 1 S.C.R. 3.

Gardner, Alex. (1994). Federal Intergovernmental Co-operation on Environmental Management: A Comparison of Developments in Australia and Canada. *Environmental and Planning Law Journal*, 11: 104.

Gertler, Franklin S. (1993). Lost in (Intergovernmental) Space: Cooperative Federalism in Environmental Protection, in Steven A. Kennett, ed., *Law and Process in Environmental Management*. Calgary: Canadian Institute of Resources Law.

Gibson, Dale. (1983). Environmental Protection and Enhancement under a New Canadian Constitution, in Stanley M. Beck and Ivan Bernier, eds., *Canada and the New Constitution—The Unfinished Agenda*, vol. 2. Montreal: Institute for Research on Public Policy.

Hanebury, Judith B. (1991). Environmental Impact Assessment in the Canadian Federal System. *McGill Law Journal*, 36: 962.

Hogg, Peter W. (1992). *Constitutional Law of Canada*, 3rd ed. Toronto: Carswell.

House of Commons Standing Committee on Environment and Sustainable Development. (1995). *It's About Our Health! Towards Pollution Prevention*. Minutes of Proceedings. Ottawa: Canada Communications Group.

Huffman, James L., and George Cameron Coggins. (1985). The Federal Role in Natural Resources Management in the United States, in J. Owen Saunders, ed., *Managing Natural Resources in a Federal State*. Toronto: Carswell.

Interprovincial Cooperatives Ltd. v. The Queen [1976] 1 S.C.R. 477.

Kennett, Steven A. (1991). *Managing Interjurisdictional Waters in Canada: A Constitutional Analysis*. Calgary: Canadian Institute of Resources Law.

_____ . (1992). *Oldman* and Environmental Impact Assessment: An Invitation for Cooperative Federalism. *Constitutional Forum*, 3: 93.

_____ . (1993a). Federal Environmental Jurisdiction after *Oldman*. *McGill Law Journal*, 38: 180.

_____ . (1993b). Interjurisdictional Harmonization of Environmental Assessment in Canada, in Steven A. Kennett, ed., *Law and Process in Environmental Management*. Calgary: Canadian Institute of Resources Law.

_____ . (1995). The Canadian Environmental Assessment Act's Transboundary Provisions: Trojan Horse or Paper Tiger? *Journal of Environmental Law and Practice*, 5: 263.

Lindgren, Richard D. (1990). Toxic Substances in Canada: The Regulatory Role of the Federal Government, in Donna Tingley, ed., *Into the Future: Environmental Law and Policy for the 1990's*. Edmonton: Environmental Law Center.

Lucas, Alastair R. (1985). Harmonization of Federal and Provincial Environmental Policies: The Changing Legal and Policy Framework, in J. Owen Saunders, ed., *Managing Natural Resources in a Federal State*. Toronto: Carswell.

_____ . (1989). *R. v. Crown Zellerbach Canada Ltd. University of British Columbia Law Review*, 23: 355.

_____ . (1990). Is "Equivalency" a Workable Solution? in Donna Tingley, ed., *Into the Future: Environmental Law and Policy for the 1990's*. Edmonton: Environmental Law Center.

Northey, Rodney. (1989). Federalism and Comprehensive Environmental Reform: Seeing Beyond the Murky Medium. *Osgoode Hall Law Journal*, 29: 127.

Oldman, 1992. See, *Friends of the Oldman River Society* v. *Canada (Minister of Transport)*.

R. v. *Crown Zellerbach*. [1988] 1 S.C.R. 401.

Rabe, Barry G. 1989. Cross-Media Environmental Regulatory Integration: The Case of Canada. *American Review of Canadian Studies*, 19: 261.

Re Canada Metal Co. Ltd. and the Queen. (1982). 144 D.L.R. (3d) 124 (Man. Q.B.)

Rehbinder, Eckard and Richard Stewart. (1985). Legal Integration if Federal Systems: European Community Environmental Law. *American Journal of Comparative Law*, 33: 371.

Saunders, J. Owen. (1985). Canadian Federalism and International Management of Natural Resources, in J. Owen Saunders, ed., *Managing Natural Resources in a Federal State*. Toronto: Carswell.

_____. (1988). *Interjurisdictional Issues in Canadian Water Management*. Calgary: Canadian Institute of Resources Law.

Standing Committee. (1995). See, House of Commons Standing Committee on Environment and Sustainable Development.

Tingley, Donna. (1990). Responding to the Challenge: An Overview of Significant Trends in Government Regulation, in Donna Tingley, ed., *Into the Future: Environmental Law and Policy for the 1990's*. Edmonton: Environmental Law Center.

Walters, Mark. (1991). Ecological Unity and Political Fragmentation: The Implications of the Brundtland Report for the Canadian Constitutional Order. *Alberta Law Review*, 29: 420.

8

INTEGRATED IMPACT ASSESSMENT: THE NEW ZEALAND EXPERIMENT

Robert V. Bartlett

The scope, complexity, and interrelatedness of environmental problems presents a difficult challenge to policymakers. Public policies have heretofore been responsive largely to particular matters of public concern. They have typically been ad hoc, sectoral, and segmental. Their administration has been charged to various agencies, each with its special mission. In consequence, governments have often acted to cross purposes. Results have too often been ineffectual and, as often, unnecessarily expensive. Incremental innovation is seldom able to affect significantly the tendencies of the larger system of public policy and administration within which it is undertaken. Inasmuch as no country has had long experience with the administration of environmental policy, a comparison of different approaches to environmental problems is useful. Direct transfers of method from one country to another may seldom be practicable, yet there may be lessons learned from the diverse experience of governments addressing similar problems. A comprehensive and radical institutional experiment in environmental policy has been initiated in the government of New Zealand. The New Zealand experiment may illuminate the effects of institutional structure on the implementation of policy. The relationships between constitutional principles, policy priorities, and administrative structures have never been clear. The problems of coping with multiple environmental trends, their causes, and their consequences justify efforts to find more effective methods of policymaking.

The term "environmental policy" encompasses several layers of meaning. It may refer to all substantive policy as it directly affects the human environment, or only to pollution and conservation policies collectively, or instead to a particular orientation of policy toward environmental protection and enhancement. At a deeper level, however, the term also implies something about the *processes* of policymaking: among other things, for example, truly environmental policymaking is significantly anticipatory, comprehensive, and integrative. Thousands of environmental laws, programs, regulations, and administrative initiatives have been adopted in the past quarter-century, but few have been intentionally designed as environmental policies in this last sense. One notable exception has been the widespread adoption of requirements for environmental impact assessment (EIA).

Yet the practice of EIA has usually fallen far short of the potential it has as a mechanism or strategy for environmental policymaking. Among the criticisms frequently leveled is that, in spite of its underlying logic and the wishful language sometimes included in statutes, directives, and declarations, EIA in practice has been much less integrative and integrated than it could be, thereby greatly limiting its ultimate policy effectiveness (e.g., Caldwell, 1991; Armour, 1991). Recent reforms in several countries, however, have had as one of their aims making impact assessment more integrated. Of particular promise and interest in this regard is the impact assessment system created as part of the wholesale reform of environmental institutions and policy processes now being implemented in New Zealand.

INTEGRATED IMPACT ASSESSMENT AS ENVIRONMENTAL POLICY

From the very first instances when the terms "environmental" and "policy" were used in policy analysis (e.g., Caldwell, 1963), several peculiar difficulties of environmental policy were identified, difficulties that decades later still pose daunting challenges for environmental policymaking. If environmental problems cannot be simply solved by technical means alone but require interrelated changes in human ethics, perceptions, and culture, then basic changes in institutions and values are a necessary objective of environmental policy. If understanding the particulars of the human environmental predicament and fashioning strategies for more enduring environmental relationships depends not just on scientific knowledge but interdisciplinary scientific knowledge, then more resources need to be committed to the environmental sciences broadly construed and more of those sciences need to be used in interdisciplinary ways in policymaking. If deleterious actions and events occur partly because policymaking is oriented mostly toward responding to crises, treating symptoms, and undertaking after-the-fact repair of damage, then more environmentally sensitive and benign policy must somehow be more anticipatory. And if key causes of environmental degradation are segmental policies and simplistic, fragmented, and compartmentalized thinking, then effective environmental policies and policymaking must be comprehensive and integrated (Bartlett, 1990a). In sum, the challenge faced by the politics and processes of environmental policymaking is not just the production of substantive environmental policies but a new approach to policymaking based on new ways of thinking, namely, ecological rationality (Bartlett, 1986, 1990b).

Achieving policy integration, then, is integral to the idea of environmental policy. Technical dimensions of policies must be integrated with the ethical and ideological. The unifying elements in the complexity of the natural world and its relationship with humans can only be understood through generation and use of integrated (that is, *inter*disciplinary) knowledge. Priority consideration of environmental values and the modeling, forecasting, and monitoring of environmental effects must be woven into routine planning and policymaking at all levels. "Shifting the focus to the policy sources" (Brundtland Commisssion, 1987, 311–313) requires not only that environmental protection be integrated into the missions of all agencies, organizations, and institutions, but that the resulting activities be coordinated with each other so as to lead to realization of environmental values.

Environmental impairment is so woven into the fabric of modern economic, political, and social systems that it would be simple-minded to think that adoption of only one mechanism, reform, or adjustment might ever fully address these challenges posed to environmental policymaking. Systemic change of this scope and magnitude calls for diverse, multiple, complementary remedies, particularly remedies that encourage social learning and further policy development. Such remedies should push modern societies toward environmentally sustainable, robust, and resilient values and institutions. Attention to the environmental problematique in the past quarter of a century has already produced a list of policy innovations and experiments that provide a basis for significant future environmental policy development. Prime among these innovations is environmental impact assessment (EIA).

First formally introduced into policy processes of the U.S. federal government by the National Environmental Policy Act of 1969, EIA of some sort is now required by numerous state and provincial governments, dozens of countries, and international development organizations. In the United States it has even become a routine business practice in instances where not formally required. In principle, EIA has considerable potential for forcing the transformation of policy institutions and processes so as to grapple better with some of the distinctive challenges of environmental policy, namely, making policy more anticipatory, more integrative, more comprehensive, more interdisciplinary, more science-based, and more directed toward cultivation of environmental values and the institutionalization of ecological rationality.

In practice, however, this potential has seldom been fully realized. Perfunctory EIA that accomplishes little to advance the integrativeness of environmental policy may still influence policy outcomes, for example, by generating and publicizing new information, by facilitating public participation, or by changing the political dynamics within and among organizations. But unless the practice of EIA itself involves an integrative, interdisciplinary approach with an integrative focus on the whole environment; unless its use is fully incorporated in policy, planning, and decision processes; and unless it is made an integral part of virtually all such processes, then its effectiveness in guiding, encouraging, and forcing environmental responsibility will be marginal.

More than two decades after the enactment of the National Environmental Policy Act (NEPA), for example, the policy effectiveness of EIA is still limited by slow and halting progress in integrating it with the policy, planning, and decision processes of agencies of the U.S. federal government. According to a policy analyst with the Council on Environmental Quality, which oversees implementation of NEPA, the absence of policy integration is a crucial failure (Clark, 1993):

Many environmental impact statements (EISs) are too long, take too long to prepare, cost too much, and many times do too little to protect the environment. Some EISs are prepared to justify decisions already made, many agencies fail to monitor during and after the project, some agencies do not provide adequate public involvement, and few agencies assess the cumulative effects of an action. . . . When the agencies prepare their own EISs, when the decisionmakers read those EISs and change the nature and scope of an action based on that analysis, then the agency is more likely to internalize NEPA's goals and policies. Those agencies that prepare their own NEPA analyses may benefit more directly from the experience and more easily instill the environmental ethic throughout their agency.

Although many countries established EIA systems in the 1970s and 1980s following the enactment of NEPA, few were willing to impose requirements as demanding as those of NEPA as it had been interpreted by the courts. But the context of greatly increased attention to environmental policy development since 1987—and the less-than-satisfactory experiences with earlier systems that often relied on discretionary, ad hoc, and add-on obligations—has led to renewed interest in several countries in accomplishing better environmental policy through impact assessment systems. For the past few years, for example, reconsideration of environmental impact assessment processes and requirements has been undertaken by several Canadian provinces and the Canadian federal government, with explicit attention to the issues of better integration (Gibson, 1990, 1993). But perhaps the single most thoroughgoing and comprehensive effort to achieve integrated impact assessment is to be found in New Zealand.

New Zealand is now implementing a set of massive institutional reforms that establish a comprehensive new framework for management of water, land, air, and other resources by re-created local and regional governments. Under these new institutional arrangements, the potential for integrated environmental policy through impact assessment is extended in at least four significant ways. First, impact assessment is integrated with planning and decision making procedures to an extent not achieved anywhere else in the world. Second, the practice of environmental impact assessment is defined in a comprehensive and integrative way, thus legislatively integrating environmental impact assessment with what are usually considered distinct forms of impact assessment, such as risk assessment, social impact assessment, and technology assessment. Third, rather than the traditional limited focus of impact assessment requirements on projects, New Zealand now requires impact assessment of all environment policies, plans, and programs of regional and local government. And fourth, land, air, water, and other resources are to be managed together in an integrated way, informed by integrated assessment of impacts of human actions.

That an impact assessment system so sweeping and bold should now be entrenched in law is a significant development in the three-decade history of environmental impact assessment. But the overall significance of these reforms for environmental policy is still largely indeterminate, as the reforms as legislated provide mostly a framework for processes and only minimal substantive policy direction. Other deficiencies in the design of this impact assessment system make it highly dependent upon discretionary interpretation, new rule making, and enforcement by current and future New Zealand governments. But the potential of EIA *in principle* with regard to grappling with some of the distinctive challenges of environmental policy can now be studied in the context of the potential of an actual evolving system *in practice*. This system should be of tremendous interest to environmental policy analysts and reformers around the world. Analysis of reforms more significant for environmental policy—whether in terms of theoretically based insight into strategic design or the possible substantive consequences of institutional choices—can hardly be imagined.

THE CONTEXT AND DYNAMICS OF ENVIRONMENTAL POLICY REFORM IN NEW ZEALAND

This new framework for environmental impact assessment, indeed, for a whole new system of environmental policy institutions and processes in New Zealand, was established by the Resource Management Act 1991. The Resource Management Act must be understood as one component of a massive, thoroughgoing, and profound reshaping of government undertaken by the Labour Party Government during its six years in power, from 1984 to 1990 (Bührs and Bartlett, 1993). Of these many policy initiatives, which collectively constituted "a period of radical change in New Zealand that has left no aspect of life untouched" (Wilson, in Holland and Boston, 1990: 8), only three directly relevant to environmental policy can be even briefly and inadequately described here. The Resource Management Act 1991 was an extension of a reorganization of environmental administration begun seven years earlier, and it also built upon a complete re-creation of local government accomplished in 1989.

Prior to 1991, environmental impact assessment in New Zealand had been prescribed its Environmental Protection and Enhancement Procedures, which came into force in 1974 and had been introduced not by statute but by cabinet minute. They applied to works and management policies of all central government departments, actions funded by central government, and actions requiring central government permits or licenses. The proponent of a proposal was required to perform an initial assessment and if this assessment determined the environment was likely to be significantly affected, a formal environmental impact report was required. Until 1987, the function of overseeing the environmental assessment process and of auditing environmental impact reports rested with a Commission for the Environment, which also had been established by cabinet without legislation in 1972.

The procedures were revised several times over a dozen years, but they retained several shortcomings—among others, they were largely discretionary, had no legal status, were poorly integrated with planning procedures, and were rarely applied to policy actions (Bührs, 1991; Murray, 1990). Without a basis in legislation, the procedures could not be enforced in courts; effectiveness and even continued existence of the procedures depended upon ongoing cabinet support. Abolishment of the procedures was repeatedly advocated by agencies that felt burdened by doing environmental impact assessment and also by the Treasury, which criticized them as unnecessary, interventionist, and costly. By the mid-1980s, efforts to produce consensus proposals for revising the procedures and giving them a statutory base foundered. Virtually no one was happy with the existing procedures (Bührs, 1991, 211), which were criticized by both advocates and opponents of the idea of a separate EIA system. In 1987 the Labour Government broadened considerably the focus of environmental and resource management reform, and the question of how to reform the EIA system was swallowed up as part of a comprehensive review of environmental and resource management statutes. This broader review was an extension of a reform program that had been underway since 1984.

With the stated primary aims being the improved efficiency of government and the economy and the improved accountability of the public service to Parliament and political executives, the Labour Government had undertaken sweeping reorganizations of the machinery of government (Boston, 1991), beginning in the area of environmental administration and later throughout the bureaucracy. Reorganization was also undertaken for the purpose of rationalizing government structure by achieving greater clarity of objectives—by separating into different agencies responsibilities for commercial endeavors, operational activities, policy advice, and regulatory and funding activities (Martin, 1990; Gregory, 1987).[1] Major changes were made in national agencies directly responsible for environmental policy and administration. The Forestry Service, the Department of Lands and Survey, the Wildlife Service of the Department of Internal Affairs, and the Commission for the Environment were abolished; created in their places were a Forestry Corporation, a Ministry of Forestry, a Land Corporation, a Department of Survey and Land Information, a Department of Conservation, a Ministry for the Environment, and a Parliamentary Commissioner for the Environment. Also particularly significant for environmental policy and impact assessment was the retrenchment of government involvement in construction and development activities, culminating in the abolishment of the once-powerful Ministry of Works and Development.

Efforts to rationalize the structure of government were not limited to the national level. After the reelection of the Labour Government in 1987, it committed itself to a fundamental review of local government as well as the review of resource and environmental management statutes generally. A single special committee, the Cabinet Committee on the Reform of Local Government and Resource Management Statutes, was established in January 1988 to be responsible for coordinating policy development for both reform efforts. The local government reform process, however, moved to the stage of legislative enactment much more quickly than did resource management law reform.

Measures implementing local government reform passed Parliament in 1988 and 1989, and all-new units of local government were established in November 1989 after local elections, although many matters of funding and function remained to be resolved. The reforms resulted in consolidation of 625 units of local government, including authorities, united councils, counties, municipalities, and districts, and special-purpose boards, into a total of 94 units: thirteen regions, 74 local districts, and seven special purpose boards. The new regional governments were assigned major responsibilities for natural resource and environmental planning and management. Further rationalization of such functions, and significant devolution from national government, was anticipated from the ongoing resource management law review process.

Resource management law reform was intended to produce legislation that would authorize and enable local governments, especially regional governments, to carry out new environmental and resource management responsibilities, some new responsibilities, and some that formerly rested with central government. Analyses and discussion documents were released in 1988, and an extensive public consultation program was conducted. A draft bill was introduced in December 1989, but the Select Committee it was referred to was unable to report back to Parliament until there was too little time for debate and passage before adjournment. After elections, however, the new National Party Government committed itself to passing the bill into law following further review and parliamentary reconsideration. The Resource Management Act was then enacted by Parliament in modified form in July 1991 to take effect on 1 October.

Appreciating this overall reform context is essential for understanding the new processes established by the act. On the one hand, the Resource Management Act is an environmental policy statute, and impact assessment is one of the several means it provides to achieve realization of that environmental policy (Morgan, 1991; Memon, 1993; Foruseth and Cocklin, 1995). The Resource Management Act as environmental policy endorses sustainable management as a fundamental purpose of resource and environmental policy and provides for application of the concept in all processes and outcomes provided for by the act. It further defines sustainable management to mean sustaining the potential of natural and physical resources to meet the needs of future generations; safeguarding the life-supporting capacity of air, water, soil, and ecosystems; and avoiding, remedying, or mitigating any adverse effects of activities on the environment. In achieving the purpose of the act all persons exercising functions and powers under it are enjoined to recognize and provide for matters of national importance, such as protection of outstanding natural features and landscapes and significant indigenous vegetation and fauna and to have particular regard to other matters such as the intrinsic value of ecosystems and maintenance and enhancement of the quality of the environment. It establishes duties and responsibilities for all persons to avoid, remedy, or mitigate adverse effects on the environment, and restricts the use of common property resources such as air and water unless expressly allowed by a plan, regulation, or resource consent. It provides for the integrated management of land, air, water, and minerals by replacing 78 statutes, regulations, and orders adopted at different times with a single coherent framework.

On the other hand, the Resource Management Act is an extension and continuation of the reform of national government and the re-creation of local government; it is "principally enabling," providing authority for its implementation to local and regional government but surprisingly few specific directives, enforcement procedures, or action-forcing mechanisms. In spite of its significant achievement with respect to design of an impact assessment system—particularly in integrating impact assessment with all making of policies, plans, and decisions, in integrating different kinds of impact assessment, and in requiring an integrated consideration of impacts on the environment as a whole—the potential of impact assessment to contribute to the achievement of sustainable management as defined in the act is constrained by some key weaknesses. Both the boldness of the innovations it encompasses and evaluation of its possible weaknesses are significant for environmental policy development beyond New Zealand.

THE PLACE OF IMPACT ASSESSMENT IN NEW ZEALAND'S NEW ENVIRONMENTAL AND RESOURCE POLICY SYSTEM

The logic of the new environmental and resource policy system is fairly straightforward. Responsibilities for many matters of environmental policy and resource management are assigned to new regional and local governments. The purposes and principles of the Resource Management Law are to be implemented through a hierarchy of formal, published policies and plans and enforced mainly through applications for consents—water permits, coastal permits, discharge permits, land use consents, subdivision consents, and so on. The central government may issue optional national policy statements on matters it deems of national importance (only a coastal policy statement is mandatory). Regional governments are required to issue regional policy statements, consistent with any national statements of government policy, that specify how the purposes of the Resource Management Law will be achieved. These mandatory regional policy statements are the foundation of the entire policy system. Regional governments may also issue regional management plans, and local district governments must issue district management plans. These plans contain specific rules—consistent with higher level policies and plans—that prohibit, regulate, or allow activities.

Impact assessment of national policy statements is not required, but impact assessment of all regional policy statements and regional and district management plans is mandatory. All resource consent applications, moreover, must be accompanied by an environmental assessment.

The Resource Management Act does not establish a distinct environmental impact assessment process, nor does it use that term. Instead, provision is made throughout the law for the evaluation of the effects on the environment of policies, plans, and proposals. Both "environment" and "effects" are defined broadly.

Environment is defined to include ecosystems, natural and physical resources, people, communities, and related social, economic, aesthetic, and cultural conditions. Effect is likewise defined in an all-encompassing way, with the law referring to, among other things, socioeconomic, cultural, visual, recreational, ecosystem, historical, spiritual, and noise effects, any risks to humans or the environment, and any discharges or emissions. Local and regional governments are required to monitor the effects of their policies and plans and to monitor compliance with resource consent conditions.

Thus the design of this environmental policy and resource management regime institutionalizes integration to a degree and extent unique to New Zealand. The basic policy decision process is designed to force an integration of government planning and decisions regarding land use, water pollution, air pollution, and waste disposal. Under this new institutional arrangement, impact assessment is required for virtually all rules and plans as well as projects, and is not an add-on requirement. Rather, impact assessment is integrated with planning, management, and regulatory procedures to a greater extent than anywhere else. And this new regime requires an integrated approach to impact assessment itself, recognizing that environmental considerations extend well beyond biophysical effects.

What are the consequences of this set of reforms? Unquestionably one of the engines of policy change built into the system is impact assessment. How the entire package of environmental policy reforms works, in terms of both procedural and substantive consequences, depends in large part on how the imbedded impact assessment system works. This raises the prior questions, then, of what is impact assessment, how is it supposed to work, and how does it work?

EVALUATION BY OTHER CRITERIA

Impact assessment as a policy strategy continues to be poorly understood (although its logic is sufficiently transparent that savvy politicians have little difficulty designing impact assessment systems that are intended to be ineffectual). Most of the thousands of people who have written about impact assessment in the last thirty years have perceived it as entailing a fairly simple set of institutional rules or mechanisms that are either automatically effective or wholly ineffective. Most policy analyses, including those done on behalf of governments in advance of adopting impact assessment requirements, have defined impact assessment as having only fairly narrow objectives, only one or two modes of policy influence, and a limited number of effects.

The idea of impact assessment may indeed be a simple one, but the way impact assessment influences policy, and the design of an effective impact assessment system, has proven to be an exceedingly complex matter. What New Zealand has achieved by designing and adopting a thoroughly integrated impact assessment system does not necessarily mean that its system will be effective in meeting the challenges of environmental policy (Wood, 1992, 1995). Any overall evaluation of an impact assessment system must be a conceptually rich one that relies on multiple perspectives and criteria (Bartlett, 1994).

In the past decade a policy literature on impact assessment has begun to emerge that allows more than superficial assessment of effectiveness, merit, or worth of an impact assessment system. Design principles—basic truths about what is necessary and sufficient for such systems to work—have been distilled from theoretically based insights and from careful comparative analysis of numerous actual EIA systems. Kennedy (1988), Ortolano, Jenkins, and Abracosa (1987), and Gibson (1990, 1993), for example, each have identified several principles for effective impact assessment.

Kennedy finds that EIA works best when there is an explicit, formal legal requirement for its application and when there are mechanisms to hold authorities accountable for using it in decision making. Ortolano, Jenkins, and Abracosa conclude that two or more of several types of formal controls—procedural controls, audit controls, judicial controls, incentive controls, direct controls—are necessary for EIA to be effective. Gibson (1990, 8) identifies eight principles for the design of an impact assessment process that will be "effective in guiding, encouraging and where necessary forcing environmental responsibility into all stages of the conception, planning and approval of environmentally significant undertakings":

1. An integrated approach must be required.
2. There must be clear and automatic application of all requirements to all significant undertakings.
3. Assessment must focus on the critical examination of purposes and comparison of alternatives.
4. Requirements must be established in law and be mandatory and enforceable.
5. The process must be open and participative.
6. The system must address implementation, with provision for monitoring and compliance enforcement.
7. The system must be designed for practical and efficient execution.
8. Impact assessment must be linked other broad policy concerns—the economy, agriculture, transportation, urban development, and so on.

Other analysts may not offer a comprehensive list of principles, but may address the importance of one or two in particular. For example, Caldwell (1989a, 1989b) concludes that effectiveness of EIA depends on a strong base in law for environmental policy—impact assessment must be explicitly linked to strong statements of policy, goals, strategies, responsibilities, obligations, or rights, with respect to which it can be action forcing.[2]

Evaluated against these criteria, the new impact assessment system in New Zealand scores high with respect to integration in all its dimensions, as discussed at length here, but also with regard to making impact assessment an explicit, mandatory legal requirement that is automatically applicable to most undertakings involving government.[4] The current New Zealand system is also embedded in a cogent statement of policy, requires examination of purposes and comparison of principles, is fairly open and participative, emphasizes monitoring, and is designed to achieve implementation efficiently.

But it is the extent to which the new impact assessment requirements are enforceable, however, that remains to be seen even several years after the adoption of the Resource Management Act. The act itself provides little formal structure or guidance for doing impact assessment, for assuring its adequacy, or for influencing its use. Local and regional councils have tremendous latitude in developing procedures, determining methods and standards, and overseeing practice for impact assessment of both their own policies, plans, and rules and the resource consent applications they must consider. Their performance to date has been highly variable (Blakeley, 1993). Many of the impact assessment provisions of the Resource Management Act depend upon prior development of a system of policies and plans, and few of them are yet operative (Gow, 1995). The only policy statement issued or planned by the current National Government is the mandatory coastal policy statement. Aside from appeal to a judicial Planning Tribunal (an institutional carry-over from the old Town and Country Planning Act) or guidance from the Ministry for the Environment, there are few mechanisms to force local and regional governments to use impact assessment in making policies, plans, and decisions. Moreover, regardless of intent, local authorities have very limited monetary and staff resources to comply with the spirit of the impact assessment requirements, a problem that is wholly unaddressed in any formal way (Dixon, 1993; Montz and Dixon, 1993).

Previously, enforcement of New Zealand's Environmental Protection and Enhancement Procedures relied on audit controls to ensure adequate impact assessment—a formal audit of the adequacy of an environmental impact report by the old Commission for the Environment. No such mechanism exists for impact assessment under the Resource Management Act (although the Parliamentary Commissioner could choose to review an impact assessment, that office does not have resources for more than a rare audit). The new system relies instead on a combination of provisions for direct involvement by the public and yet unclear judicial controls by the Planning Tribunals. (Impact assessment documents under the Resource Management Act are not themselves justiciable; the Planning Tribunal can confirm, amend, or cancel decisions and it can order changes to any policy statement or plan, but given the Planning Tribunal's origins and background in land use planning law, it can hardly be expected to focus on regulating impact assessment requirements per se.) The Ministry for the Environment is granted broad authority by the Resource Management Act for procedural controls, incentive controls, and direct controls, but the exercise of that authority is wholly discretionary under the law. By the end of 1995 it had issued only general, nonbinding guidance.

So, notwithstanding its accordance with most of the principles that have been identified in the policy literature as prerequisite for effective environmental impact assessment, there is considerable potential for New Zealand's new impact assessment system to founder on the shoals of implementation and enforcement.

Integration has been declared and innovatively provided for in the framework created by the Resource Management Act, but its achievement is far from inevitable.

CONCLUSION

New Zealand in its recent environmental policy reforms has gone further than any other country in creating an impact assessment system consistent with the strong imperative for integration that is implicit in the very term environmental policy. Evaluation of this new system also reveals the extent to which New Zealand reformers may have learned from some of the inadequacies of their own EIA experience and that of other countries. A number of principles for the design of an effective impact assessment system, as identified by policy scholars, are reflected in the New Zealand legislation now being implemented. But some deficiencies can be identified as well: the new framework is extremely flexible, existing guidance is general, and mandated action-forcing mechanisms are few. These inadequacies could be rectified, but only at the discretion of the central government through the substantial powers reserved to it in the Resource Management Act. Doing so would require considerable vision, will, and even timing. Meanwhile, environmental policy analysts have the opportunity in New Zealand to learn from something rare in the brief history of environmental impact assessment: the formative influence of institutionalized impact assessment on a whole system of re-created local and regional governments—governments coming of age under a mandate to *make* environmental policy *routinely*, by way of integrated impact assessment.

New Zealand's integrated impact assessment reforms hardly are transferable as a whole to other nations, each with different traditions and different political systems—even if desirable, political realities such as federalism, judicial review, and separation of powers make it difficult to imagine other nations adopting New Zealand's reforms unmodified, embedded in a single unified environmental and resource management statute. And the New Zealand system has its identifiable weaknesses that could be addressed. But the integrative character of impact assessment in New Zealand is something others may wish to watch, learn about, and emulate. A certain challenge of environmental policy in the twenty-first century is making the processes of environmental policy anticipatory, comprehensive, and integrative—and thus truly environmental. Part of the future can be glimpsed in New Zealand now.

NOTES

1. These reforms generally succeeded in putting many of the functions performed by state organizations on a commercial basis, requiring agencies to charge on a full-recovery basis for a wide range of goods and services. An attempt was made to separate commercial and noncommercial activities of departments, with commercial activities assigned to public corporations and many of public corporations subsequently sold (privatized).

2. Even so, Caldwell has also noted that this declaration of policy must be binding on those charged with execution of the policy and must have priority overriding other competing policies, or else it will be less than fully effectual. Hence, Caldwell suggested that to the extent that the National Environmental Policy Act has been ineffective, the only permanent remedy is an amendment to the U.S. Constitution (Caldwell, 1989b).

3. Local and regional government that is, to which many responsibilities formerly resting with central government have been delegated. Impact assessment under the Resource Management Act is largely optional for central government. Central government activities are still technically governed by a version of the Environmental Protection and Enhancement Procedures, but requirements of the procedures have been largely ignored in recent years. When the Ministry for the Environment was established in the mid-1980s, a "reporting function" was given to the Ministry. To ensure that environmental implications of policy proposals would be considered by the Cabinet in making decisions, all proposals with significant environmental implications submitted to the Cabinet or its committees are required to be accompanied by a report from the Ministry for the Environment. This procedure has worked modestly well, but its status is legally precarious and there are inherent limitations to the degree of integration it forces upon the central government (Bührs, 1992).

REFERENCES

Armour, Audrey. (1991). "Impact Assessment and the Planning Process," Impact Assessment Bulletin, 9 (4): 27–33.

Bartlett, Robert V. (1986). "Ecological Rationality: Reason and Environmental Policy," *Environmental Ethics*, 8 (Fall 1986): 221–239.

_____ . (1990a). "Comprehensive Environmental Decision Making: Can It Work?" in *Environmental Policy in the 1990s: Toward a New Agenda*, ed. Norman J. Vig and Michael E. Kraft. Washington, DC: CQ Press, pp. 235–254.

_____ . (1990b). "Ecological Reason in Administration: Environmental Impact Assessment and Administrative Theory," in *Managing Leviathan: Environmental Politics and the Administrative State*, ed. Robert Paehlke and Douglas Torgerson. Peterborough, Ontario: Broadview Press, pp. 81–96.

_____ . (1994). "Evaluating Environmental Policy Success and Failure," in *Environmental Policy in the 1990s: Toward a New Agenda*, 2nd ed., ed. Norman J. Vig and Michael E. Kraft. Washington, DC: CQ Press, pp. 167–187.

Blakeley, Roger. (1993). "Variable Performance by Councils," *Environment Update* (newsletter of the Ministry for the Environment), no. 32 (April), p. 2.

Boston, Jonathan. (1991). "Reorganizing the Machinery of Government: Objectives and Outcomes," in *Reshaping the State: New Zealand's Bureaucratic Revolution*, ed. Jonathan Boston, John Martin, June Pallot, and Pat Walsh. Auckland: Oxford University Press, pp. 233–267.

Brundtland Commission [World Commission on Environment and Development]. (1987). *Our Common Future*. New York: Oxford University Press.

Bührs, Ton. (1991). "Working within Limits: The Role of the Commission for the Environment in Environmental Policy Development in New Zealand." Unpublished Ph.D. dissertation. Auckland: University of Auckland.

_____ . (1992). "Giving the Environment the Swerve," *Terra Nova*, no. 14 (March 1992): 33–35.

Bührs, Ton, and Robert V. Bartlett. (1993). *Environmental Policy in New Zealand: The Politics of Clean and Green?* Auckland: Oxford University Press, 1993.

Caldwell, Lynton K. (1963). "Environment: A New Focus for Public Policy?" *Public Administration Review*, 23 (September): 132–139.

_____ . (1989a). "Understanding Impact Analysis: Technical Process, Administrative Reform, Policy Principle," in *Policy through Impact Assessment: Institutionalized Analysis as a Policy Strategy*, ed. Robert V. Bartlett. Westport, CT: Greenwood Press, pp. 7–16.

_____ . (1989b). "A Constitutional Law for the Environment: Twenty Years with NEPA Indicates the Need," *Environment*, 31 (10): 6–11.

_____ . (1991). "Analysis-Assessment-Decision: The Anatomy of Rational Policymaking," *Impact Assessment Bulletin*, 9 (4): 81–92.

Clark, Ray. (1993). "The National Environmental Policy Act and the Role of the President's Council on Environmental Quality," *The Environmental Professional*, 15 (1): 4–6.

Dixon, J. (1993). "The Integration of EIA and Planning in New Zealand: Changing Process and Practice," *Journal of Environmental Planning and Management*, 36: 239–251.

Foruseth, Owen, and Chris Cocklin. (1995). "An Institutional Framework for Sustainable Resource Management: The New Zealand Model," *Natural Resources Journal*, 35 (Spring): 243–273.

Gibson, Robert B. (1990). "Basic Requirements for Environmental Impact Assessment Processes: A Framework for Evaluating Existing and Proposed Legislation." Unpublished paper. Waterloo, Ontario, Canada: Department of Environment and Resource Studies, University of Waterloo.

_____ . (1993). "The Zen of Environmental Assessment: Canadian Experience and the Eight Paths to Enlightened Process Design," *The Environmental Professional*, 15 (1): 12–24.

Gow, Lindsay. (1995). "NZ's Integrated Environmental Approach Impresses US Audiences," *Environment Update* (newsletter of the Ministry for the Environment), no. 44 (July), p. 4.

Gregory, Robert. (1987). "The Reorganization of the Public Sector: The Quest for Efficiency," in *The Fourth Labour Government: Radical Politics in New Zealand*, ed. Jonathan Boston and Martin Holland. Auckland: Oxford University Press, pp. 111–133.

Holland, Martin and Jonathan Boston. (1990). "Introduction," in *The Fourth Labour Government: Politics and Policy in New Zealand*, 2nd ed., ed. Martin Holland and Jonathan Boston. Auckland: Oxford University Press, pp. 1–9.

Kennedy, William V. (1988). "Environmental Impact Assessment in North America, Western Europe: What Has Worked Where, How, and Why," *International Environment Reporter*, 11 (13 April): 257–262.

Kurian, Priya A. (1995). "Gender and Environmental Policy: A Feminist Evaluation of Environmental Impact Assessment and the World Bank." Unpublished Ph.D. dissertation. West Lafayette, IN: Purdue University.

Martin, John. (1990). "Remaking the State Services," in *The Fourth Labour Government: Politics and Policy in New Zealand*, 2nd ed., ed. Martin Holland and Jonathan Boston. Auckland: Oxford University Press, pp. 123–139.

Memon, P. Ali. (1993). *Keeping New Zealand Green: Recent Environmental Reforms.* Dunedin, New Zealand: University of Otago Press.

Montz, Burrell and Jennifer E. Dixon. (1993). "From Law to Practice: EIA in New Zealand," *Environmental Impact Assessment Review*, 13: 89–108.

Morgan, Richard K. (1991). "Approaches to Environmental Impace Assessment under the Resource Management Act," in *Implementing the Resource Mangement Act*, ed.

Richard K. Morgan, P. Ali Momon, and Mary Anne Miller. Dunedin: University of Otago Environmental Policy and Management Resource Center.

Murray, Anne C. (1990). *Environmental Assessment: The Evolution of Policy and Practice in New Zealand.* Master's Essay, Centre for Resource Management, University of Canterbury and Lincoln University, Christchurch, New Zealand.

Ortolano, Leonard; Jenkins, Bryan; and Ramon P. Abracosa. (1987). "Speculations on When and Why EIA Is Effective," *Environmental Impact Assessment Review*, 7: 285–292.

Wood, Christopher. (1992). "Strategic Environmental Assessment in Australia and New Zealand," *Project Appraisal*, 7(3): 143–149.

_____ . (1995). *Environmental Impact Assessment: A Comparative Review.* Essex, U.K: Longman Scientific and Technical.

9

PROSPECTS FOR INTEGRATED ENVIRONMENTAL POLICY

Odelia Funke

Because of the interrelating cross-media character of many environmental problems, development of comprehensive but coherent policies for their abatement or management is difficult. This is particularly true where, as in the United States, there has been a strong tendency toward focus on single-issue aspects of complex problems. Nowhere has this problem of policy and program integration more been difficult than in the EPA. Question: should the Congress legislate to establish effective intra-agency integration and departmental reorganization if necessary to its achievement? Or is this task so complex and subject to change with new findings that its attainment should be left primarily to administrative agencies, relying more heavily on the states? This chapter uses the lead contamination issue to illustrate the obstacles to integration of policy and procedure even for a single environmental pollutant. Given the holistic and ramifying character of environmental problems, how can appropriate policies and regulations be developed in a political system characterized by sectoral, specialized structure and special interest clientele? At the time of this writing, the effects of elevating the EPA to a cabinet-level department cannot fully be foreseen. The expansion of EPA to the administration of nonregulatory responsibilities will doubtless bring new problems of policy to this agency. Problems of program integration may increase unless EPA is authorized to devise and adapt more effective integrative procedures.

In its early years, the Environmental Protection Agency (EPA) was busy trying to address imminent environmental threats—burning rivers and belching stacks signal clear and immediate problems. Over the years it became increasingly obvious that controlling pollutants medium by medium was either moving pollutants around (rather than getting rid of them), inefficiently regulating the same pollutants through a chain, or failing to target the best sources to control. Environmental problems cannot be differentiated into distinct media categories, and fragmented approaches are therefore expensive and ultimately ineffective. Scholars and practitioners recognize that effective environmental protection demands an integrated approach, and have been searching for mechanisms to facilitate integration.[1]

Focusing on a problem or pollutant across program boundaries (air, water, soil, toxic chemicals) encourages the Agency to do a better job of defining substantive criteria and setting priorities. This process helps identify unresolved issues, data and technical gaps, and what can and cannot be done. It is more likely to identify cost-effective options for a given plant or chemical. A multimedia perspective also tends to make overlaps in jurisdiction obvious earlier and thus enhances the likelihood that offices will act to resolve their policy and regulatory differences. Articulating clear policy objectives, including implementation, provides a basis for coordination of roles, and gives agencies a better chance to integrate programs across offices and levels of government.

While there is a general awareness of the need for holistic strategies, creating organizational and legal structures and appropriate processes to achieve this end are formidable tasks. The EPA consists of a group of programs that have functioned almost as fiefdoms, built around a dozen media-specific statutes, with differing standards for taking action. Each of these programs also has its work teams, and its own congressional and private sector clientele. National and state programs have been created without much cross-media attention, and attempts to integrate often run into difficulty in complying with media-specific statutory requirements as well as difficulties in breaking down institutional barriers. Integration would require developing new ways of understanding and addressing issues, and training professionals to deal with cross-media programs.

In an organization that is structurally and legally organized around media programs, a cross-media approach puts administrative and sometimes legal stress on the system. It takes a great deal of organizational effort to pull together individuals from various programmatic, administrative jurisdictions to work effectively on a multimedia issue within the agency. Joint responsibility and ownership of analysis and recommendations—which are critical to successfully moving a strategy through the agency—can be difficult to establish across program lines; even getting all of the paperwork done is a formidable task. (As a practical matter, one office has to act as catalyst and take responsibility for overall planning and management.) When several offices have some jurisdiction and programmatic interests at stake, the task of consensus-building through the hierarchy is complicated and time-consuming at best. In the short term, there is invariably institutional resistance to new processes and approaches. Statutory requirements can be significant impediments. Integration across agencies and levels of government is an even more formidable undertaking. It is not surprising that EPA has not given this kind of attention and analysis to many issues.

This chapter seeks to illustrate the need for and difficulty of integration. "Integration" can refer to a variety of things: ultimate goals or objectives, methodologies or proximate objectives (how to rank problems, choose protection strategies, assess chemicals or establish research objectives), as well as planning and management approach.[2] The primary focus here is on integrated management, including policy and implementation, and not on ultimate goals or how issues are selected in the first place. The chapter looks first (and quickly) at some earlier attempts toward integrated environmental policy at EPA, and then considers one effort started under the Reilly/Habicht administration at EPA (1989–1992) in greater detail. It argues that EPA's multimedia Lead Strategy, formally announced in February 1991, offers an excellent case, demonstrating the need for better coordination and the barriers to successful integration, even with leadership that is dedicated to cross-media policy making. Finally, there is a brief discussion of EPA attempts to coordinate with the Organization for Economic Cooperation and Development (OECD) on this same issue. While integrated policy on the international level is beyond political reach, at least for now, efforts to coordinate programs are underway, and these efforts illustrate some of the difficulties of fashioning integrated programs.

EARLY INTEGRATION ATTEMPTS—
THE TOXIC SUBSTANCES CONTROL ACT

By 1976, when Congress passed the Toxic Substances Control Act (TSCA), it was clear that an integrating mechanism for environmental policy was necessary. TSCA represented a pioneering effort to integrate on the basis of controlling chemicals across media, including manufacturing, production, distribution, and disposal. TSCA was designed to be a flexible tool, which gives the EPA broad authority and responsibility for: collecting and disseminating information about production and use of chemicals, including possible adverse effects; screening and assessing the safety of chemicals in commerce or chemicals planned for commercial distribution; requiring testing; limiting or prohibiting specific uses of chemicals, or even banning a chemical entirely.[3]

The act includes very broad authority to take action when the agency finds "unreasonable risk" (section 6), while at the same time requiring the administrator to consider other authorities, both within EPA and in other agencies (section 9). The EPA Administrator has discretion to judge whether a risk could be addressed adequately using those other authorities, in which case TSCA should not be used. The same section of TSCA encourages consultation between agencies regarding problems of mutual interest or responsibility. If TSCA functioned smoothly, it would stimulate cooperation and integration among programs, and between agencies. The reality has been far from optimal.[4]

This statute, like all other major legislation, embodied compromises. The effect of these compromises has significantly impeded (some say crippled) the intended integrative function. From the time TSCA was written, there has been disagreement over whether it should function as a comprehensive authority, or whether its role should be limited to a "gap filler." Clearly section 9 limits EPA's authority under TSCA. Some emphasize that the discretion it gives to the administrator entails considerable latitude to decide that TSCA authority would be more effective or efficient for a given problem, and therefore the appropriate tool. Conservative interpretations of TSCA authority have reasoned that referral should be the norm, but when a chemical would have to be referred to several different agencies for resolution, it might best be addressed under the single authority of TSCA.[5] The debate continues.[6] Statutory responsibilities overlap and there are no clear processes or mechanisms for resolving the territorial issues emphasized by section 9. Available resources, differing judgments about risk or comparative importance, and turf considerations all affect an agency's willingness to take on a task—or have another agency do so. Other agencies surely do not want the appearance of inaction or indifference to what EPA defines as a problem.

Another ongoing debate is whether TSCA is more important as a regulatory authority or as a mechanism to collect, analyze and share information. This touches on issues such as the appropriate constraints on information sharing posed by the need for business confidentiality, and the practical limitations on TSCA regulatory authority given the demanding (some think impossible) cost-benefit balancing required by the statute. Arguments for TSCA's potentially powerful regulatory role were significantly undermined by the 1991 Fifth Circuit Court of Appeals decision on asbestos. Despite a massive and very expensive EPA effort lasting over ten years to assess chemical risk and evaluate use and market information, the Court found that EPA had not sufficiently considered all relevant costs and tradeoffs before banning asbestos.[7]

The limit of EPA authority under TSCA is not solely a legal issue. There are political and practical considerations that cannot be ignored. Two experiences under TSCA in the 1980s will illustrate this point. In the early 1980s, EPA embarked on an inter-agency, cross-media project to address chlorinated solvents in a comprehensive fashion, with TSCA acting as the focal point within EPA. The chlorinated solvents project proved a very difficult undertaking. Intra-agency squabbles and policy debates slowed the project and required unforeseen time and effort to resolve. Coordinating with other agencies also proved cumbersome and time-consuming. The project was finally declared "done" in spring of 1991, though some outstanding issues and chemicals still remained for future attention. Those involved give the project mixed reviews. Some remark that the effort was a mistake, not worth the time and trouble it took. Others think that, despite the acknowledged difficulties and high resource costs, the project was worthwhile. They argue that any such pioneering effort is bound to take extraordinary commitment. The real benefit lies in having learned from the process, and having created some patterns and precedents for cooperative ventures in the future. Whether future attempts run smoothly because of the lessons learned remains to be seen. Such hard-earned lessons must be utilized to be valuable, and cross-media projects are still far from common.

A second experience was developing the Comprehensive Assessment and Information Rule (CAIR). The Office of Pollution Prevention and Toxics (OPPT, the office administrating TSCA) pushed this rule in the mid-1980s as a powerful information-gathering tool that could both gather a broad array of information efficiently for federal agencies, and prevent duplication which is costly to industry. It was touted as a powerful but more precise tool, one that could serve various programs efficiently. OPPT had an uphill battle designing and promulgating this rule, and the office continued to grapple with it for a number of years.[8]

There were several notable difficulties. OPPT invited other EPA offices and other agencies to include their information needs in CAIR. OPPT felt some obligation to screen information items to avoid duplication and make sure they were reasonable and technically sound. Potential users considered whether they would lose flexibility or authority by using a regulatory tool administered by another office. They also faced the need to fashion generic questions that they could justify. OPPT was willing to expend resources to collect information for others, but had to worry about how to comply with the information collection requirements under the Paperwork Reduction Act and associated "burden hours" accounting (administered by the Office of Management and Budget, OMB) for the comprehensive rule they envisioned. Another major problem was that parts of industry were strongly opposed. Industry feared that, rather than providing an efficient and streamlined tool, CAIR would create a mechanism for massive intrusion and make such information demands all too easy.

The EPA tried to address these concerns, stressing the goal of nonduplication and that questions would have to be justified; the agency promised to pilot the questionnaire, to start on a modest scale and expand it by increments, and to evaluate early results. These promises notwithstanding, there was still a great deal of industry opposition. This opposition together with the institutional resistance and sheer difficulty of designing the rule slowed the project and eventually pressured OPPT into paring the scope dramatically. Opponents gathered support in Congress. After spending considerable resources over several years, OPPT has very meager results to show for its efforts. The issues were under discussion for several years, and there were numerous attempts to design fixes to CAIR. But CAIR was viewed by many as a white elephant, and the eventual solution was to set the rule and its goals aside as unachievable. As part of a regulatory reform initiative announced by President Clinton in 1995, OPPT decided to remove CAIR from the *Code of Federal Regulations*—after using it only once to collect information. Unlike the Chlorinated Solvents project, not even the most optimistic can see this effort as a success, nor do there seem to be any valuable lessons learned that will help integration efforts in the future.

NEW COMMITMENT TO INTEGRATION EFFORTS

Under the Reilly/Habicht administration at EPA, cross-media integration first became a predominant theme.[9] Commitment to this goal was manifest in several initiatives designed to bring about a gradual cultural change within EPA's overall legal and organizational lines. The strong Reilly/Habicht goal of breaking down program barriers was a consistent theme in speeches and in high-level agency meetings. For at least some of the biggest issues, they insisted upon the importance of integrated planning by pressing cross-media questions and in some cases delayed decisions pending resolution of cross-media concerns. The Office of Research and Development was charged to conduct several cross-media studies; the agency's research agenda started highlighting more cross-media issues. Delaying decisions and committing funds in the name of integration were critical signals to program managers of their determination to move the agency toward more integrated policies.

The Reilly/Habicht administration also tried to incorporate cross-media issues and initiatives into the budgetary process. This budgetary push encouraged offices to seek issues of mutual interest across program areas as a way to increase funding. Given the amount of work within each program that is deemed to be nondiscretionary, any office's flexibility to add items to coincide with work in other offices is quite limited. If a chemical or issue is not a priority under a particular statute, the program responsible for that statute is not very likely to initiate a project just because it is important in other offices, other media. On the other hand, there are always overlapping projects on chemicals of concern across EPA offices. The budget initiative to fund cross-media efforts resulted in some reordering of priorities within offices. Minimally, if offices coordinate efforts on issues they are already working on, the agency can minimize duplication of research efforts or development of conflicting policies among offices. The budget initiative created some incentive to foster cooperative ideas and contacts across program lines.

The boldest and most countercultural initiative was the attempt to form "cluster groups" for targeted policies and regulations. The Reilly/Habicht administration wanted to select about a dozen high-visibility, complex projects for which work was underway in different program offices, and cluster the various program projects into a single oversight workgroup. The goal was to facilitate review and insure consistency and overall effectiveness. How to define clusters proved a difficult issue in itself. In the case discussed here (lead), a single contaminant provided the focus; a related set of pollutants, an industry, or a pollution receptor could likewise provide a clustering principle. The system was further differentiated by outlining degrees of workgroup centralization. A *loose* cluster would be formed by workgroup members representing their own office's interests, coordinating to make sure offices would keep each other informed and avoid inconsistent policies. A *tightly* integrated project would require program offices to designate qualified individuals for a central workgroup where they were to represent an agency view rather than their own office's interests. The central workgroup would play an active policy role in advising individual programs and guaranteeing an integrated approach, including, for example, the priority and sequence for rule-making across programs. Program priorities and the chain of accountability for workgroup members makes this approach extremely difficult under the current legal and organizational framework. A third cluster model falls between the loose and tight models. There were never more than a few cluster workgroups underway, and none embodied the degree of integration characterized by the highly centralized model.

The process begun under the Reilly/Habicht administration has continued. Clinton's Administrator, Carol Browner, has endorsed cross-media efforts. Because her new team of political appointees was very slow to arrive, her approach to integration took many months to emerge. Clearly, creating a cross-media culture within EPA will be a slow process that will require continued attention from one administration to the next. The ultimate question is whether truly integrated environmental policy is possible without a statutory framework (including removing current statutory barriers).

Integration of the Lead Strategy: A Multifaceted Problem

The most successful cluster experiment for integrating program policies and activities has been the lead project. Lead provides an excellent example of the need for and problems of cross-media integration. It is a persistent and highly toxic pollutant that contaminates air, water, soil, and incinerator ash, and may create disposal problems in sludge and landfills. Lead has multiple routes of entry, and affects a wide spectrum of organs and systems. It is toxic to both humans and animals, but is particularly hazardous for infants and small children. There is no known threshold level; researchers are finding a continuum of lead-engendered neurotoxicity in children at lower and lower levels. Hazards from lead range from minor neurological effects, which often include decrements in intellectual function, to significant neurological disorders, including permanent brain damage; at very high doses, it can cause death. In 1991, researchers estimated that about 400,000 babies are born with elevated blood lead levels each year, and that 3–4 million children have elevated levels.[10]

Several important federal actions have had dramatic effects on reducing lead exposures across age and income groups.[11] Beginning in the 1970s, EPA started a series of actions to phase out lead in gasoline. By 1994, levels of lead in gas were .05 percent of the amount used in 1970, the peak year. Between 1975 and 1984, national ambient lead concentrations dropped by about 75 percent.[12] Between 1976 and 1990, lead in gas was reduced 99.8 percent.[13] The phasedown of lead in gasoline was not the only important factor in blood lead reductions. Other federal actions were a ban on lead in house paint (Consumer Product Safety Commission, CPSC), on lead solder and pipe for drinking water systems (EPA), on lead solder in food and beverage cans (Food and Drug Administration, FDA), as well as a blood screening program (Centers for Disease Control, CDC). As of November 1991, lead-soldered food and beverage cans were no longer manufactured in the United States. In 1995, FDA replaced its voluntary ban with a regulatory ban, which includes imported cans. The percentage of children with elevated levels of lead in their blood has steadily declined over the past two decades, and average levels have declined as well. By the early 1980s, the problem seemed to be on the verge of resolution. We now know that it was not. Despite major control initiatives, lead risks from past uses of lead have not sufficiently abated.

Aside from the fact that new information has pushed levels of concern steadily downward, the problem remains primarily because of residual lead in the environment from a long history of past uses. As is the case with many environmental pollutants, past practices have adverse consequences far into the future. We stopped most of the lead emissions from automobiles and dramatically reduced ambient lead levels, but we still have soil contaminated from past emissions. The majority of current high exposures in the United States are attributable to historic depositions of lead rather than current uses.[14] The single largest source of elevated blood lead levels, and the dominant source of extremely high blood lead levels (over 25 ug/dl)[15] comes from lead-based paint—particularly from paint dust in houses and yards. Although lead is no longer used in house paint, old layers of lead-based paint deteriorate into dust, which children inhale. They also get it on their hands, then into their mouths. In short, typical infant and small child behavior leads to high exposure when they are in and around buildings with deteriorating lead-based paint.[16]

How to clean up deteriorating paint poses a number of complex technical and methodological problems; abatement is an extremely expensive and resource-intensive proposition, which has received increasing attention over the past few years. But even addressing this tangle of issues still would not by itself take care of the problem of elevated blood lead levels in children. Studies have demonstrated that contaminated dust can be tracked or blown in from outside, recontaminating the house.[17] Soil is suspected of being a significant source of high exposures, not only because deteriorated lead-based paint has contaminated soils as well as houses, but also as a result of leaded gas emissions from motor vehicles (and, in some areas, point source emissions) over the years. Soil abatement would constitute an even larger undertaking than paint removal, requiring potentially massive expenditures for uncertain benefits. In abated units—those houses and soils where lead contamination is removed—the debris raises new risk issues. In some cases it has to be treated as hazardous waste. Attempts to clean up lead might wind up pushing it from one medium to another. Further, any abatement efforts have to be undertaken with care. Removal exposes workers to potentially high risks. Removing lead would in some cases release large amounts of lead dust and create more of a hazard for building inhabitants than leaving it in place and managing it. And removing paint from walls is not effective without removing the dust, inside and outside, that has been contaminated from ground-up paint chips and gasoline. An integrated approach demands that we sort through the various sources and routes of exposure and set priorities.

Another aspect of continuing risks is that, since lead is a stable element, it does not degrade in the environment. Lead in products does not always or necessarily entail exposures of concern during use—lead acid storage batteries, for example, present no known risk during use. However, some argue that all lead is of concern, because after disposal it will eventually be dispersed into the environment (by leaching into groundwater, for example). It is debatable whether all lead will eventually present risks, but it is clear that controlling lead in one medium does not guarantee protection, if it is deposited in another medium, where it can pose a hazard. One example is that combusting lead in municipal waste incinerators (even if emissions are tightly controlled) leaves ash, which can present risks for workers nd perhaps the environment. Drinking water provides another example of the omplexity of eliminating lead contamination. Lead can be removed from drinking vater, but that does not solve the largest portion of the drinking water problem, vhich is attributable to old lead service pipes, to lead fittings, fixtures, and solder hat contaminate water after it leaves the public water works.[18]

Federal agencies have continued to assess current lead uses and exposures nder various statutory authorities. A 1992 federal statute addressing lead-based •aint (see below) channeled much of EPA's resources and efforts toward this xposure route. In-place lead is clearly the largest source of risk, and abatement onstitutes a major focus of federal attention. The federal government has a clear ole in assessment of the problem and evaluation of abatement techniques, efficacy, nd costs. The federal effort is oriented toward evaluation, technology assessment, ducation, and training, rather than conducting actual abatements (aside from a few •ilot cleanup efforts). Federal agencies are not anxious to take on a massive batement program. EPA's experience with asbestos removal demonstrated the erious problems inherent in a federally managed abatement program. State or local ction would probably be more efficient and effective than a federal mplementation program.[19] Close coordination between technical and public health xperts on the federal and local levels is essential to the success of any large-scale ead abatement program, particularly given the potential dangers posed by abatement activities. EPA is supporting a decentralized approach with a grant •rogram to states.

Integration of the Lead Strategy: The Players

Controlling unacceptable lead risks crosses not only internal EPA media •oundaries, but also involves other agencies' areas of responsibilities and •xpertise. In fiscal year 1991 (FY91), the three key agencies—EPA, and the)epartments of Housing and Urban Development (HUD) and Health and Human Services (HHS)—were all working on their own strategies. They were drafted ndependently, though there was some staff-to-staff review and communication, ind they did not agree in all important points.[20] They did, however, agree that lead ixposures continue to present risks that should be addressed and that children are •articularly vulnerable. OMB's role should be mentioned in this context. Before egulatory agencies can publish important policy documents, they must be eviewed by OMB. OMB tries to assure cost-effective, compatible, nonduplicative •rograms across the federal government. In the case of lead, OMB understandably ias had a keen interest, because of the huge costs associated with abatement and urisdictional overlaps. Any rule-making developed by EPA or other federal igencies is also reviewed by OMB. (OMB has its own views, which it presses on)ther agencies in the review process.) Although CDC (which is part of HHS) is a ionregulatory agency and might publish a strategy without OMB approval, igencies require the support of the White House budget office to implement •rograms. An integrated federal approach clearly must take OMB into account, as ts concerns can delay, redirect, or even dismantle federal agency plans.

As the strategies evolved, jurisdictional issues became obvious. In some cases there are overlapping jurisdictions, in some cases one agency is given exclusive authority, and in others no agency has clear responsibility. Lead in food cans or cosmetics and probably chinaware, for example, is the sole responsibility of FDA. CPSC has jurisdiction over consumer products, but EPA may also regulate them.[21] EPA has responsibility for controlling industrial emissions to air, water, and soil, including disposal and incineration; for setting drinking water standards, and for assessing many uses, from printing inks to lead fishing sinkers to storage batteries, not covered by other agencies. CDC has expertise and experience in areas such as blood lead screening and laboratory accreditation. The National Institute for Standards and Testing (NIST, formerly the Bureau of Standards, Department of Commerce) usually evaluates techniques and technologies for measuring lead levels and instruments used in abatement, though EPA has been involved in some of these activities too. The Occupational Safety and Health Administration (OSHA) has joined the effort to oversee worker protection issues. The military, the Army in particular, is actively engaged in these issues, as they manage many buildings, including housing and other family facilities contaminated with lead paint. Abatement requirements for buildings and soil pose significant technical, management, and budget challenges, especially if contaminated materials must be disposed of as hazardous waste. Each of these agencies has somewhat different perspectives and goals, and undoubtedly has something to win or lose depending upon what lead policy is established by the federal government.

For some major aspects of the problem, such as cleanup of urban soils or houses, no agency has wanted to claim jurisdiction. Congress gave HUD the authority and responsibility to address *public* housing contaminated with lead-based paint about twenty-five years ago (in the 1971 Lead-Based Paint Poisoning Prevention Act). HUD was later charged with developing a "comprehensive and workable plan" for abating contamination in private housing as well. Congress charged EPA (in 1988) with providing technical assistance to HUD.[22] These responsibilities entail assessment and planning, not necessarily implementation. By 1992, HUD had not been able to resolve evaluation and planning issues associated with how best to abate public housing, and the private housing stock presented even greater costs and challenges. As noted earlier, lead-based paint abatement is confounded with soil cleanup issues in urban housing. No agency was anxious to own this set of problems. In 1992, Congress gave EPA primary responsibility (under the Residential Lead-Based Paint Hazard Reduction Act of 1992, known as Title X of TSCA) for lead paint abatement in private housing. This statute, administered by OPPT, highlights the need to clarify soil contamination issues for abatement sites. Within EPA, the Superfund program sets soil concentration standards to guide cleanups of hazardous waste sites. After years of delay they set guidelines for lead and now plan to set regulatory (i.e., required) limits after 1995. But OPPT needs to address paint abatement issues specifically, and is therefore developing lead soil standards under TSCA—which might well differ from the Superfund soil standards for lead.

The need for coordination goes beyond the executive branch. Congress has shown a strong interest in the lead problem, especially in the early 1990s, as demonstrated by numerous congressional hearings and the introduction of several lead bills (in both Houses) during this time. Mandating a single-chemical approach by statute will not necessarily solve integration problems, however. Several versions of draft legislation included specific, narrowly defined requirements, so that the agency would have to act even if it found that the requirements had the wrong risk priority, set impossible deadlines for action, or vested responsibility in the wrong agency (exacerbating the overlaps and potential conflicts). When detailed policy is set by Congress, not an agency, some solutions are bound to be unworkable. If Congress sets clear general policy goals, a politically accountable regulatory agency, with its technical capabilities, is better equipped than Congress to develop detailed policy.

Early versions of the major bill (sponsored by Senator Reid) in 1990–1991 contained impossible deadlines and allocated some responsibilities to EPA that could best be handled elsewhere. Hill staff conferred with various interests, however, and modified many of these provisions toward a more feasible set of requirements, including reassigning responsibilities to agencies with the corresponding expertise. Competition among congressional committees for oversight authority in the early 1990s threatened to complicate integration efforts even further, particularly given the visibility and appeal of reducing lead exposures to children. On the other hand, congressional action can provide clear directives, and legislative deadlines create a powerful incentive to force resolution of substantive issues, jurisdictional struggles, and technical problems that otherwise would cause long delays. After much discussion among players, and lobbying from various interests, legislation did emerge (Title X of TSCA), but it was far narrower in scope than Reid's bill.

Federal agencies have tried to coordinate research with the private sector as well. The lead industry in particular, but also paints and coatings companies, have been intensely interested in federal government lead policies, and in finding efficient ways to address in-placed lead contamination (and adverse attention on their companies). Lead mining and smelting industries have been very active, and have influenced such important issues as how to treat/handle smelter slag and whether there should be mandatory battery recycling. A large and vocal set of nonindustry private sector organizations also joined the debate. This is a topic that stirs passions, particularly since small children are the primary victims of poisoning. The medical profession has taken uncommon interest in lead as a health hazard. Unions are concerned about worker exposures. The research community, both inside and outside government, has its own agenda, which does not always coincide with that of federal policymakers. National environmental organizations have been active; many local organizations around the country, and the media, are also watching these issues.

Integration by the federal government across all of these arenas is very important—but insufficient for effective policymaking regarding lead. Many state and local authorities already have programs that should be taken into account by federal policy. Several of states have adopted legislation to address lead poisoning issues, though many are awaiting EPA regulations under Title X. Local authorities, public health and housing officials especially, have a stake in decisions about the national program. The scope and nature of the problem (that is, primarily abatement) make it clear that solutions must be chosen and implemented primarily at the local level. Policies and programs at the federal (and even international) level can be important as a context for state and local action.

The rest of the chapter is devoted to considering how EPA has attempted to manage its lead activities within the context of other federal agencies' efforts, OMB policy, congressional activities, state and local programs and needs, and industry and other private sector interests. Reference to international coordination is addressed here too, to shed additional light on the difficulty of shaping a holistic approach to complex environmental issues.

National Integration Activities

Before EPA gained increased responsibility for lead under Title X, it already had a significant role, not only in supporting HUD, but also in a number of other activities to reduce lead risks. EPA regulates lead under several separate statutes. Aside from past controls on leaded gasoline, the two most significant regulations are National Ambient Air Quality Standards (NAAQS) under the Clean Air Act, and a Maximum Contaminant Level for lead in drinking water under the Safe Drinking Water Act.[23]

At the start of the integration efforts in 1989, under the guidance of EPA's Deputy Administrator Habicht, EPA began making an unprecedented effort to integrate and coordinate lead planning across its various offices and statutes. EPA's managers were aware that only a cross-media approach would produce a workable and reasonable program for reducing risks from current and future uses of lead. Two EPA lead advisory panels urged an integrated approach, to guarantee a comprehensive and consistent program.[24] The need for integrated planning across government sectors was particularly obvious for remedial activities. Continuing personal interest and commitment by EPA's former administrator and deputy administrator to fashioning a lead strategy and to the success of the cluster concept helped keep the initiative on track. Thus, the efforts expended in 1989–1992 to build coordination and cross-media perspectives laid a good foundation for Title X responsibilities.

As a practical and managerial matter, how did EPA go about fashioning an integrated policy? The deputy administrator designated a single office (the Office of Pesticides, Prevention and Toxic Substances, OPPTS) and one senior manager (the Deputy Assistant Administrator of OPPTS) as overall coordinator for the Lead Strategy. Actual management responsibility resided with the Office of Pollution Prevention and Toxics (OPPT), under OPPTS. OPPT formed an agency-wide workgroup that met regularly for over a year to: (1) develop an EPA strategy, (2) keep all interested offices informed of lead activities across EPA and in other agencies, and (3) identify and resolve (or elevate) issues of policy, timing, etcetera. Research is an important component for setting priority and selecting methods. One of the accomplishments of the lead cluster workgroup was the creation of an agency-wide research plan in 1991 (still operational in 1995), an unprecedented agreement among programs and with the Office of Research and Development on a research agenda for lead. The expectation was that this process would yield research results to help regulatory and implementation decisions.

Aside from the umbrella workgroup, a number of other, functionally autonomous workgroups continued, or began working on specific projects. Each workgroup was set up and chaired by the office administering the particular statute under discussion. For the cluster to operate, the system has depended upon overlapping workgroup membership to link issues and guarantee communication. The expertise required for different activities has varied; individuals do not have the expertise or time to participate in all activities, and thus linkage has not been perfect.

As overall project manager, OPPT expended considerable time and effort trying to keep informed of significant issues and projects. Under Habicht, OPPT set up periodic meetings and mailings as well as the umbrella workgroup to inform other offices. OPPT held quarterly meetings with Habicht to report on project status, seek policy directives, and solicit help in resolving major problems, especially issues with outside agencies. The Browner administration has continued the efforts for an integrated lead program. (Browner's commitment to integration is also evidenced in the Common Sense Initiative, a cross-programmatic, multimedia initiative in six industrial sectors.) Program office coordination continues, but with fewer meetings and much less oversight by top level managers. EPA's administrator and deputy have had little direct engagement on lead cross-office issues. The optimistic interpretation is that little high-level intervention is now needed, because patterns have been established. But, more important to long-term integration, offices have now created channels of communication and a habit of staff cooperation. One can conclude that coordination is occurring and senior management no longer needs to intervene to guarantee it. It should also be noted that several of the major rule-making activities in other EPA offices were completed or dropped, and therefore the stakes are considerably reduced for those players. In that sense, the good news is not entirely conclusive.

In addition to organizational and managerial mechanisms for integration, EPA has pursued substantive approaches. The complexity, technical difficulty, and expense of lowering blood lead levels pushes the agency to use risk as an integrative principle. When faced with such a complicated, multi-faceted problem—one calling for abatement as well as control of current production and/ or uses, and a means of preventing future uses that might prove too risky—the most prudent public policy is to address the worst (and fixable) risks first. That the preponderant threat comes from historic depositions, and that formidable technical issues and the costs are associated with their removal, emphasizes the need for determining what is doable and fashioning a strategy based on reducing the largest risks first. Risk can act as an integrating factor by encouraging the agency to sort out and set priorities across media, and between current and historic uses; it can help align federal agencies around a set of goals and objectives, including implementation issues.

Yet another factor for targeting agency action has been to focus on geographic areas of high risk.[25] Neither EPA nor other federal agencies can deal effectively with all of these problems and issues at the same time. Even though there seems to be general agreement on what the biggest problems are (old housing in urban areas, with poor and minority areas at greatest risk; old water distribution systems and/or solder in some areas), it is far from clear how to address them. And there is not consensus on how broad the problem is. Remedial action presents a huge area of uncertainty, regarding how much in-place paint and soil should be removed, how to establish criteria for case-by-case judgments, and how quickly the government can proceed, given current knowledge. But some high-risk areas require special assistance under virtually any approach. EPA has worked on methods to identify "hot spots" to help all levels of government focus their implementation activities. More refinement of these tools is needed to target action.

With the enactment of Title X, OPPT had to focus its attention to meeting tight deadlines for addressing the highest risk lead exposures—in other words, those from lead-based paint and dust. EPA is charged to work with HUD, CPSC, CDC, NIOSH (National Institute of Occupational Safety and Health), OSHA, HHS, and NIEHS (National Institute of Environmental Health and Safety). EPA's most significant new responsibilities were that it must: promulgate rules identifying lead-based paint hazards and contamination levels for lead in soil and dust; promulgate a rule on disclosure of lead-based paint hazards during real estate transactions; develop training and certification programs for workers; develop certification programs for laboratories; and establish state program requirements. Based on a current study, worker training may be expanded to cover a greater variety of renovation and remodeling workers. A task force convened to consider ways to influence financial institutions (lenders, insurers) to increase pressures for lead abatement, and issued a report on its findings. The principal agencies have accomplished a high level of interaction, joint planning, and program cooperation. One manifestation is a jointly funded lead hotline to provide the public with a broad range of information about lead issues and about government programs. EPA has also initiated a grant program to help states implement their own lead abatement programs.

Title X differed from several earlier congressional bills on lead in that it has a narrower focus, and the jurisdictional lines it created did not add to the confusion regarding roles and expertise within the federal government. Responsibilities under Title X built on existing cooperative arrangements, especially the inter-agency task force that had been meeting for years to address lead-based paint abatement. The act did establish tight deadlines, and EPA has not met those deadlines. By the end of 1995, EPA expects to complete rule-making on training and certification of lead paint abatement workers, on the real estate disclosure requirements, and on requirements for prerenovation notification. Final lead hazard standards, including levels for paint in soil and dust, are projected for 1997.

As noted earlier, EPA has already issues Superfund guidelines suggesting a tiered approach for evaluating lead in soil.

As a ground-breaking effort, the Lead Strategy cluster has been a qualified success. Though progress has been slow, coordination and cooperation across agency turf lines has improved over the past several years. Inter-agency coordination has also proved rather successful. Those who have taken part are hopeful that a cultural change is gradually beginning that will provide a basis for additional cross-media planning in the future.

INTERNATIONAL ASPECTS OF INTEGRATION

Greater integration of environmental policy would also provide benefits for addressing many problems across borders. The cultural, legal, political, practical, and bureaucratic barriers that bedevil integration efforts in the United States are mirrored at the international level. But since there is no authority to force individual players to act against their real or perceived interests, at the international levels even more than domestically, persuasion is a critical component. Coordination appears to be feasible for some range of issues, and cooperative efforts for chemical management have increased over the past several years. But genuine integration requires a commitment that goes beyond the current political will of nation states. Given the very different kinds of exposures in different countries, and their relative importance, and more importantly, the diverse ways in which risk is perceived in various cultures, integrated environmental management might be a reasonable goal only for limited, critical circumstances. Enhanced coordination, including more systematic sharing of data, might be the appropriate international goal in most cases.

EPA has participated in several international environmental efforts over the past decade. The Montreal Protocol to phase out CFC use is one example of successful coordination, where states agreed to accept limitations that made sense only if policies were linked to provide guarantees and some equity of burden. In this case there was widespread (though not universal) belief that the stakes are very high. This conviction helped negotiators press for an agreement.

Other chemicals in commerce do not pose the urgent need felt with CFC reduction. There is nonetheless a growing awareness that real benefits can result from cooperative efforts. Harmonizing risk reduction programs for existing chemicals is an attractive goal, in that chemicals are marketed across national borders. Some chemicals are highly mobile in the environment, and testing chemicals is both time-consuming and expensive. OPPT is participating in a program with OECD nations to reach consensus on the hazard of some chemicals in commerce, and also to agree on how to define minimum data requirements for screening chemicals (screening information data set, or SIDS). OECD nations are seeking better agreement on chemical testing principles, so that test results might be shared and the costs can be distributed.

Scientists often disagree on how to define chemical toxicity. Thus, the effort to build consensus in the international arena has been quite complicated. And agreeing on the toxicity of a chemical or pollutant in no way guarantees integrated policies. Nations often differ substantially on how to deal with a chemical, even based on a similar evaluation of its toxicity. Risks can differ dramatically depending upon the volumes to which people and the environment are exposed, and how a chemical is produced, used, or stored. Since use and exposure patterns vary, one should not expect nations to have similar priorities or choose the same risk management solutions. Further, chemical controls depend upon the economic importance of the chemical, and the feasibility of substitution. Perceptions of "risk" differ, and what is unacceptable in one country might be acceptable in another. Finally, the time horizons nations use for assessing risk are not uniform. Policy based only on current evidence of risks can differ radically from policy based on long-term considerations, including eventual leaching of pollutants into the ecosystem. All of these factors push in the direction of disparate rather than integrated policies.

In 1990s, the Council of the OECD adopted a Decision-Recommendation on the Cooperative Investigation and Risk Reduction of Existing Chemicals. The focus was human health and environmental risk reduction among member nations. OECD intended that nations share strategies, and that in cooperating and facilitating harmonization of programs, technical barriers to trade might also be prevented. Comparative analyses and the exchange of information about risk reduction strategies might facilitate cooperation and provide the foundation for more consistent programs across borders, which would be mutually beneficial.[26]

As EPA was struggling to write its multimedia strategy for lead risk reduction, coordinating with the many other U.S. government players, OECD nations decided to address lead risks. Lead was one of five chemicals chosen by member countries in 1991 for an initial pilot project on cooperative risk reduction. The United States took a prominent role in providing information. Canada, Australia and Germany joined with the United States to form an OECD clearing house to collect additional information from member countries and their industries. These countries produced a monograph based on the information gathered.

The attempt to form consensus is a long process, involving many rounds of discussion and review. After several years, OECD nations have identified areas of mutual concern. During this time, OECD was able to take advantage of information provided by individual member countries and by other international bodies addressing lead toxicity: at the May 1994 meeting of the U.N. Commission on Sustainable Development, governments reached decisions and recommendations on human health impacts from lead exposure and urged further reduction efforts; also in 1994, international experts for the International Programme on Chemical Safety developed a risk assessment on lead.[27]

OECD member nations agree that lead is highly toxic, especially to infants and small children, that it has widespread uses, and is persistent in the environment. Even with substantial agreement on toxicity and most of the uses/exposures of primary concern, member nations differ on what to target, or how. Another issue to resolve is the specificity and degree of commitment sought. In the case of lead, if OECD can reach a consensus beyond the general intention to reduce lead risks, nations are most likely to agree that methods for addressing exposures of concern should be left up to each nation. Each state would then decide whether to pursue voluntary or required approaches, or some mixture of policy alternatives, depending upon national circumstances.

In 1993, OECD published a report, "Risk Reduction Monograph No. 1: Lead." Ten nations offered statements, to reflect their overall sense of the lead problem.[28] More than a dozen countries provided information for the report. The purpose of this report was to: summarize information regarding releases of lead to the environment, and the associated environmental and human exposures and perceived risks; describe actions taken or intended to reduce risks, and identify the risk reduction benefits sought. Because of its harmful effects to both human health and the environment, and its ability to bioaccumulate, Norway, Sweden, and Denmark support a broad lead phase out, starting with applications resulting in the most dangerous exposures and those for which there are already known substitutes. These nations define the goal as eliminating lead uses. They reason that, since lead persists and remains toxic in the environment, loadings should minimized. Even though exposures and therefore risks are not currently demonstrable from all lead uses, lead products will eventually end in waste and thereby will be dispersed in the environment.[29]

Most nations focus on human health problems, and particularly on known exposure routes resulting in risk. Their stated goal is not to phase out all uses of lead, or necessarily to reduce the amount of lead used in products, but to reduce exposures to lead and to reduce risks, as measured in blood lead levels. They agree that *some* lead products, processes, and uses can and should be replaced or controlled to provide adequate human health protection. Nations do not all define the same blood lead levels as indicative of risk, or requiring intervention. Among those nations that focus on reducing or eliminating known risks, there is significant diversity, not only because they define levels of concern differently, but also because the principal routes of exposure differ from country to country. In the United States, for example, most exposures of concern arise from past uses of lead; safe containment or abatement is therefore the biggest issue. In other nations, current uses (such as leaded gasoline) or production facilities are very significant sources of exposure.

The diversity of problems and the relative efficacy of proposed solutions is illustrated by Mexico's position. Mexico recognizes that it has a significant problem with lead toxicity and it has participated in OECD's lead project. Mexico has noted that lead paint (eliminated by 1938 in Mexico) is not as large a problem for them as it is in other OECD member countries; lead glazed pottery is a significant source of exposure. Mexico will not simply eliminate these glazes, however. Pottery production is a traditional activity closely linked to the Indian cultures that Mexico's government wants to protect and preserve. Because pottery production is scattered, it would be difficult to control through government action in any case. And pottery is a source of income and employment for very poor sectors of the society. Mexico must design a policy that meets these cultural and economic objectives while diminishing risks from lead glazes.

In 1995, Mexican officials supported a voluntary action plan by the lead industry, but later decided to support the idea of an OECD Council Act to formalize the commitment of states to take. In a highly industrialized country like the United States, a voluntary program for highly toxic sources might be criticized as too slow or not fully effective in protecting human health. In Mexico, on the contrary, a voluntary program might look more efficient and effective in that it can bring immediate reductions. Aside from the time it takes to put regulations into effect, in developing countries circumstances such as a lack of enforcement capacity, corruption, poor access to technologies, and insufficient education and training can diminish regulatory effectiveness. Voluntary programs, according to some, have proved useful in Mexico.[30] The effectiveness of such programs is, of course, subject to debate. The willingness of states to depend primarily on industry initiatives, whether for political or practical reasons, clearly varies.

Further, there are still debates about exposure routes. Some take the position that the evidence of exposure from certain uses is insufficient and caution that those uses should not be "over controlled."[31] These controversies often stalemate public policy decisions within nations, and similarly affect consensus on the international level. Environmental effects are particularly controversial. The adverse effects of lead shot are not universally recognized as unacceptable, for example. The efficacy of lead in some products makes it very difficult to ban lead in those uses, particularly if human exposure is not a direct concern. The attempt to ban lead fishing sinkers has met widespread opposition within the United States.

Nations are aware of the economic impacts of banning lead uses. Lead has very desirable qualities for which substitutes are not always readily available. And substitutes can be more expensive, which can result in public resistance to banning a product (lead sinkers, for example). Nations producing lead-containing commodities must balance their policy position with concerns about losing markets; banning lead uses could disadvantage a supplier nation if other producers do not follow the same policy. Another important element is the power of the lead industry in some nations. The lead industry has been quite effective in convincing nations to focus concern on specific sources with known exposures rather than lead production in general. In many cases exposures arise from past uses rather than current lead uses. Second, primary uses of concern are those associated with human health risks more than environmental loadings. The focus on current human exposures considerably narrows the likelihood that nations will attempt to curtail the lead industry.

Crafting international lead policies is complicated by many of the same factors that make it difficult to pursue a unified national policy. Each nation has multiple sectors involved (various industries, health care professionals, consumers and environmental activists as well as government), and also various agencies or bureaus with a stake in how policy is formulated and which bureaucratic elements assume leadership. Coordinating issues and policies among the many players is difficult at best; when interests are in conflict, it may be impossible. Without a coherent domestic policy, any nation's position at an international forum such as OECD is likely to be fragmentary.

The international arena introduces yet another layer of complications and players (foreign affairs experts, international trade groups and interest groups, for example) that must be included in policy development.[32] In the OECD, consensus and mutual interest form the basis for policy. Where there is no authoritative voice, the lowest common denominator usually forms the basis for international action.

Nations clearly have different interests at stake. Supplier nations have different concerns from consumers; nations might not have the wealth or technical capability to abandon lead in some products, and targets for risk reduction will depend not only on exposure but on the cost and difficulty of reducing those exposures; as in the case of Mexican pottery, cultural goals can also affect policy alternatives. As nations negotiate their positions and attempt to reach common ground, each will be aware that commitments or statements of principle regarding risk reduction will differentially affect industries and consumers in the various member countries. Beliefs (or suspicions) regarding the true motives of other nations also plays a role in international agreements.

During 1995, a draft OECD document offered by the United States and the European Commission proposed a goal of minimizing exposures, and emphasized the importance of reducing exposures to children and women of childbearing age. It targeted several sources for reductions: phasedown of lead in gasoline; virtual elimination of exposures to lead in children's products and from solder, caps, or coated sheets in food or beverage containers; reducing exposure in paints; restricting exposure from ceramic ware or crystal, or from drinking water systems; and restricting workplace exposures. Several preventive principles were also proposed in the document, such as preventing exposures during abatement activities and maximizing recycling of lead products.

The draft embraced elements to encourage international consensus. Members can endorse a very flexible approach to risk management, which allows individual states to set priorities, policies, and programs. Thus, risk reduction may rely on either standard-setting or voluntary approaches. Some time frame might be defined to report back on plans or progress, but the agreement would probably avoid specific commitments. If member states cannot forge agreement on these general targets and principles, compromises may satisfy specified concerns. In an earlier 1995 draft, Australia noted concern that the proposal was "driven by the lead substitution principle," and did not allow for country tailoring of the program.[33] Versions later in 1995 seem to have addressed those concerns. Some participants might withhold concurrence unless certain items are removed from the proposed list of risk reduction targets. Or, OECD might specifically endorse cost-benefit analysis as a basis for action, which would tend to delay action against lead without evidence of actual harm. Member nations might share models for assessment, but it would be surprising if OECD reached consensus on a model or models for conducting assessments. If nations cannot compromise differences, OECD might be left with only the general intention to pursue risk reduction and to share information.

What form should an agreement take? How authoritative should the agreements be (that is, what kind of pronouncement is made and by whom)? The areas of substantial agreement have been stymied by the unwillingness of a couple of nations to formalize the agreement at the highest OECD level, with a council act. A council act is the most authoritative kind of pronouncement OECD makes. That is, completely separate from the policies countries are willing to endorse is the question of how the OECD consensus should be articulated. A council act, which would indicate a strong policy and dedication to lead risk reduction, gained the support of most member nations in 1995. But others insisted on something less formal, less prescriptive and not including real commitments. Voices of strong opposition do not want OECD to set this kind of precedent. Still others support a council statement, but believe it is appropriate only for the transboundary issues.

A single dissenting voice in OECD might be persuaded to join the consensus, or abstain. But two or more dissenting votes can block action. As a result, as of late 1995, there was a serious breakdown of the OECD risk reduction process for lead. The principal players were considering their options and possible approaches to bring about consensus. The United States has made clear that it wants an agreement embedded in a council act. Another OECD meeting, planned for early 1996, might provide a forum for some resolution. The limits of agreement on lead will help define the boundary between coordination and integration for international environmental management.

CONCLUSIONS

Integration can be a frustrating and time-consuming responsibility. It is difficult to gain and keep the resources needed for either domestic or international coordination, upon which any integration effort depends. Integrated approaches can be seen by program managers as requiring unnecessary and self-imposed restraints. Managers fear integration will exacerbate the tension and slowness of the policymaking process by requiring coordination at every step with multiple actors, rather than the typical mode of activity, where a designated program controls the issues, brokering policy differences and often not consulting with other interested parties until very late in the process. But integrated efforts, as noted earlier, have clear benefits, especially domestically: integration encourages clearer and earlier definition of roles, of differences in assumptions or policy approach, and of where the gaps lie.

Over the years, EPA has expended considerable resources pursuing issues only to be stalemated in controversies at the end. Given EPA's experience with issues arising from duplicative activities and with substantive or methodological disagreements, managers should be open to integrative approaches. On both a domestic and an international level, EPA seems to have begun a slow cultural change toward more integrated policymaking.

Domestically, integration might in theory be substantially accomplished through legislative means, by creating a unified environmental statute. Congress might enact a law promoting integrated approaches that avoids the section 9 shortcomings of TSCA, and goes further in emphasizing the cross-media nature of environmental problems. An integrated policy goal has never been set legislatively; indeed, the current fragmented statutory framework often seems to frustrate coordination. Under the current statutory and organizational framework, we have many—sometimes conflicting—goals, many ways of defining problems and alternative solutions, and great difficulty in setting priorities rationally. Having a unified environmental law that takes a multimedia, prevention approach (rather than a single-media, end-of-pipe approach) sounds like a very reasonable and desirable solution; the idea reemerges periodically. In the midst of a severe barrage of criticism of and attacks on EPA in 1995, a former (Republican) administrator endorsed this idea: "The nation needs a new, single, unified environmental statute supervised by a single authorizing committee and a single appropriations committee in each house of Congress. Not the 12 laws and 70 committees we now have." He went on to recognize how difficult this goal seems, but no more "impossible" than the current assignments under which EPA labors.[34]

The prospects for fashioning such a piece of legislation, with all of the various interests involved, is quite small, however. It would require a fundamental shift in current lines of power and influence on Capitol Hill, and between Capitol Hill and outside groups (public and private sector). Expertise and influence built over the years on certain statutes would be jeopardized; similarly, power in EPA would shift. Those who stood to lose might well oppose such a dramatic change. As for the substance of any unified legislation, Congress could not include a level of detail comparable to existing environmental statutes, and Congress is unlikely to write a general statute, leaving vast areas of discretion to EPA. Indeed, the trend over the past ten to fifteen years has been to decrease EPA discretion. Prior to the 1994 congressional elections, the complex power shifts necessary to support a unified environmental statute seemed all but impossible. The dramatic shifts signaled by the 1994 election, and the possibility of additional significant changes in congressional power balances after the 1996 election, makes previously unlikely events more plausible. And the extreme threats against EPA might make that power structure more amenable to radical change as well. Thus it may be that a largely new congressional majority could enact a simplified, integrated environmental statute. But even if old power structures do not stand in the way, other concerns nonetheless make it unlikely. The new congressional representatives are ideologically even more suspicious of EPA than their predecessors. They may well make fundamental changes (many have been suggested since the 1994 election), but there is no indication that they would give greater policy discretion to EPA, as a unified environmental law would require. In short, from both a political and substantive perspective, unified cross-media legislation still seems a distant goal.

Of course, the challenge of integration goes beyond EPA. Even assuming EPA continues to move toward cross-media strategies, the Lead Cluster makes clear that integration across EPA is a necessary but insufficient goal. Cross-government coordination is critical for a number of global issues already at our doorstep. In addition to well-publicized international environmental issues such as acid rain,

CFCs, deforestation of the tropics, and global warming, the United States is attempting to forge coordinated policies in other areas, such as chemical testing and lead controls. Before the United States can take a seat at international meetings to discuss global issues, we need to have a U.S. position; individual U.S. agencies must reach some agreement. As the European Union moves toward greater integration, the economic and political pressure for the United States to coordinate internally, in order to negotiate externally, will increase. Increased communications among agencies on topics of mutual concern, supplemented on an ad hoc basis for emergency issues, might move the federal government closer toward the integrated policy. Federal agencies are groping to establish mechanisms to deal with global environmental issues—where the State Department and other nonenvironmental entities are additional players that must be taken into account. Progress in managing policy development and implementation is slow and piecemeal, but some policy-building processes are emerging.

The international opportunities and needs for integration add another level of complexity. Some issues require international cooperation to prevent or effectively manage them. In other cases (such as chemical testing), efficiency or the equitable sharing of burdens pressures the United States to seek international agreements. The struggle to set a national agenda is a prerequisite to effective international policy, but surely cannot guarantee it. Efforts to negotiate issues among nations have increased and will probably continue to do so, because of greater awareness of both economic and ecological transborder effects. Agenda 21 from the U.N. Conference on Environment and Development (UNCED) in Brazil highlighted the global aspects of environmental protection, which are compelling when viewed over the long term. Integration at the international level proceeds even more slowly and uncertainly. Legislation cannot force progress in this arena, but only collective recognition of the need for better coordination.

The message is clear: integrated environmental management is essential if we are to maintain the environment for sustained, long-term use. Unfortunately we have not yet figured out how to implement this truth in the EPA or national policy processes—and at the same time we are being overtaken by the pressing need for international integration. The responsibility for stewardship of natural resources must be recognized and shared across national boundaries. A small but quickly growing voice is calling for policies that recognize the connections between environmental protection and sustainable economic growth, between environmental protection and national/international security.[35] As the World Commission on Environment and Development report noted:

Until recently, the planet was a large world in which human activities and their effects were neatly compartmentalized within nations, within sectors (energy, agriculture, trade), and within broad areas of concern (environmental, economic, social). These compartments have begun to dissolve. . . . There has been a growing realization in national governments and multilateral institutions that it is impossible to separate economic development issues from environment issues; many forms of development erode the environmental resources upon which they must be based, and environmental degradation can undermine economic development. . . . The next few decades are crucial. The time has come to break out of past patterns. Attempts to maintain social and ecological stability through old approaches to development and environmental protection will increase instability.[36]

Clearly, we have much to do.

NOTES

1. One writer notes that the benefits of integrated environmental management "are so evident, after even the most superficial examination, that one wonders why implementation appears so difficult. The more obvious benefits are: (1) Long-term protection of the resource; (2) Enhanced potential for nondelecterious multiple use; (3) Reduced expenditure of energy and money on conflicts over competing uses and the possibility of redirecting these energies and funds to environmental management; (4) More rapid and effective rehabilitation of damaged ecosystems to a more usable condition (more ecosystem services provided); (5) Cost effectiveness." See John Cairns, Jr., "The Need for Integrated Environmental Systems Management," in John Cairns, Jr. and Todd V. Crawford, eds., *Integrated Environmental Management* (Chelsea, MI: Lewis Publishers, Inc., 1991), p. 5. Despite his view that the issue is very obvious, in a later chapter, the author expresses a great deal of pessimism about the near-term prospects for integration: "I fear that enormous irreparable environmental destruction will be required for the development of the necessary social and political will. Multiple catastrophes may have to occur on a global scale to motivate the politicians and general public. [H]istory indicates that no substantive action will be taken until the crisis is unmistakable to even the most unobservant people." Cairns, "Future Needs," *Integrated Environmental Management*, p. 184.

2. Cairns, for example, offers the definition "proactive or preventive measures that maintain the environment in good condition for a variety of long-range sustainable uses." *Integrated Environmental Management*, p. 5. Others focus on means or elements of integration. Integration might be achieved through using clear risk criteria or risk reduction strategies. These ideas have been widely discussed, and are the topic of several major EPA reports since 1987: "Unfinished Business: A Comparative Assessment of Environmental Problems, Overview Report" (Washington: U.S.EPA, February 1987); and EPA's Science Advisory Board Reports, "Future Risk: Research Strategies for the 1990s" (Washington, DC: U.S. EPA, September 1988), and "Reducing Risk: Setting Priorities and Strategies for Environmental Protection" (Washington, DC: U.S. EPA, September 1990). For discussion of risk as an integrator, see Milton Russell, "Integrated Environmental Management," *Journal of the Air Pollution Control Association*, 36(4) (April 1986): 361–363; and Daniel J. Fiorino, "Can Problems Shape Priorities? The case of Risk-Based Environmental Planning," *Public Administration Review*, 50 (January/February 1990): 82–90.

3. TSCA 6(a) is thought to contain the broadest authority. It gives EPA authority from requiring public notice and labeling, to record-keeping; to prohibiting or limiting manufacture, processing, distribution, or certain uses; to controlling disposal, "[i]f the Administrator finds that there is reasonable basis to conclude the manufacture, processing, distribution in commerce, use or disposal of a chemical. . . . presents or will present an unreasonable risk."

4. For a strong indictment of TSCA implementation, see Cynthia Ruggerio, "Referral of Toxic Chemical Regulation under the Toxic Substances Control Act: EPA's Administrative Dumping Ground," *Boston College Environmental Affairs Law Review*, 17(1) (Fall 1989): 75–122. See also, "What Ever Happened to the Toxic Substances Control

Act?" Hearing Before House Environment, Energy and Natural Resources Subcommittee of the Committee on Government Operations, October 3, 1988 (Washington, DC: U.S. Government Printing Office, 1989). Terry Davies, who has been active in environmental policy and a force behind the TSCA, as well as a scholarly observer, has noted that the TSCA's promise has not been fulfilled; Gary G. Rabe, *New Perspectives On Pollution Control: Cross-Media Problems* (Washington, DC: Conservation Foundation, 1985), p. 2.

5. Section 9 orders EPA to consider other existing statutory authorities (inside or outside EPA) and defer to those other authorities if "in the Administrator's discretion" the risk "may be prevented or reduced to a sufficient extent by action taken under a Federal Law not administered by the Administrator" (section 9(a)) or by actions taken under other EPA authorities (section 9(b)). In addition to formal referral under section 9(a), section 9(d) calls for consultation with other relevant federal agencies. Under the Reagan administration, EPA took a very conservative view of its discretionary authority, interpreting section 9(a) as compelling referral in most cases for chemicals covered by other statutes. See, for example, "An Evaluation of EPA's Use of Referrals under TSCA Section 9," a 1990 report by The Cadmus Group, Inc., for EPA; and Memorandum from Gerald Yamada, EPA Acting General Counsel, to Lee Thomas, EPA Administrator, "Section 9(a) of the Toxic Substances Control Act," June 7, 1985.

6. According to Terry Davies, the White House and most influential members of Congress agreed that TSCA should only be a "gap filler." He sees the section 9 referral language as a very strong limit on EPA authority under TSCA. See "The United States: Experiment and Fragmentation," in Nigel Haigh and Frances Irwin, eds., *Integrated Pollution Control in Europe and North America* (Washington:, DC Conservation Foundation, 1990), p. 55. In Ruggerio's view, "Although section 9 was intended to prevent jurisdictional overlap and inefficient use of administrative resources, it has instead become an escape hatch for the EPA to avoid regulatory responsibility." "Referral," p. 77.

7. *Corrosion Proof Fitting* v *US EPA*, 947 F.2d 1201 (5th Cir. 1991).

8. In considering the nature of OPPT's attempt to provide leadership under TSCA for *internal* EPA integration, Jurgen Schmandt appropriately noted that, after early analytic efforts, nothing happened. OPPT "instead of leading program integration, became preoccupied with the TSCA-mandated control of new chemicals, and assigned low priority to the integrated toxic program." See Jurgen Schmandt, "Managing Comprehensive Rule Making: EPA's Plan for Integrated Environmental Management," *Public Administration Review*, 45(2) (March/April 1985): 309–318. Failure to bring about cross-program integration under TSCA was not due solely to OPPT motivations and priorities, of course. Other people and organizations had a stake in this issue and certainly influenced the outcome. Aside from these dynamics, there are other reasons why organizations do not embark on changes easily. Reorganizing work units in the name of rationality and efficiency might create unforeseen problems, including the disruption of good work teams. See Neil S. Grigg, "Is Integrated Environmental Management Feasible?" *Journal of Professional Issues in Engineering*, 109(2) (April 1983): 71–80.

9. It should be noted that actions under TSCA have not been the only integration efforts. There have been R&D efforts; EPA has worked on integrated assessment of some industries (e.g., see Timothy M. Barry, "Integrated Environmental Management: A Pilot Study of the Pulp and Paper Industry," *UNEP Industry and Environment*, [April/May/June 1987]: 29–34; EPA conducted a multiyear, multicity study of air toxics (see Craig S. Koralek et al., "Area Sources and Toxic Pollution: A Method For Estimating and Distributing Emissions Within a Geographic Area," presented a the 78th Annual Meeting of the Air Pollution Control Association, June 16–21, 1985).

10. There is an extensive research literature on lead toxicity, particularly regarding effects on children. For a good overview, see Herbert L. Needleman and David Bellinger, "The Health Effects of Low Level Exposure to Lead," *Annual Review of Public Health*, 12 (1991): 111–40. Some other important sources are: Agency for Toxic Substances Disease Registry, "The Nature and Extent of Lead Poisoning in Children in the United States: A Report to Congress" (Atlanta, GA: Public Health Service, U.S. Department of Health and Human Services, July 1988); EPA Office of Air and Radiation, "Air Quality Criteria for Lead and Addendum" (Washington, DC: U.S. EPA, 1986); EPA Office of Air and Radiation, "Review of the National Ambient Air Quality Standards for Lead: Assessment of Scientific and Technical Information," also called "Staff Paper" (Washington, DC: U.S. EPA, September 1989); CASAC Committee of the Science Advisory Board, "Report of the Clean Air Scientific Advisory Committee on Its Review of the National Ambient Air Quality Standards for Lead" Report to EPA's Administrator (Washington, DC: CASAC, Spring 1989); Lynn Goldman, M.D., American Academy of Pediatrics, Testimony on Lead Poisoning, before the U.S. Senate Subcommittee on Toxic Substances, Environmental Oversight, Research and Development of the Committee on Environment and Public Works, June 27, 1990. H. Needleman, "The Persistent Threat of Lead: A Singular Opportunity," *American Journal of Public Health*, 79(5) (May 1989): 643–645; and Herbert L. Needleman, et al., "The Long-Term Effects of Exposure to Low Doses of Lead in Childhood," *New England Journal of Medicine*, 322(2) (January 11, 1990): 83–88.

11. For an analysis of recent data, see D. J. Brody, J. L. Pirkle, R. A. Kramer, K. M. Flegal, T. D. Matte, E. W. Gunter, D. C. Paschal, "Blood Lead Levels in the US Population," *Journal of the American Medical Association (JAMA)*, 272(4) (July 27, 1994): 277–283; and J. L. Pirkle, D. J. Brody, E. W. Gunter, R. A. Kramer, D. C. Paschal, K. M. Flegal, T. D. Matte, "The Decline in Blood Lead Levels in the United States," *JAMA*, 272(4) (July 27, 1994), pp. 284–291.

12. See Session B, "Issue Paper for OECD Workshop on Lead: The Use of Lead Additives in Gasoline," U.S. paper presented at the "OECD Workshop on Lead Products and Uses," September 12–15, 1994, Toronto, Canada. See also, Victor Kimm, Environmental Protection Agency, Testimony before the U.S. Senate Subcommittee on Toxic Substances, Environmental Oversight and Research and Development, March 8, 1990; and EPA Document, "Final Regulatory Impact Analysis: Costs and Benefits of Reducing Lead in Gasoline," February 1985.

13. J. L. Pirkle et al., "The Decline in Blood Lead Levels in the United States," cited above, p. 289.

14. EPA concluded in 1991 that the principal pathways of highest risk are: (1) deteriorated lead-based paint, (2) soil contamination, especially in urban areas, and (3) remaining low-level, widespread exposures—especially in drinking water, largely because of in-place lead in plumbing fixtures and pipes. See EPA's "Strategy for Reducing Lead Exposures," February 1991.

15. CDC established this level of concern in 1984; CDC lowered their definition of blood lead poison level twice in twelve years prior to 1991. In 1991, CDC lowered the number again—to a 4-tier classification with 10 ug/dl as the new level for toxicity.

16. After several partial statutory bans starting in 1971, CPSC took action, banning all leaded paint in housing in 1977. For a brief chronology, see the Environmental Defense Fund (EDF), "Legacy of Lead: America's Continuing Epidemic of Childhood Lead Poisoning," March 1990, pp. 29–30. EDF contrasts U.S. action (starting in 1971) to the Europeans, many of whom banned interior paint in 1921.

17. The CASAC Report noted that "airborne lead serves not only as a source of inhalation exposures, but. . . . deposits on soil and plants becoming a potential source for intake into the body." See CASAC, "Report of the Clean Air Scientific Advisory Committee," cited above, p. 3. The Department of Housing and Urban Development's "Comprehensive and Workable Plan for the Abatement of Lead-Based Paint in Privately Owned Housing: Report to Congress" (Washington, DC: HUD, December 1990) emphasizes the interrelation. Findings in the three-city demonstration project EPA sponsored also make this interrelationship evident (a point made by Dr. Robert Bornschein of the University of Cincinnati in his Testimony before the Senate Subcommittee on Toxic Substances, Environmental Oversight and Research and Development, March 8, 1990). A related, but even vaguer, concern exists regarding the contribution furniture, drapes, rugs, etcetera, make to continued risks after lead-based paint is removed.

18. See *Federal Register* Preamble to EPA's final drinking standard for lead, 56FR26460 (June 7, 1991).

19. EPA's Lead Strategy clearly stated the view that the federal program should not include implementation. Nor has HUD (charged by Congress with assessing lead paint contamination in housing) recommended a massive federal program; see HUD's "Comprehensive and Workable Plan," cited above. Planning remediation (lead-based paint or lead plumbing especially) must take into account the privacy of people's homes. Some of EPA's lead activities, public outreach for drinking water in particular, were designed to stimulate action by others—state and local governments, private industry, and other federal agencies. Further, because local authorities will probably oversee abatement activity, EPA's research strategy has included technology transfer.

20. Because of its broad authority, EPA's was the most comprehensive; see "Strategy for Reducing Lead Exposures," cited above. HUD's "Comprehensive and Workable Plan," cited above, and the Department of Health and Human Services' (HHS) "Strategic Plan for the Elimination of Childhood Lead Poisoning," (Washington, DC: HHS, February 1991) both focus on lead-based paint.

21. Sections 3 and 9 of TSCA draw boundaries for TSCA authority. TSCA section 3 excludes a variety of chemical substances; section 3(2)(B)(vi) clearly excludes "any food, food additive, drug, cosmetic, or device." EPA has found this exclusion to be rather clear and noncontroversial. Section 9, as noted above, has been a continual source of ambiguity and sometimes heated debate.

22. This activity has broad-based federal participation. A task force on lead-based paint, co-chaired by EPA and HUD, includes many agencies. By the late 1980s, HUD was being widely criticized for its slow response, and some sought to move the responsibility away from HUD. For example, EDF's Report, "Legacy of Lead," cited above, referred to HUD's "intransigent failure" and "abysmal" performance; EDF suggested that EPA and HHS have primary roles. Senator Reid's Bill, S.391, would have given EPA overall responsibility for the lead paint abatement program. Authority given to EPA under the Residential Lead-Based Paint Hazard Reduction Act of 1992 was surely in part a response to the general perception that HUD could not be relied upon.

23. After several years of intense controversy, EPA promulgated a revised drinking water standard in June 1991. Work on the revised NAAQS was ongoing for several years; the rule revision was first delayed considerably to devote resources to enforcement of the existing standard (which was expected to yield greater risk reduction), then formally dropped from the schedule in October 1993. Some other lead activities underway in 1991 were: new source performance standards for lead emissions from municipal waste combustors (completed FY91); 2two revisions to the combustor rule underway for Pb, cadmium, and mercury emissions (under and over 250 tons of pollutant/year—which were

combined into a single effort in late 1992 and proposed in 1994); review of the rule for secondary smelters; review (and appropriate revisions) of state implementation plans/ attainment status; controlling corrosivity in drinking water systems, and delivering training programs to protect drinking water supplies; pilot study on urban soil contamination and abatement; TSCA regulatory investigations regarding battery recycling (dropped in September, 1991), lead solder uses (dropped in 1995), brass plumbing fittings (not yet proposed by 1995), nonresidential lead-based paint, and significant new uses (effort focused on fishing sinkers in addition to solder and fittings—and sinkers proposal raised a storm of criticism that stalled action in 1995); an ongoing research program, including studies to evaluate various exposure routes (including soil), bioavailability through various routes, and "low tech" abatement procedures; limiting use and disposal of lead-contaminated sewage sludge; identifying major sources of lead in municipal solid wastes; controlling lead discharges to surface waters; review/cancellation of lead-containing pesticides. These activities were under a variety of EPA authorities. In addition to the Clean Air Act (CAA), Safe Drinking Water Act (SDWA) and TSCA, regulatory authorities include the Clean Water Act (CWA), Resource Conservation and Recovery Act (RCRA), Federal Insecticide, Fungicide and Rodenticide Act (FIFRA), and the Superfund Amendments and Reauthorization Act (SARA).

24. CASAC, "Report of the Clean Air Scientific Advisory Committee," cited above, p. 2; and Joint Study Group on Lead, "Review of Lead Carcinogenicity and EPA Scientific Policy on Lead" (Washington, DC: U.S. EPA, December 1989) p. 2.

25. EPA Senate testimony on June 27, 1990s was that "lead contamination comes from a variety of sources, which tend to be geographically dispersed. Finding workable solutions to the array of geographic problems is therefore difficult; solutions need to track the dispersed, geographical nature of the problem. We must target our efforts to concentrate first on those areas which present the greatest risk to the largest numbers of people." See Kimm's Testimony, cited above, p. 3, and EPA's Lead Strategy.

26. For background information and a fuller description of the OECD Lead Project, see OECD, "Risk Reduction Monograph No. 1: Lead," (Paris: Environment Directorate, OECD, 1993), pp. 9–23.

27. These two sources are referenced in the "US/EU Proposal for a Council Act on Lead Risk Reduction Measures," April 28, 1995, a draft OECD decision-recommendation document. The final document, adopted in February 1996, adopted a similar set of risk reduction measures, but in the form of a Ministerial Declaration rather than an OEC Decision Document. The Ministerial Declaration commits members to act, but is not a binding agreement.

28. Australia, Canada, Denmark, Norway, France, Germany, Sweden, Switzerland, the United Kingdom, and the United States provided national positions. OECD, "Risk Reduction Monograph No. 1: Lead," cited above, Ch. 4.

29. Denmark, Sweden, and Norway all state their goal as phasing out lead uses (Ibid., Ch. 4). In addition to their OECD positions, they have undertaken a joint initiative by signing a Ministerial Declaration of the Third International Conference on the Protection of the North Sea, which includes a commitment to reduce lead emissions by 70 percent by the end of 1995, compared to a 1985 baseline. Through the Baltic Marine Environment Commission Denmark, Finland and Sweden have agreed to reduce lead emissions by 50 percent by the end of 1995, using a 1987 baseline (Ibid., p. 21).

30. This position on the proposal to adopt a Decision Document or a Voluntary Action Plan to reduce lead risks was communicated to EPA from Mexico City (Instituto Nacional de Ecologia Unidad de Proyecios Especiales) in June 1995. The Mexican government's official position at meetings in February 1996 was to support risk reduction activities, but

request technical assistance to meet its national goals. The February 1996 Ministerial Declaration invites industry to develop voluntary programs.

31. Differing assessments of some exposure routes are evident in the papers presented at the 1994 OECD lead workshop. OECD, "OECD Workshop on Lead Products and Uses," September 12–15, 1994, Toronto, Canada.

32. Letter from the Color Pigments Manufacturers Association, Inc. (CPMA), to an EPA official illustrates the complexity. This trade association represents color pigment manufacturers in Canada, Mexico, and the United States, accounting for 95 percent of color pigment production in these three countries, and also foreign pigment manufacturers with sales in these three countries. CPMA has product committees to represent many types of pigment categories, including a Lead Chromate Committee. They wrote to EPA to clarify past uses of lead additives (lead carbonate and lead sulfate) in low-cost residential paint, and distinguish these additives from lead chromate as defined by their industry—though lead chromate pigments have "varying amounts of lead sulfate sealed within the solid crystal composition of the pigment." CPMA urged EPA to edit the proposed OECD language to capture this distinction and specifically NOT phase out lead chromate pigments. CPMA letter from J. Lawrence Robinson, President, to Mr. Bill Hanson, Office of Pollution Prevention and Toxics, U.S. EPA, June 15, 1995.

33. John Crighton, Assistant Secretary, Australian Department of Foreign Affairs & Trace, Letter to Dr. G. del Bino, Directorate General XI, OECD, March 21, 1995.

34. William D. Ruckelshaus, "Stopping the Pendulum," Remarks presented at the Environmental Law Institute, Washington, DC, October 18, 1995.

35. See, for example, the writings of Lynton K. Caldwell, a prophetic voice in this area, *In Defense of Earth* (Bloomington, IN: Indiana University Press, 1972); see also, Lester R. Brown, "Redefining National Security," *Worldwatch Paper 14* (Washington, DC: Worldwatch Institute, 1977). In the late 1980s, as the cold war ended, new attention was directed toward environmental security concepts. Michael Renner, "National Security: The Economic and Environmental Dimensions," *Worldwatch Paper 89* (Washington, DC: Worldwatch Institute, 1989); Jessica Tuchman Mathews: "Redefining Security," *Foreign Affairs*, 68(2) (Spring 1989): 162–177; and Hilary F. French, "Partnership for the Planet: An Environmental Agenda for the United Nations," *Worldwatch Paper 126* (Washington, DC: Worldwatch Institute, 1995). Numerous books and chapters were published in the early 1990s exploring these issues. During the Clinton administration the federal government has acknowledged the linkage between environmental protection and security in several national security documents: Office of Science and Technology Policy, *National Security Science and Technology Strategy* (Washington, DC: OSTP, September 1995); *A National Security Strategy of Engagement and Enlargement* (Washington, DC: U.S. Government Printing Office, July 1994); *National Security Strategy of the United States* (Washington, DC: U.S. Government Printing Office, 1991). DOD has shown considerable interest in how environmental security concerns should affect their policies and strategies. The Wilson Center, part of the Smithsonian Institution, initiated a two-year seminar on environmental security in 1994.

36. World Commission on Environment and Development, "From One Earth to One World: An Overview by the World Commission on Environment and Development," *Our Common Future* (New York: Oxford University Press, 1987), pp. 4, 3, 22.

10

INTERNATIONAL OPINION AT THE CENTURY'S END: PUBLIC ATTITUDES TOWARD ENVIRONMENTAL ISSUES

Riley E. Dunlap

At the end of the twentieth century globalizing trends in commerce, travel, communication, information, and environmental risks have begun to affect popular opinions regarding the environment. Awareness of risks in a changing environment is now appearing in most countries—in less-developed economies as well as in industrialized states. Opinion surveys indicate that environmental trends are becoming transnational and even global issues. Concerns over climate change, stratospheric ozone depletion, acidic precipitation, transportation and disposal of hazardous materials, desertification and degradation of agricultural and grazing land, deforestation, and water supply and quality are appearing in many counties although the particular cause of concern varies among countries, for example, sea-level rise in some island states, desertification in Africa and the Middle East, and air pollution in industrialized countries. Nongovernmental organizations (e.g., IUCN/World Conservation Union) and intergovernmental agencies (e.g., U.N. Environment Programme) have contributed significantly to raising public awareness and concern over environmental change. But concern among the public at large appears to exceed that of their governments. Public officials tend to focus on issues affecting them in the present and near future—for example, issues of defense, taxation, commerce, employment, crime, civil disorder, and economic trends generally. Even so, environmental issues have been growing in number and in salience. Opinion surveys, national legislation, and international agreements confirm the trend.

Analyses of international environmental policymaking have emphasized the roles played by governmental organizations and regimes and other transnational actors such as multinational corporations, scientific bodies, and international environmental organizations (Caldwell, 1984; Haas et al., 1993). Less comprehensive cross-national studies of environmental policymaking have typically focused on the roles of national governments, green parties, and ecological movements (Kamieniecki, 1993). Although both international and cross-national analyses increasingly acknowledge the vital role played by citizens via their participation in nongovernmental organizations (Caldwell, 1992), typically only small percentages of any nation's public belong to environmental NGOs. Thus, there is clearly a need to augment the growing body of information on environmental NGOs active around the world (Fisher, 1993) with data on public perceptions and opinions concerning environmental issues.

Public opinion is widely regarded as a potentially significant factor in the development and implementation of effective environmental policies, for at a minimum supportive public opinion provides a valuable resource within policymaking arenas (Dunlap, 1995; Stern et al., 1995). However, the absence of data from nations outside of Europe and North America has made it impossible to assess public opinion toward environmental issues at anything approximating the international level. In light of the increasingly global nature of environmental problems, and the consequent need for international cooperation to solve them, the time has come to extend our knowledge of the public's view of environmental problems and policies from Europe and the United States to other parts of the world (Dunlap and Scarce, 1991; Hofrichter and Reif, 1990).

Developing effective policies for environmental protection at the international level is inherently difficult, given the varying interests of differing nations and interest groups, but it will be made more so if levels of citizen awareness of environmental problems and support for environmental protection differ dramatically across nations—as is widely assumed to be the case. This chapter addresses this issue by reporting results from a unique survey designed to help fill the existing void in knowledge of international public opinion toward environmental issues. It will pay particular attention to a number of issues relevant to international environmental policymaking.

Conventional wisdom, both among social scientists (e.g., Beckerman, 1974; Inglehart, 1990) and society at large (Elmer-Dewitt, 1992), has long held that concern for the environment is limited primarily to residents of the wealthy industrialized nations, primarily in the Northern Hemisphere, as those who live in the poorer, Southern Hemisphere nations are assumed to be too preoccupied with economic survival to be able to worry about environmental quality. This may have been true back in 1972, when the U.N. Conference on the Human Environment was held in Stockholm, but it seems implausible in the current era of worldwide activism on behalf of the environment (Durning, 1989; Finger, 1992; McCormick, 1989). Yet, it may be that residents of the northern, industrialized nations remain *more* concerned about environmental problems than do those of the less economically developed (and primarily southern) nations.

Conventional wisdom also holds that the perceptions of the roots of the global environmental problematique, and of how it ought to be mitigated, differ dramatically between residents of the wealthy nations and those of the poorer nations (Elmer-Dewitt, 1992). These differences were certainly apparent at the

1992 UN Conference on Environment and Development in Rio de Janeiro, where the governments of poorer nations emphasized the importance of "development" and those of the richer nations that of "environment" (to the neglect of development), and the means of achieving "sustainable development" remained ambiguous (Haas et al., 1992; White, 1992; Vaillancourt, 1993). Did this North-South division at the "Earth Summit" reflect a chasm in perceptions of environmental problems and how they ought to be solved between those who live in rich nations and those who live in poorer nations? If so, the future for international environmental policymaking will prove highly problematic.

To examine possible differences in public perceptions of environmental problems the George H. Gallup International Institute conducted an unprecedented international environmental opinion survey in early 1992. Gallup's "Health of the Planet" (HOP) survey included twenty-four nations covering a wide range of economic levels and geographic regions. Results from the survey allow for an examination of both key elements of conventional wisdom: that public concern over environmental quality is much higher in the richer nations, and that views of the causes and solutions of environmental problems differ dramatically between residents of the rich and poor nations.

After describing the nature of the Gallup survey in more detail, I will summarize briefly the results concerning public perceptions of the seriousness of environmental problems across the nations, focusing on possible differences between wealthy, industrialized and poorer, less-industrialized nations. I will then report in detail the results of the most policy-relevant items in the HOP survey, beginning with the perceived causes of, and solutions for, environmental problems within each nation. Next will come several items dealing with the linkage between environment and development that are highly relevant to debates surrounding sustainable development: the relative responsibility of rich and poor nations for the world's environmental problems; the major contributor to environmental problems within the poorer, developing nations; and the actions that the industrialized nations should take in order to help developing nations protect their environments. Finally, I will examine two items dealing with support for an international environmental agency, a topic of particular relevance in the present context. Taken together, these results should provide crucial insights into points of convergence, and possible divergence, in public opinion toward environmental problems and policies among citizens from a diverse range of countries, including both very wealthy and very poor nations.

INFORMATION ON SURVEY METHODOLOGY

Timed to coincide with preparations for the 1992 Earth Summit in Rio de Janeiro, the HOP survey was coordinated by the George H. Gallup International Institute and conducted by the worldwide network of Gallup affiliates (who donated over $1 million dollars in data collection and tabulation costs). The selection of countries was dependent upon the availability of a Gallup affiliate (or willing partner) and funding and two dozen nations were included (Dunlap et al., 1993a, 1993b). While poorer, less-developed nations are consequently underrepresented, the intent was *not* to conduct a worldwide survey whose results could be generalized to the entire world. Rather, our goal was to survey citizens in a wide range of nations, in terms of both geographic location and level of economic development, and thereby go beyond existing cross-national environmental surveys that have been limited primarily to Europe or North America. We were reasonably successful in this goal, covering a greater number and wider range of nations than have ever been included in an environmental opinion survey.[1] The result is that we can provide the first reasonable test of conventional wisdom concerning North-South, rich-poor variation in public perceptions of environmental issues.

Table 10.1 shows the twenty-four nations that were included in the HOP, classified by levels of national affluence as measured by per capita GNP in 1992 U.S. dollars (World Bank, 1994). European and North American nations are clearly overrepresented, while Asian and especially African nations are underrepresented. Nonetheless, although eleven of the nations fall into the World Bank's "high income" category, the other thirteen include a wide range of "low" to "medium" income nations. Thus, there is sufficient variation to allow for meaningful comparisons between citizens of wealthy and poor nations in terms of their views of environmental and development issues.

The survey covered a wide range of environmental issues that appear to be of relevance to all types of nations, drawing upon extensive reviews of existing studies (e.g., Dunlap and Scarce, 1991). The affiliates were responsible for translating the questionnaire into the appropriate language(s) for their nations, and then the Gallup International Institute had them "back-translated" into English to ensure comparability. The surveys were conducted in early 1992 via face-to-face, in-home interviews (thus minimizing problems of illiteracy) with nationally representative samples in all nations but India. In India rural areas were underrepresented, and thus caution must be used in generalizing the results to the nation as a whole. The sample sizes are shown in Table 10.1, most from about 1,000 to 1,500. Samples in this size range should be accurate within approximately plus or minus three percentage points of the national populations.

PERCEPTIONS OF THE SERIOUSNESS OF
ENVIRONMENTAL PROBLEMS

As noted earlier, it has long been assumed that residents of economically poor nations are not very concerned about the state of the environment because they are confronted with far more pressing problems such as adequate food and shelter. The HOP began with a number of items focusing on the perceived seriousness of environmental problems and personal concern over such problems, and the results were quite surprising. Contrary to conventional wisdom, we found that residents of the poorer nations often express greater concern over the state of the environment

Table 10.1
GNP per Capita and Sample Size by Nation

Country[1]	GNP/capita	Sample size
Low Income		
India	310	4,984
Nigeria	320	1,195
Philippines	770	1,000
Poland	1,910	989
Turkey	1,980	1,000
Russia	2,510	964
Chile	2,730	1,000
Middle Income		
Brazil	2,770	1,414
Hungary	2,970	1,000
Uruguay	3,340	800
Mexico	3,470	1,502
Korea	6,790	1,500
Portugal	7,450	1,000
High Income		
Ireland	12,210	928
Great Britain	17,790	1,105
Netherlands	20,480	1,011
Canada	21,970	1,011
Finland	21,970	770
Germany (West)	23,030	1,048
United States	23,240	1,032
Norway	25,820	991
Denmark	26,000	1,019
Japan	28,190	1,434
Switzerland	36,080	1,011

[1]GNP per capita and income categories are from World Bank (1994).

than do their counterparts in the wealthier nations.[2] These results can be summarized very briefly by reporting Pearson correlation coefficients between national-level (aggregate) scores on the various HOP items and national affluence, as measured by per capita GNP. In each case the attitudinal variables are coded so that a high score reflects public concern about the quality of the environment, and therefore conventional wisdom would predict *positive* correlations between all of the measures and per capita GNP.[3]

Early in the interview we gave respondents a list of six national problems, including environment, and asked them to rate the seriousness of each. Surprisingly, there is a slight (but not statistically significant) negative relationship (r = -.17) between GNP/capita and the rating of environment—meaning that citizens in the poorer nations tend to rate environmental problems as somewhat more serious than do those in the wealthy nations. Of course, residents of poorer nations also rate the other problems—hunger and homelessness, crime and violence, poor health care, high cost of living and racial/ethnic/religious prejudice and discrimination—as more serious than do their counterparts in wealthy nations. Consequently, a measure of the perceived seriousness of environmental problems *relative* to the other problems was positively and significantly related to GNP/capita (r = .70, P < .001). Although one can debate which measure, the absolute or relative rating of the seriousness of environmental problems, is the better indicator of environmental concern, the results for subsequent items are less debatable.

Following the above items and an explanation of exactly what we meant by "environment," respondents were asked to rate the quality of the environment at the community, national and world levels. Residents of the poorer nations are significantly more likely to rate the quality of their community and national environments as "fairly bad" or "very bad" (r = -.58, P < .01 and r = -.63, P < .001, respectively), while residents of the wealthier nations are significantly more likely to rate the world environment negatively (r = .47, P < .05). These results suggest that people in the poorer nations are very aware that their local and even national environments have been seriously degraded, and see them as significantly worse in quality (often appropriately so) than do their counterparts in the wealthy nations.

A similar pattern occurred when we asked respondents to rate the seriousness of six potential local-level environmental problems (e.g., air and water pollution) in their own community and then to do the same for seven worldwide environmental problems such as rainforest destruction and ozone depletion. People in poorer nations rate the community-level problems as far more serious than do those in the wealthier nations (r = -.56, P < .01), but there is virtually no difference in their rating of worldwide environmental problems (r = .07, n.s.). While it might not be surprising that people in poor countries are more likely to see their local air and water as more polluted than do those in wealthy nations, it is quite surprising that the former are about as likely as the latter to see global environmental problems as serious.

The HOP also inquired about the perceived health effects of environmental problems, in the past (ten years ago), at present, and in the future (over the next twenty-five years). People in poorer nations are more likely to see environmental problems as health threats at all three times, although the relationships are significant only for the present (r = -.70, P < .001) and future (r = -.54, P < .01) time frames. (For past health effects, r = - .29, n.s.)

Given the significantly greater levels of concern expressed over local environmental problems, particularly their health effects, among residents of the poorer nations, it may not be so surprising that citizens in these nations also expressed a higher level of concern over environmental problems in general. A standard question asking respondents to indicate "how concerned are you personally about environmental problems" finds that personal concern is significantly higher (r = -.50, P < .05) among residents of the poorer nations than among those of the wealthier ones—perhaps the most striking contradiction to conventional wisdom found in the HOP.

Overall, then, the HOP results on perceptions of environmental problems reveal that concern about the state of the environment is clearly not limited primarily to residents of the wealthy, industrialized nations of the Northern Hemisphere as was once widely believed. Citizens in the less economically developed nations are much more likely to see their local environments as degraded, somewhat more likely to see their national environments as in poor shape, but not all that much less likely to see world environmental problems as very serious than are citizens in the wealthier nations. Whereas the specific environmental problems that are of most concern vary, and people in poorer nations tend to be especially concerned about their local environments, concern about environmental quality is distributed across a wide range of nations and is not confined to the wealthy, industrialized nations. Indeed, more often than not the HOP finds that citizen concern about environmental problems is negatively associated with national affluence, in direct contradiction to conventional wisdom.

Clearly environmental quality is no longer a "post material" value that is of concern only to those who have met their material needs and can afford to worry about a high "quality of life." Rather, a habitable environment has come to be seen as a basic need in its own right, and the HOP results suggest that people in the poorer nations are keenly aware of the dependence of their well-being on the quality of the environments they inhabit. The assumption that a lack of widespread public concern over environmental quality within the nonwealthy nations of the world poses a barrier to international environmental policymaking is certainly not validated by the HOP results.

ATTITUDES TOWARD ENVIRONMENTAL POLICY ISSUES

Not only has far more attention been paid to environmental issues in the international arena since the 1972 Stockholm conference, but there has been some progress toward the recognition that international development and environmental protection are two sides of the same coin, rather than separate issues (Caldwell, 1984: 6, Haas et al., 1992, 9). In fact, the official name of the Earth Summit, the U.N. Conference on Environment and Development, signifies this trend. Stimulated by the work of the Brundtland Commission set forth in *Our Common Future* (World Commission on Environment and Development, 1987), the goal of "sustainable development" has been put forth as a means of integrating economic development and environmental protection—particularly within the less economically developed nations.

Nonetheless, the nature of sustainable development, and the means of achieving it, remain ambiguous and the subject of considerable controversy (Lele, 1991; Redclift, 1992). This was quite apparent at the Earth Summit, where policy debates revealed a huge chasm between governments of the rich and poor nations in terms of their views of the relationship between international economic development and the protection of environmental quality (Sachs, 1993; White, 1992). Although the HOP survey was designed well before the Earth Summit, an effort was made to examine citizens' views of a wide range of issues related to the environment and development linkage, along with other policy-relevant issues such as the perceived causes and preferred solutions of national-level environmental problems and public opinion regarding the creation of an international agency designed to implement environmental protection policies.

Causes and Solutions of Environmental Problems within Nations

Since the emergence of environmental quality as a social problem, there has been much debate over the crucial causes of, and appropriate solutions for, environmental problems (see, e.g., the literature reviewed in Dunlap et al., 1994). Although public preferences for various solutions have been the subject of numerous surveys (Dunlap and Scarce, 1991), little attention has been given to public perceptions of the causes of environmental problems—even in the United States and Europe. For this reason the HOP included a number of questions on the perceived causes of environmental problems—within respondents' own nations, in the world as a whole, and in the nonindustrialized nations. I'll begin with perceived causes at the national level, then focus on preferred solutions for national problems, before turning to the international domain.

To elicit public perceptions of the causes of environmental problems at the national level, HOP respondents were read "a list of possible causes of our nation's environmental problems," and then asked to indicate "how much you think [each] contributes to the environmental problems here in our nation." The list contained half-a-dozen items tapping the most widely mentioned sources of environmental problems, including over-population, technology, institutions, and individuals (Dunlap et al., 1994). In terms of institutions, we included both "business and industry—they care more about growth than protecting the environment" and "government—it does not place enough emphasis on protecting the environment," while for individuals we included both "lack of education—people just don't know what to do to protect the environment" and "waste—individuals use more resources than they need and throw away too much." Table 10.2 shows the percentages saying that each factor contributes "a great deal" to environmental problems within respondents' nations.

Across the twenty-four nations, respondents are most likely to point to business and industry as the major contributor to their nation's environmental problems, with majorities in eighteen nations seeing business and industry as contributing a great deal to environmental problems. Next most likely to be perceived major causes are technology (seen as contributing a great deal by majorities in sixteen nations) and waste (rated a major contributor by majorities in fourteen nations). Lack of education and poor government are rated fourth and fifth in terms of contributing a great deal to environmental problems, and over-population is least likely to be viewed as a major cause. The high level of blame

Table 10.2
Perceived Causes of National Environmental Problems[1]

Country	Percentage saying each contributes "a great deal"					
	Over-population	Government	Individual Waste	Lack of Education	Business and Industry	Technology
Low Income						
India	74	43	47	61	56	43
Nigeria	51	51	52	63	61	47
Philippines	65	48	66	54	61	64
Poland	7	39	36	38	69	69
Turkey	56	54	57	75	69	62
Russia	17	5	55	47	68	62
Chile	28	27	54	66	71	59
Middle Income						
Brazil	30	47	58	61	70	60
Hungary	12	27	37	28	64	56
Uruguay	17	45	34	68	77	63
Mexico	64	52	69	68	72	69
Korea	32	50	61	41	73	58
Portugal	26	36	46	61	66	61
High Income						
Ireland	13	37	57	47	61	53
Great Britain	25	37	60	39	65	53
Netherlands	12	12	31	8	40	20
Canada	12	38	68	42	62	53
Finland	5	20	40	15	49	31
Germany	32	40	68	30	68	53
United States	36	45	73	53	69	50
Norway	6	18	47	21	47	34
Denmark	4	16	44	15	35	24
Japan	11	29	41	23	46	35
Switzerland	20	19	56	17	44	34

[1]Respondents were asked: "Now I'm going to read a list of possible *causes* of our nation's environmental problems. As I read each item, please tell me how much you think it contributes to the environmental problems **here in our nation**—a great deal, a fair amount, not very much, or not at all? (a) Overpopulation—there are too many people using up resources; (b) Our government—it does not place enough emphasis on protecting the environment; (c) Waste—individuals use more resources than they need and throw away too much; (d) Lack of education—people just don't know what to do to protect the environment; (e) Business and industry—they care more about growth than protecting the environment; (f) Technology—the way products are made uses too many resources and creates too much pollution."

placed on business and industry is consistent with previous surveys in the United States and Europe (Dunlap and Scarce, 1991).

In general, citizens in the lower-income nations are more likely to rate the various factors as contributing a great deal to their nation's environmental problems than are those in the high-income nations, with the exception of waste by individuals. In fact, when per capita GNP is correlated with aggregate-level ratings of each of the causes across the nations (coded as "a great deal" = 4, "a fair amount" = 3, "not very much" = 2, and "not at all" = 1), individual waste is the only causal factor that is positively correlated with national affluence ($r = .28$, n.s.). Ratings of all of the other five possible causes are negatively related to affluence, with the correlations between per capita GNP and the various causal factors being -.43 ($P <$ .05) for over-population (a correlation that is dampened by the low ratings given by Polish and Russian citizens); -.52 ($P < .01$) for government; -.73 ($P < .001$) for lack of education; -.60 ($P < .01$) for business and industry; and -.64 ($P < .001$) for technology. It is particularly important that population is more likely to be seen as contributing to environmental problems within lower-income nations such as India, the Philippines, Turkey, and Nigeria, which do in fact have rapidly growing populations. There is little evidence that citizens in nations with purported "population problems" deny the causal impact of over-population on environmental problems.

The above question was followed by one dealing with possible solutions for national environmental problems: "Here are some actions our government could take to help solve our nation's environmental problems. Keeping in mind that there are costs associated with these actions, tell me—for each one I read—whether you would strongly favor, somewhat favor, somewhat oppose or strongly oppose this action." Three of the items deal explicitly with laws and regulations, one is aimed at business and industry, one at individual citizens and one—banning the sale of products that are unsafe for the environment—has implications for both individuals and industry. The other three actions are supporting scientific research, providing family planning, and limiting exports of natural resources.

Table 10.3 shows the percentages saying they "strongly favor" each of the six actions. Not surprisingly, government support for scientific research to control pollution receives the strongest endorsement, as majorities in twenty-two of the twenty-four nations strongly favor this action. This is followed by banning the sale of harmful products (receiving majority support in twenty-one nations) and stronger laws for business and industry (receiving such support in nineteen nations), both of which are compatible with the previously noted emphasis placed on the role of business and industry in causing environmental problems. Less popular are laws aimed at individual citizens, the provision of family planning, and banning the export of natural resources. The overall low rating of the latter may partially reflect the fact that many of the nations do not export substantial amounts of their natural resources, while the relatively low rating of family planning coincides with the lack of emphasis placed on over-population as a cause of environmental problems within most of the individual nations. From a policy standpoint, it is important to note that stronger laws on both industry and

Table 10.3
Preferred Solutions for National Environmental Problems[1]

Country	*Laws on Industry*	*Laws on Citizens*	*Family Planning*	*Research*	*Limit Exports*	*Ban Products*
Low Income						
India	69	60	71	55	34	51
Nigeria	79	70	65	80	51	72
Philippines	68	66	69	70	54	74
Poland	54	53	41	53	40	49
Turkey	76	74	69	75	52	74
Russia	84	77	21	66	61	66
Chile	73	65	49	73	42	78
Middle Income						
Brazil	82	77	73	78	52	66
Hungary	51	39	20	48	24	50
Uruguay	83	83	77	80	55	89
Mexico	71	72	71	74	60	73
Korea	79	60	31	76	44	65
Portugal	66	67	36	54	34	56
High Income						
Ireland	68	58	45	66	32	68
Great Britain	67	42	50	67	32	65
Netherlands	65	45	20	54	19	57
Canada	68	50	33	61	35	68
Finland	38	31	13	57	16	44
Germany	74	49	36	67	31	69
United States	57	44	51	59	41	62
Norway	44	44	18	51	18	56
Denmark	44	43	13	58	14	59
Japan	48	24	4	47	11	47
Switzerland	47	37	17	55	17	62

Percentage saying "strongly favor" each

[1]Respondents were asked: "Here are some actions our government could take to help solve our nation's environmental problems. **Keeping in mind that there are costs associated with these actions,** please tell me—for each one I read—whether you would strongly favor, somewhat favor, somewhat oppose, or strongly oppose this action. (a) Make stronger environmental protections laws for business and industry; (b) Make laws requiring that all citizens conserve resources and reduce pollution; (c) Provide family planning information and free birth control to all citizens who want it to help reduce birth rates; (d) Support scientific research to help find ways to control pollution; (e) Limit exports of our natural resources in other nations; (f) Ban the sale of products that are unsafe for the environment."

individuals, banning environmentally harmful products, and support for scientific research are favored (combining "strongly" and "somewhat" favor) by large majorities in all twenty-four nations.

It is apparent from Table 10.3 that all of the proposed solutions are more likely to be strongly favored by citizens of the poorer nations than by their counterparts in the wealthy nations, and these patterns are confirmed by correlational analyses. With the exception of banning the sale of unsafe products, support for each potential solution (coded as "strongly favor" = 4, "somewhat favor" = 3, "somewhat oppose" = 2, and "strongly oppose" = 1) is significantly negatively correlated with national affluence: $r = -.61$ ($P < .01$) for stronger laws for business and industry; $r = -.80$ ($P < .001$) for stronger laws for individual citizens; $r = -.76$ ($P < .001$) for family planning; $r = -.46$ ($P < .05$) for scientific research; and $r = -.77$ ($P < .001$) for limiting exports of natural resources. In the case of banning unsafe products, $r = -.22$ (n.s.).

Overall, then, the HOP finds that residents of the poorer nations are more favorable toward a wide range of potential solutions, including family planning, for their nations' environmental problems than are residents of the wealthier nations. These results are consistent with the earlier-noted tendency for residents of the poorer nations to see environmental problems (at least at the local and national levels) as more serious than do their counterparts in the wealthier nations, and certainly contradict the assumption that citizens of the poorer, less-industrialized nations are not supportive of environmental protection efforts. Indeed, they express more support than do the residents of the wealthy, industrialized nations.

Responsibility for World Environmental Problems

An especially controversial issue that emerged with preparations for the Earth Summit, and continues in debates over sustainable development, concerns the relative contributions of the rich and poor nations to the world's environmental problems.[4] In particular, spokespersons for the less-developed nations point to the disproportionate levels of resource consumption and pollution production in the richer countries, while spokespersons for the latter have suggested that poorer nations contribute greatly to environmental problems—via high population growth, weak environmental regulations and use of outmoded technologies (White, 1992; Elmer-Dewitt, 1992). Do citizens around the world hold sharply contrasting views on the issue of relative responsibility for world environmental problems? To examine this issue the HOP asked respondents, "Which do you think is more responsible for today's environmental problems in the world— industrialized countries, developing countries, or do you think they are both equally responsible?" The results are shown in Table 10.4.

Overall, the results provide little evidence to suggest that the citizens of rich and poor nations are sharply divided on the issue of responsibility for world environmental problems. In ten countries, covering all income levels, majorities choose "both equally responsible," and in five more pluralities do so, making this the most popular choice in fifteen nations. In eight countries, citizens are most

Table 10.4
Responsibility for the World's Environmental Problems[1]

| | *Percentage who think each is responsible*[2] | | |
| | Industrialized | Developing | Both |
Country	Nations	Nations	Equally
Low Income			
India	31	13	46
Nigeria	32	18	37
Philippines	30	14	54
Poland	45	57	39
Turkey	40	13	38
Russia	28	6	55
Chile	37	9	50
Middle Income			
Brazil	32	8	56
Hungary	28	9	56
Uruguay	38	5	49
Mexico	37	37	23
Korea	33	37	23
Portugal	37	3	52
High Income			
Ireland	40	4	46
Great Britain	37	6	50
Netherlands	53	2	40
Canada	37	3	57
Finland	58	5	33
Germany	54	4	36
United States	29	4	61
Norway	65	3	26
Denmark	64	5	26
Japan	41	11	28
Switzerland	46	5	46

[1]Respondents were asked: "Now, thinking about the world, which do you think is more responsible for today's environmental problems in the world—industrialized countries, developing countries, or do you think they are both equally responsible?"

[2]Percentages do not add to 100 because the categories of "not sure" and "refused" are not reported.

likely to blame industrialized nations. However, six of these (including the only five where majorities take this position: the Netherlands, Germany, Denmark, Finland, and Norway) are themselves industrialized nations. Ironically, the sole nation in which a plurality places the blame on developing nations is Korea, itself one of the most rapidly developing countries in the world. The other nations in which at least 10 percent place the blame on developing nations include the low-income countries of Nigeria, India, the Philippines, Chile, and Turkey, as well as Japan.

Thus, citizens of the rich and poor nations do not seem as polarized as widely assumed when it comes to assigning responsibility for world environmental problems. Residents of the highly industrialized nations tend to recognize their greater contribution to these problems, whereas residents of the less-developed countries are likely to acknowledge a share of the blame. In fact, when national affluence is correlated with a dichotomous measure of responsibility, coded as "industrialized nations" = 1 and "developing nations" or "both equally" = 0, the coefficient is .64 (P < .001), indicating that residents of wealthy nations are significantly more likely to attribute responsibility to industrialized nations than are residents of poorer nations. Given that the highly industrialized nations have, in fact, had far greater impact on the global environment than have the less-developed nations (see, e.g., White, 1992), the HOP results suggest that residents of the middle- and low-income nations hold relatively charitable opinions of the situation.

Contributors to Environmental Problems in Developing Nations

A related issue, which has also been the object of much controversy, is the source of environmental degradation *within* the less-developed nations themselves. Some see these problems as stemming mainly from forces outside of these countries, especially the exploitation of their resources by multinational companies for the purpose of supplying the high-consumption lifestyles of the industrialized nations (Sachs, 1993). Others point to conditions within the less-developed nations, particularly their rapidly growing populations, as the primary contributor to their environmental problems (Elmer-Dewitt, 1992; White, 1992). We examined perceptions of this issue by asking, "How much do you think each of the following contributes to environmental problems in developing countries: Consumption of the world's resources by industrialized countries? Multinational companies operating in developing countries? Over-population in these developing countries?" The percentages responding "a great deal" for each are shown in Table 10.5.

Overall, there is a modest tendency for more blame for developing nations' environmental problems to be placed on their "population problem" than on the industrialized nations or multinationals, as the former is the most highly rated factor in fourteen of the nations. In fact, in all of the high-income countries except Japan,[5] citizens assign most responsibility to over-population. However, people in these countries also place a good deal of responsibility on industrialized nations and multinationals as well. Furthermore, respondents in India, Nigeria ,and the Philippines (the three poorest nations in the survey) also place the most emphasis on over-population, while majorities in Turkey and Mexico assign a great deal of responsibility to over-population. In fact, among the low- and middle-income nations, only the three Eastern European countries and Korea place little blame on over-population. The result is that there is a modest, but insignificant, correlation

Table 10.5
Perceived Contributors to Environmental Problems in Developing Countries[1]

	Percentage who say each contributes "a great deal"		
	Consumption		*Over-population*
	by Industrialized	*Multinational*	*in Developing*
Country	*Countries*	*Companies*	*Countries*
Low Income			
India	36	30	61
Nigeria	47	47	55
Philippines	44	41	52
Poland	25	21	17
Turkey	64	39	52
Russia	28	26	18
Chile	43	37	37
Middle Income			
Brazil	46	45	37
Hungary	14	13	19
Uruguay	48	50	43
Mexico	55	51	54
Korea	42	41	29
Portugal	54	50	41
High Income			
Ireland	43	43	46
Great Britain	45	43	54
Netherlands	12	16	32
Canada	43	44	50
Finland	49	42	57
Germany	60	55	62
United States	41	35	50
Norway	57	53	60
Denmark	34	35	42
Japan	38	25	22
Switzerland	33	34	52

[1]Respondents were asked: "How much do you think each of the following contributes to environmental problems in developing countries—a great deal, a fair amount, not very much, or none at all? (a) Consumption of the world's resources by industrialized countries; (b) Multinational companies operating in developing countries; (c) Overpopulation in these developing countries."

(r = .29) between national affluence and seeing over-population as a major contributor to environmental problems within developing nations (coded as "a great deal" = 4, "a fair amount" = 3, "not very much" = 2, and "none at all" = 1), and this is likely due to the very low emphasis placed on it by the Poles and Russians.

Surprisingly, residents of the poorer nations are no more likely to place the blame for developing countries' environmental problems on the wealthy, industrialized nations than are residents of the latter nations ($r = -.02$, n.s.). Finally, when it comes to the contribution of multinational corporations, citizens in the high-income nations are a bit more likely to see them as causing environmental problems in developing nations than are citizens in the low-income nations, although the relationship is not statistically significant ($r = .29$).

In short, even when the focus is restricted to environmental problems within the developing nations, citizens from around the world do not seem as heavily polarized over the roles of the rich and poor nations as might be assumed from conflicts at the Earth Summit. Combined with the results of the prior question on responsibility for worldwide environmental problems, these responses suggest that at least in the nations covered by the HOP, residents of poor, Southern nations and those of rich, Northern nations do not hold dramatically differing views of the sources of environmental problems—whether worldwide or within their own nations. There is little evidence of a strong tendency for the poor to blame the rich, and vice versa, with residents of the low-income nations being especially generous in their assessments on the roles of the wealthy nations and multinational corporations. In general, there tends to be widespread acceptance of mutual responsibility for environmental problems across all types of nations.

Achieving Sustainable Development

The growing use of the concept of "sustainable development" reflects increasing awareness of the fact that environmental protection should be coupled with recognition of the need for continuing economic development, at least among the nonwealthy nations of the world (Lele, 1991). While achieving ecologically sound economic development will require major changes within all types of nations (especially both production and consumption practices in wealthy nations), the special problems faced by poor countries in protecting their nation's environmental quality while pursuing economic growth is, in fact, the aspect of sustainable development that has received the most attention. A major policy issue surrounding discussions about achieving sustainable development within the less-developed nations has been the importance of assistance from the richer nations, and the failure of the latter to offer significantly more aid was a major failure of the Earth Summit (Jordan, 1994).

There are a variety of ways in which the wealthy nations might assist poorer nations to protect their environments while nonetheless pursuing economic development. Several prominently mentioned efforts were examined in the HOP via the question shown in Table 10.6, which asks respondents whether they favor or oppose five differing actions that "industrialized countries might take if they were to give help in some way" and which one would *best* help. The table shows the percentage that "strongly favors" each type of action as well as those choosing each as the single best action.

Not surprisingly, the noncontroversial action of providing educational information is the most popular action overall, being *strongly* favored by majorities in twenty-two of the twenty-four nations. This is closely followed by supplying

Table 10.6
Actions Industrialized Countries Might Take to Help Developing Countries and
Action That Would Best Help

		Percentage saying "strongly favor" each[1] and percentage choosing each as best action[2] (in parentheses)			
Country	Education	Technology	Model Laws	Family Planning	Cancel Debt
Low Income					
India	70(41)	57(22)	53 (9)	66(14)	149 (7)
Nigeria	82(22)	81(24)	73(11)	66 (5)	76(24)
Philippines	72(37)	72(23)	62(12)	69 (9)	65(18)
Poland	52 (7)	67(49)	49 (4)	33 (1)	60(23)
Turkey	9(29)	70(17)	68(13)	68 (4)	76(28)
Russia	71(14)	68(37)	55 (9)	28 (3)	37(16)
Chile	73(37)	70(28)	54(14)	45 (5)	58(11)
Middle Income					
Brazil	87(30)	85(11)	76 (7)	62 (9)	79(36)
Hungary	46(13)	49(43)	37 (7)	36 (6)	34(20)
Uruguay	86(22)	87(19)	83(12)	71(12)	76(31)
Mexico	70(21)	70(21)	69(21)	70(10)	70(17)
Korea	66(21)	74(51)	58(12)	33 (2)	42 (8)
Portugal	66(43)	61(27)	58(11)	42 (3)	51(11)
High Income					
Ireland	73(39)	71(10)	56(15)	57(12)	50(14)
Great Britain	61(27)	60(24)	45 (5)	64(20)	39(13)
Netherlands	56(27	57(32)	51(10)	57 (9)	31(11)
Canada	66(42)	54(21)	55(15)	54(11)	30 (7)
Finland	58(27)	50(29)	38(12)	62(20)	30 (4)
Germany	55(26)	50(13)	44(15)	59(23)	32(14)
United States	63(41)	48(20)	49(15)	57(13)	23 (5)
Norway	69(34)	55(19)	43 (6)	67(14)	49(18)
Denmark	64(35)	46(16)	36(12)	62(21)	35 (6)
Japan	48(17)	48(37)	24(13)	23 (5)	18 (2)
Switzerland	59(24)	47(20)	32(10)	59(26)	38(18)

[1]Respondents were asked: "Protecting the environment is difficult for any country, but especially for developing countries. I'm going to read you a list of actions industrialized countries might take if they were to give help in some way. For each, tell me how strongly you favor or oppose each of the following—strongly favor, somewhat favor, somewhat oppose, strongly oppose. Encourage industrialized countries to . . . (a) Provide developing countries with information to help educate citizens about environmental protection; (b) Supply technology and equipment to control pollution and cope with environmental problems; (c) Provide model environmental laws to put appropriate restrictions on business and industry; (d) Supply family planning information to lower birth rates and manage population problems; (e) Cancel some of the foreign debt owed by developing nations so this money can be put into environmental protection."

[2]Repondents were asked: "Which *one* of these actions by industrialized countries do you think would *best* help developing countries deal with their environmental problems—educational materials, supply technology and equipment, provide model environmental laws, supply family planning information, or cancel some foreign debt?" Percentages do not add to 100 because the categories of "not sure" and "refused" are not reported.

technological assistance (strongly favored by majorities in nineteen nations) and the provision of family planning information (strongly favored by majorities in seventeen nations). Providing model laws for business and industry, which might be seen as less readily transferable to the poorer nations, receives majority support in fourteen nations. Finally, the cancellation of foreign debt, no doubt the most controversial of the five actions, receives strong support from majorities in only ten nations. It should come as no surprise that this action is most popular in the low-income nations, next most popular in the middle-income, and least popular in the high-income nations that would be writing off the debts. Residents of Ireland and Norway, among the latter, give most support to this action, while those in Japan and the United States are the least favorable.

A striking feature of the results in Table 10.6 is that there is strong support for nearly all of the actions across most of the countries. In fact, when the percentages "moderately" favoring the actions are added to those "strongly" favoring them (reported in the table), all five actions are favored by majorities in *every* nation. Such results reflect a broad-based awareness of the necessity of wealthier nations providing assistance to the less-developed nations to help the latter protect their environments.

It should come as no surprise that, overall, residents of the poorer nations express even more favorability toward most of these policies—especially debt cancellation—than do those of the wealthier nations. There is a negative correlation between national affluence and favorability (coded as "strongly favor" = 4, "somewhat favor" = 3, "somewhat oppose" = 2, and "strongly oppose" = 1) for four of the five policies: -.54 (P < .01) for educational assistance; -.75 (P < .001) for technological assistance; -.79 (P < .001) for model laws; and -.70 (P < .001) for debt cancellation. The exception is family planning, support for which increases very slightly with national affluence (r = .12, n.s.)—again, largely due to the low support it receives among Poles and Russians.

In order to get a better sense of citizen priorities for sustainable development policies, we next asked respondents to indicate "Which one of these actions by industrialized countries do you think would best help developing countries deal with their environmental problems?" and repeated the list of items used in the prior question. The figures within the parentheses in Table 10.6 show the percentage choosing each item as the single "best" action. Again, education is the most preferred action, followed by technological assistance. Family planning continues to receive considerable support among residents of most of the high-income nations, but much less so as the single best action among those in low-income nations. The reverse is the case for debt cancellation. In fact, when per capita GNP is correlated with the percentage in each nation choosing each action as the best one (coded as "1" if chosen, "0" if not), family planning and debt cancellation are the only two for which the correlations are significant: r = .67 (P < .001) for the former, and r = -.50 (P < .05) for the latter.

In sum, the results in Table 10.6 reveal widespread support across all nations for the general idea that industrialized nations should provide assistance to developing nations to help the latter protect their environment, but differences emerge in the emphases given to various proposals—especially when it comes to the single best action. Citizens in the low-income nations are understandably more likely to favor all of the actions, with the exception of family planning, significantly more than are citizens in the high-income nations. Even though all of the actions entail some financial assistance, it is obvious that residents of the high-income nations are less supportive of the most obviously costly action—debt cancellation—than they are of the others. Thus, while the HOP results suggest that in most countries the public recognizes the need for wealthy nations to provide assistance to poorer ones in order to help the latter protect the quality of their environments, translating this supportive climate into concrete economic assistance will no doubt remain a difficult task (Jordan, 1994).

Attitudes Toward an International Environmental Agency

Another issue that has received considerable attention in recent years is the importance of strengthening international mechanisms for protecting the environment (Caldwell, 1992). The growing recognition of the global dimensions of environmental problems has led to the establishment of several international environmental conventions and treaties (Haas et al., 1993), but little progress has been made in setting up effective regulatory agencies designed to ensure their implementation. This is not surprising, as international regulatory bodies pose major challenges to traditional notions of national sovereignty. To examine public attitudes toward an international environmental agency the HOP asked two questions, one dealing with the funding for such an agency and the other dealing with the granting of authority to it. The questions and results are shown in Table 10.7.

The first column shows the percentages saying they either "strongly favor" or "somewhat favor" their own national government "contributing money to an international agency to work on solving global environmental problems." As the table shows, there is considerable support for funding such an agency, with majorities in every nation at least somewhat in favor of this. These majorities range from a high of 90 percent in Finland and 89 percent in Great Britain and the Netherlands to a low of 56 percent in Brazil. Overall there is a modest tendency for support (coded as "strongly favor" = 4, "somewhat favor" = 3, "somewhat oppose" = 2, and "strongly oppose" = 1) to increase with national affluence (r = .29, although the relationship is not statistically significant). This comes as no surprise given the greater economic resources of the wealthier nations.

When respondents were next asked if they "favor or oppose giving an international agency the authority to influence [their] government's policy in environmentally important areas," there was somewhat less enthusiasm. Although majorities favor this in every nation, they are often only slim majorities—noticeably smaller than in the case of providing funding for such an agency. And, as was the case in terms of funding, there is somewhat less enthusiasm for granting

Table 10.7
Support for Contribution to an International Environmental Agency and for Giving Authority to the Agency

	Percentage saying "strongly favor" and "somewhat favor"	
Country	*Contributing Money to Agency[1]*	*Giving Authority to Agency[2]*
Low Income		
India	75	57
Nigeria	73	69
Philippines	75	64
Poland	78	70
Turkey	75	60
Russia	76	72
Chile	69	53
Middle Income		
Brazil	56	63
Hungary	84	71
Uruguay	61	55
Mexico	77	61
Korea	82	74
Portugal	83	73
High Income		
Ireland	79	70
Great Britain	89	73
Netherlands	89	74
Canada	77	71
Finland	90	74
Germany	82	78
United States	73	63
Norway	82	65
Denmark	78	52
Japan	78	65
Switzerland	79	71

[1]Respondents were asked: "Would you favor or oppose our government contributing money to an international agency to work on solving global environmental problems—strongly favor, somewhat favor, somewhat oppose, or strongly oppose?"
[2]Respondents were asked: "Would you favor or oppose giving an international agency the authority to influence our government's policy in environmentally important areas—strongly favor, somewhat favor, somewhat oppose, or strongly oppose?"

authority to an international environmental agency among residents of the less-developed nations than among their counterparts in the rich nations, although the relationship is even weaker (r = .20, n.s.).

Taken together, these results reveal a substantial degree of support for the establishment of an international agency designed specifically to deal with environmental problems. Strong majorities in most nations support their government funding such an agency (although they tend to be smaller among the low-income nations, as one would expect), and at least slim majorities are in favor of granting such an agency some degree of authority in the environmental affairs of their own nation. While it is impossible to judge in the absence of trend data, these results likely reveal a major shift in public recognition of the importance of dealing with environmental problems at the international level compared to a decade or two ago. (This support seems consistent with the widespread perception of world environmental problems as very serious as documented above.) Although there is a bit less support for an international agency among residents of the lower-income nations than among their counterparts in wealthy nations, this is understandable given that such an agency has been portrayed as providing a means by which the wealthy nations can increase their control over the resources of the nonindustrialized world (Sachs, 1993).

SUMMARY AND CONCLUSIONS

As was the case for perceptions of the seriousness of environmental problems, the results of the HOP survey do not reveal major differences between citizens in the wealthy and poor nations in terms of attitudes toward environmental policy issues. While there are some differences in emphases, there is certainly no lack of support for environmental protection among those living in poorer nations. Indeed, residents of the poor nations are more supportive of a broad range of policies to deal with their nations' environmental problems than are their counterparts in the wealthy nations. Residents of the wealthy nations tend to accept a good deal of responsibility for world environmental problems, while those in poorer nations do not absolve themselves of blame. Similarly, when it comes to environmental problems within the less-developed nations, there is a fairly similar tendency for both consumption among industrialized nations and over-population in developing nations to be seen as contributing factors. There is little evidence overall that citizens of the rapidly growing, poor nations downplay the impact of their population growth while blaming the wealthy nations for the bulk of the world's environmental problems.

When we turn to policy actions designed to help the less-developed nations protect their environments, we find fairly broad support across all nations and stronger support for most actions among the lower-income nations. The closest thing we find to a cleavage between residents of wealthy, Northern nations and those of poorer, Southern nations is in the latter's greater support for assistance (including debt cancellation) to developing nations. Residents of lower-income nations are understandably more favorable than their counterparts in the high-income nations toward wealthy nations providing economic assistance to poorer nations for sustainable development. Finally, there is relatively broad support across all types of nations for an international agency empowered to enforce environmental protection regulations, albeit somewhat less in the poorer countries.

Thus, although there are obviously some differences in opinion, overall the HOP did not find residents of the wealthy, industrialized nations to hold drastically differing views of the relative contributions of rich and poor nations to environmental problems—nor of policies for dealing with such problems—than do residents of poorer, less-developed nations. The huge chasm that often separated leaders from the wealthy nations and those from the developing and poor nations that was apparent among world leaders at Rio de Janeiro does not emerge among the general publics of two dozen nations around the world included in the HOP.

Those who see worldwide environmental problems as serious, and environmental protection as a major international goal, will likely take heart from the findings of Gallup's Health of the Planet survey. No longer is concern about environmental quality limited to those who in live in the wealthy, industrialized nations of the Northern Hemisphere—if it ever was. Clearly the assumption that outside the rich nations there is little public support for environmental protection is in error. Not only are people in low- and middle-income nations concerned about environmental quality (as reflected by their widespread participation in environmental NGOs as well as the HOP results), I personally find their diagnoses of problems and prescriptions for solutions as being quite generous toward those of us in the wealthy nations (who enjoy the fruits of our historically disproportionate use of the world's resources). At this point, I think it is fair to argue that the willingness of our nations to provide adequate assistance to poorer nations is far more of a barrier to global environmental protection than is limited awareness or concern among the citizens of those nations.

NOTES

1. The most comprehensive effort prior to Gallup's HOP survey was a sixteen-nation survey conducted by Louis Harris and Associates for UNEP in 1988 and 1989. However, in most of the nations included in that study the samples were quite small (ranging from 300 to 600), resulting in large sampling errors. Further, in the nonindustrialized nations the samples were typically limited to residents of large urban areas, and consequently the results cannot be generalized to the adult populations of those nations. For these and other reasons the Harris survey has been viewed critically by social scientists (Stycos, 1994) and virtually ignored.

2. Frequency distributions for most of the items discussed in this chapter can be found in Dunlap et al. (1993b), and for all of the HOP items in Dunlap et al. (1993a). It should be noted that there may be minor differences in the percentages reported in this chapter and those in earlier reports due to extensive data cleaning after the HOP data were transferred to Washington State University.

3. For a detailed description of the measurement of the various attitudinal variables see Dunlap and Mertig (1995). It should be noted that the correlations reported in this chapter differ slightly from those in Dunlap and Mertig (1995) because 1990 data on per capita GNP was used in the analyses reported in the latter, whereas 1992 data were used in the analyses for this chapter.

4. For a wide range of reviews of the Earth Summit, see Haas et al. (1992); Levy (1993); Jordan (1994); Rogers (1993); Sachs (1993); and Vaillancourt (1993).

5. Caution should be used when viewing the percentages reported for Japan, because there is often a much higher frequency of "nonresponse" ("no answer" or "unsure") in Japan. If these nonresponses were omitted (which is the case for the national-level correlational analyses) it would often boost the percentages reported for Japan much more than for most nations. See Dunlap et al. (1993a) for data on nonresponses to each item.

REFERENCES

Beckerman, W. (1974). *Two Cheers for the Affluent Society.* New York: St. Martin's.

Caldwell, L. K. (1984). *International Environmental Policy: Emergence and Dimensions.* Durham, NC: Duke University Press.

———. (1992). "Globalizing Environmentalism: Threshold of a New Phase in International Relations," in R. E. Dunlap and A. G. Mertig, eds., *American Environmentalism: The U.S. Environmental Movement, 1970–1990.* Washington, D.C.: Taylor and Francis, pp. 63–76.

Dunlap, R. E. (1995). "Public Opinion and Environmental Policy," in J. P. Lester , ed., *Environmental Politics and Policy.* Durham, NC: Duke University Press, pp. 63–114.

Dunlap, R. E., G. H. Gallup, Jr., and A. M. Gallup. (1993a). *Health of the Planet.* Princeton, NJ: Gallup International Institute.

———. (1993b). "Of Global Concern: Results of the Health of the Planet Survey." *Environment,* 35 (November): 7–5, 33–39.

Dunlap, R. E., L. A. Lutzenhiser, and E. A. Rosa. (1994). "Understanding Environmental Problems: A Sociological Perspective," in B. Burgenmeier, ed., *Economy, Environment and Technology: A Socio-Economic Approach.* Armonk, NY: M. E. Sharpe, pp. 27–49.

Dunlap, R. E., and A. G. Mertig. (1995). "Global Concern for the Environment: Is Affluence a Prerequisite?" *Journal of Social Issues,* 51(4) (Winter 1995): 121–137.

Dunlap, R. E., and R. Scarce. (1991). "The Polls—Poll Trends: Environmental Problems and Protection." *Public Opinion Quarterly,* 55: 651–672.

Durning, A. (1989). "Mobilizing at the Grassroots," in L. Brown et al., eds., *State of the World 1989.* New York: Norton, pp. 154–173.

Elmer-Dewitt, P. (1992). "Rich vs. Poor: Summit to Save the Earth." *Time* (June 1): 42–58.

Finger, M. (1992). "The Changing Green Movement—A Clarification." *Research in Social Movements, Conflicts and Change, Supplement* 2, 229–246.

Fisher, J. (1993). *The Road from Rio: Sustainable Development and the Nongovernmental Movement in the Third World.* Westport, CT: Praeger.

Haas, P. M., R. O. Keohane, and M. A. Levy (eds.). (1993). *Institutions for the Earth.* Cambridge, MA: MIT Press.

Haas, P. M., M. A. Levy, and E. A. Parson. (1992). "Appraising the Earth Summit: How Should We Judge UNCED's Success?" *Environment,* 34 (October): 6–11, 26–33.

Hofrichter, J., and K. Reif (1990). "Evolution of Environmental Attitudes in the European Community." *Scandinavian Political Studies* 13: 119–146.

Inglehart, R. (1990). *Culture Shift in Advanced Industrial Society*. Princeton, NJ: Princeton University Press.

Jordan, A. (1994). "Financing the UNCED Agenda: The Controversy over Additionality." *Environment*, 36 (April):16–20, 26–34.

Kamieniecki, S. (ed.). (1993). *Environmental Politics in the International Arena: Movements, Parties, Organizations, and Policy*. Albany: State University of New York Press.

Lele, S. M. (1991). "Sustainable Development: A Critical Review." *World Development*, 19: 607–21.

Levy, M. A. (1993). "UNCED: Mileposts Along the Road from Rio," *Environment*, 35(June): 4–5, 43–45.

Louis Harris and Associates, Inc. (1989). *Public and Leadership Attitudes to the Environment in Four Continents*. New York: Louis Harris and Associates.

McCormick, J. (1989). *Reclaiming Paradise: The Global Environmental Movement*. Bloomington: Indiana University Press.

Redclift, M. (1992). "The Meaning of Sustainable Development." *Geoforum*, 23: 395–403.

Rogers, A. 1993. *The Earth Summit: A Planetary Reckoning*. Los Angeles: Global Press.

Sachs, W. (ed.). (1993). *Global Ecology: A New Arena of Political Conflict*. Atlantic Highlands, NJ: Zed.

Stern, P. C., T. Dietz, G. A. Guagnano, and L. Kalof. (1995)."Values, Beliefs, and Proenvironmental Action: Attitude Formation Toward Emergent Attitude Objects: The Social Construction of Environmental Concern." *Journal of Applied Social Psychology*, 25(18) (September): 161–163.

Stycos, J. M. (1994). *Population and the Environment: Polls, Policies, and Public Opinion*. EPAT/MUCIA Working Paper 15. Madison: EPAT/MUCIA Research and Training, University of Wisconsin.

Vaillancourt, J. G. (1993). "Earth Summits of 1992 in Rio." *Society and Natural Resources*, 6: 81–88.

White, R. R. (1992). "The Road to Rio or the Global Environmental Crisis and the Emergence of Different Agendas for Rich and Poor Countries." *International Journal of Environmental Studies*, 41: 187–201.

World Bank. (1994). *World Development Report 1994: Infrastructure for Development*. New York: Oxford University Press.

World Commission on Environment and Development. (1987). *Our Common Future*. New York: Oxford University Press.

INDEX

ABOUT THE CONTRIBUTORS

AUDREY M. ARMOUR is Associate Professor and Associate Dean in the Faculty of Environmental Studies, York University. She has also served on the Science Advisory Board of the International Joint Commission on Great Lakes water quality and as President of the International Association for Impact Assessment.

ROBERT V. BARTLETT is Associate Professor of Political Science at Purdue University. He has published numerous scholarly articles and book chapters on environmental policy and politics, and is the author or editor of several books, including *The Reserve Mining Controversy: Science, Technology, and Environmental Quality*, and *Policy Through Impact Assessment: Institutionalized Analysis as a Policy Strategy*, and (with Ton Bühers) *Environmental Policy in New Zealand: The Politics of Clean and Green?*

LYNTON K. CALDWELL is Arthur F. Bentley Professor Emeritus of Political Science and Professor Emeritus of Public and Environmental Affairs at Indiana University. He has authored numerous books and articles on public policy, international science and technology, and environmental policy, and has served on many scientific advisory boards and commissions and played a major role in drafting the U.S. National Environmental Policy Act of 1969. He has undertaken many assignments abroad, including co-directorship of the United Nations Public Administration Institute for Turkey and the Middle East.

RILEY E. DUNLAP is Boeing Distinguished Profession of Environmental Sociology at Washington State University, where he has studied environmental activism and attitudes since 1972. He is president of the International Sociological Association's Research Committee on Environment and Society, and co-editor of *American Environmentalism* and *Public Reactions to Nuclear Waste*.

ODELIA FUNKE is a political scientist with over fifteen years of experience in environmental policy at the U.S. Environmental Protection Agency. She currently manages a group with responsibility for projects and polices related to public access in the Office of Pollution Prevention and Toxics. Her research interests include issues in political theory and environmental policy.
U.S. Environmental Protection Agency

STEVEN KENNETT is a Research Associate with the Canadian Institute of Resources Law at the University of Calgary. His areas of research and publication include environmental assessment, energy law and regulation, constitutional law, water resource management, federalism, and environmental law and policy. He is the author of *Managing Interjurisdictional Waters in Canada: A Constitutional Analysis.*

KERRY KRUTILLA is Associate Professor of Public and Environmental Affairs at Indiana University. He has received the Josiah Charles Trent Award for International Studies, and the 1992 Policy Article Prize from the Center for International Food and Agricultural Policy, University of Minnesota.

TAE JOON LAH is a doctoral candidate in the School of Public and Environmental Affairs at Indiana University. He holds a B.A. Degree (1989) and an M.A. Degree (1991) in public administration from Yonsei University, Korea, and an M.P.A. Degree (1994) from the Maxwell School, Syracuse University.

ROSEMARY O'LEARY is Associate Professor of Public and Environmental Affairs at Indiana University, Previously she was on the faculty of the Department of Public Administration at the Maxwell School of Citizenship and Public Affairs at Syracuse University. She has won five national research awards and has published over fifty scholarly articles and three books in the areas of environment and natural resources policy, public management, law and public policy, and bureaucratic politics, and is currently Chair of the Public Administration Section of the American Political Science Association.

J. OWEN SAUNDERS is Executive Director, Canadian Institute of Resources Law, and Adjunct Professor in the Faulty of Law at The University of Calgary. His published research includes work on such topics as natural resources law and policy, domestic and international environmental law, and international trade law.

ROY W. SHIN is Professor of Public Policy and Political Economy at the School of Public and Environmental Affairs, Indiana University, Bloomington. His current research focuses on the cross-national analyses of regional economic adjustment strategies and he as written extensively on comparative and environmental aspects of economic development.

LAURA A. STROHM, Assistant Professor at the Monterey Institute of International Studies, focuses her research on trade and environment, the transfer of environmental risk, and international organizations and conventions. She worked for the International Union for the Conservation of Nature (IUCN) in Gland, Switzerland, and in soil conservation and watershed management in California.

ISBN 1-56720-079-6

90000>

EAN

9 781567 200799

HARDCOVER BAR CODE